# CIMA

## NEW SYLLABUS
## PRACTICE & REVISION KIT

Intermediate Paper 5

## Business Tax

BPP Publishing
*January 2001*

First edition January 2001

ISBN 0 7517 3831 X

**British Library Cataloguing-in-Publication Data**
A catalogue record for this book
is available from the British Library


Published by

BPP Publishing Limited
Aldine House, Aldine Place
London W12 8AW

www.bpp.com

Printed in Great Britain by W M Print
45 – 47 Frederick Street
Walsall
West Midlands WS2 9NE

We are grateful to the Chartered Institute of Management Accountants for permission to reproduce past examination questions. The answers to past examination questions have been prepared by BPP Publishing Limited.

**CONTENTS**                                                                    *Page number*

**BPP** PUBLISHING

## Question and answer checklist/index

The headings in this checklist/index indicate the main topics of questions, but questions often cover several different topics.

**Preparation questions**, listed in italics, provide you with a firm foundation for attempts at exam-standard questions.

Questions preceded by ★ are **key questions** which we think you must attempt in order to pass the exam. Tick them off on this list as you complete them.

Questions set under the old syllabus *Business Tax* papers are included where their style and content are similar to those which will appear in the Paper 5 exam. A date (11/00, say) after the question refers to an old syllabus paper.

**BPP** PUBLISHING

## Question and answer checklist/index

# TOPIC INDEX

Listed below are the key Paper 5 syllabus topics and the numbers of the questions in this Kit covering those topics.

If you need to concentrate your practice and revision on certain topics or if you want to attempt all available questions that refer to a particular subject (be they preparation, exam-standard or case study/scenario-based questions), you will find this index useful.

| Syllabus topic | Question numbers |
|---|---|
| Self assessment/payment of corporation tax | 3, 4, 15, 61, 62 |
| Schedule D adjustments | 5, 6, 7, 8, 9, 57, 58 |
| Capital allowances on plant and machinery | 11, 13, 57, 59 |
| Industrial buildings allowances | 10, 11, 12, 60 |
| Shadow ACT | 2, 13, 14, 39, 43, 44, 46, 47, 59 |
| Computation of corporation tax payable | 1, 2, 4, 13, 14, 34, 57, 59 |
| Loan relationships | 14, 15, 34, 46, 57, 58, 60 |
| Corporation tax losses | 16, 17, 39, 41 |
| Benefits in kind | 24, 25, 26, 27, 28, 56, 58, 60 |
| PAYE and NICs | 25, 56, 58, 60 |
| Group relief | 30, 31, 32, 34, 42 |
| Overseas aspects of corporate tax | 32, 43, 44, 45, 46, 47, 48, 61 |
| VAT | 32, 33, 40, 45, 48, 51, 52, 53, 59, 61, 62, 63 |
| Chargeable gains groups | 35, 36, 37, 38, 39, 40, 62 |
| Computing chargeable gains/allowable losses | 19, 20, 21, 22, 23, 36, 37, 38, 55, 62 |
| Chargeable gains: rollover/holdover reliefs | 19, 22, 23, 35, 36, 37, 38, 55, 62 |
| Chargeable gains on shares and securities | 19, 20, 21, 22, 23, 36, 38, 55 |
| Financing through debt or equity | 15 |

BPP PUBLISHING

## THE EXAM PAPER

### Format of the paper

|  |  | Number of marks |
|---|---|---|
| Section A | Objective test questions | 14 |
| Section B | One compulsory scenario style question | 46 |
| Section C | Two questions from four | 40 |
|  |  | 100 |

Time allowed: 3 hours

### Analysis of the pilot paper

The analysis below shows the topics included in the Pilot paper for *Business Tax* .

*Section A*
7 objective test questions worth 2 marks each

*Section B*

2    Scenario style question involving the computation of a CT liability, payment dates and CTSA obligations.

*Section C*

3    Calculation of benefits in kind. PAYE code numbers.
4    Capital allowances on plant and machinery. Industrial buildings allowance.
5    Chargeable gains including holdover relief.
6    Double tax relief. Controlled foreign companies.

This paper forms mock exam 2 at the end of the Kit, so only an outline of its contents is shown here.

### The examiner

The examiner is Thomas Docherty. He has been setting the old syllabus examinations for many years. He wrote an article entitled 'Reformation of corporation tax' for the March 2000 edition of *CIMA student*. We recommend you read this article.

Syllabus guidance notes for the 2001 Business Tax examinations have been published in the December 2000 edition of *CIMA Insider*. It is very important that you read these guidance notes.

# WHAT THE EXAMINER MEANS

The table below has been prepared by CIMA to help you interpret exam questions.

| Learning objective | Verbs used | Definition |
|---|---|---|
| **1 Knowledge**<br>What you are expected to know | • List<br><br>• State<br><br>• Define | • Make a list of<br><br>• Express, fully or clearly, the details of/facts of<br>• Give the exact meaning of |
| **2 Comprehension**<br>What you are expected to understand | • Describe<br><br>• Distinguish<br>• Explain<br>• Identify<br><br>• Illustrate | • Communicate the key features of<br><br>• Highlight the differences between<br>• Make clear or intelligible/state the meaning of<br>• Recognise, establish or select after consideration<br>• Use an example to describe or explain something |
| **3 Application**<br>Can you apply your knowledge? | • Apply<br>• Calculate/compute<br>• Demonstrate<br><br>• Prepare<br>• Reconcile<br>• Solve<br>• Tabulate | • To put to practical use<br>• To ascertain or reckon mathematically<br>• To prove the certainty or to exhibit by practical means<br>• To make or get ready for use<br>• To make or prove consistent/compatible<br>• Find an answer to<br>• Arrange in a table |
| **4 Analysis**<br>Can you analyse the detail of what you have learned? | • Analyse<br><br>• Categorise<br>• Compare and contrast<br><br>• Construct<br>• Discuss<br>• Interpret<br>• Produce | • Examine in detail the structure of<br><br>• Place into a defined class or division<br>• Show the similarities and/or differences between<br>• To build up or complete<br>• To examine in detail by argument<br>• To translate into intelligible or familiar terms<br>• To create or bring into existence |
| **5 Evaluation**<br>Can you use your learning to evaluate, make decisions or recommendations? | • Advise<br><br>• Evaluate<br><br>• Recommend | • To counsel, inform or notify<br><br>• To appraise or assess the value of<br><br>• To advise on a course of action |

## HOW TO PASS PAPER 5

### Revising with this Kit

*A confidence boost*

To boost your morale and to give yourself a bit of confidence, **start** your practice and revision with a topic that you find **straightforward**.

*Diagnosis*

Several banks of **objective test questions** are included within this Kit. Use these questions as a **diagnostic tool**: if you get lots of them wrong go back to your BPP Study Text and do some revision; if you get the majority of them right, move on to any **preparation questions** included for the syllabus area. These provide you with a firm foundation from which to attempt exam-standard questions.

*Key questions*

Then try as many as possible of the **exam-standard questions**. Obviously the more questions you do, the more likely you are to pass the exam. But at the very least you should attempt the **key questions** that are highlighted in the questions and answer checklist/index at the front of the Kit. Even if you are short of time, you must prepare answers to these questions if you want to pass the exam - they incorporate the key techniques and concepts underpinning *Business Taxation* and they cover the principal areas of the syllabus.

*No cheating*

Produce **full answers** under **timed conditions**; practising exam technique is just as important as recalling knowledge. Don't cheat by looking at the answer. Look back at your notes or at your BPP Study Text instead. Produce answer plans if you are running short of time.

*Imagine you're the marker*

It's a good idea to actually **mark your answers**. Don't be tempted to give yourself marks for what you meant to put down, or what you would have put down if you had time. And don't get despondent if you didn't do very well. Refer to the **topic index** and try another question that covers the same subject.

*Ignore them at your peril*

Always read the **Pass marks** in the answers. They are there to help you.

*Trial run for the big day*

Then, when you think you can successfully answer questions on the whole syllabus, attempt the **two mock exams** at the end of the Kit. You will get the most benefit by sitting them under strict exam conditions, so that you gain experience of the four vital exam processes.

- Selecting questions
- Deciding on the order in which to attempt them
- Managing your time
- Producing answers

## Tackling objective test questions

Of the total marks available for this paper, objective test questions comprise 14 per cent.

The objective test questions (OTs) in your exam contain four possible answers. You have to **choose the option that best answers the question**. The three incorrect options are called distracters. There is a skill in answering OTs quickly and correctly. By practising OTs you can develop this skill, giving you a better chance of passing the exam.

You may wish to follow the approach outlined below, or you may prefer to adapt it.

*Step 1.*    Skim read all the OTs and identify what appear to be the easier questions.

*Step 2.*    Attempt each question - **starting with the easier questions** identified in Step 1. Read the question thoroughly. You may prefer to work out the answer before looking at the options, or you may prefer to look at the options at the beginning. Adopt the method that works best for you.

*Step 3.*    Read the four options and see if one matches your own answer. Be careful with numerical questions, as the distracters are designed to match answers that incorporate common errors. Check that your calculation is correct. Have you followed the requirement exactly? Have you included every stage of the calculation?

*Step 4.*    You may find that none of the options matches your answer.

- Re-read the question to ensure that you understand it and are answering the requirement

- Eliminate any obviously wrong answers

- Consider which of the remaining answers is the most likely to be correct and select the option

*Step 5.*    If you are still unsure make a note and continue to the next question. You have an average 3.5 minutes per objective test question. Some questions will take you longer to answer than others. Try to reduce the average time per question, to allow yourself to revisit problem questions at the end of the exam.

*Step 6.*    Revisit unanswered questions. When you come back to a question after a break you often find you are able to answer it correctly straight away. If you are still unsure have a guess. You are not penalised for incorrect answers, so **never leave a question unanswered!**

After extensive practice and revision of OTs, you may find that you recognise a question when you sit the exam. Be aware that the detail and/or requirement may be different. If the question seems familiar read the requirement and options carefully - do not assume that it is identical.

## Tackling scenario based questions

Part B of your examination will contain a compulsory scenario based question.

Start by reading the question through carefully so that you know what you are required to do. Remember that there are presentation marks for this question, so if the requirements ask for a letter make sure you produce a letter, etc.

If the question is broken down into parts make sure that you allocate your time spent on each part carefully. Do not spend too long on any one area.

If possible, ensure you attempt any marks that you find easy first. This will boost your confidence. You can then look at the harder aspects of the question.

## Topics no longer in the syllabus

Are you taking Paper 5 because you **failed old syllabus Paper 12** *Business tax*? If this is the case, be aware that the following topics are no longer in the syllabus.

     (i)   Income tax computations
    (ii)  Schedule D Case I basis of assessment for individuals
   (iii)  Calculation of capital gains for individuals
   (iv)  Capital gains tax taper relief for individuals

You will need to take great care if you have an old syllabus textbook as much of the coverage will relate to the above topics.

We recommend that you purchase a copy of the BPP Study Text that was written specifically for Paper 5 *Business Taxation*. The Paper 5 Text is also fully up to date for the Finance Act 2000.

# USEFUL WEBSITES

The websites below provide additional sources of information of relevance to your studies for *Business Tax.*

- www.bpp.com

  This website provides information about the courses and publications offered by BPP.

- www.cimaglobal.com

  This website provides a wealth of information about CIMA's examinations.

- www.inlandrevenue.gov.uk

  This website includes information covering all aspects of tax and national insurance.

## SYLLABUS MINDMAP

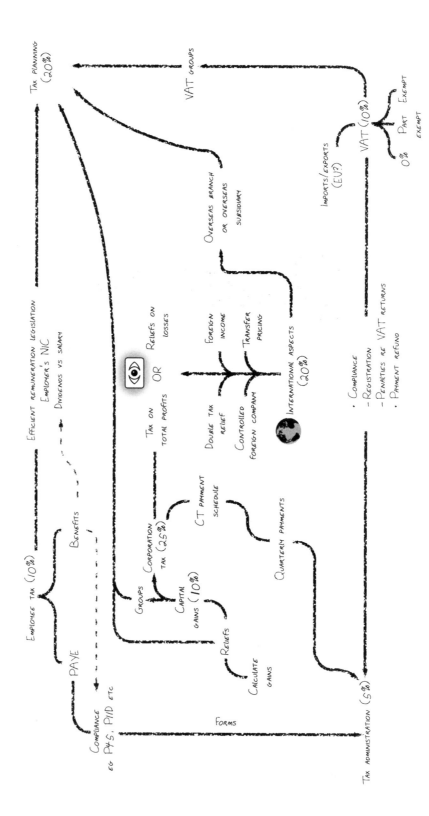

# Questions

**Corporate tax**

Questions 1 to 18 cover corporate tax, the subject of Part A of the BPP study text for paper 5.

## 1   PREPARATION QUESTION: CORPORATION TAX COMPUTATION

Abel Ltd, a UK trading company with no associated companies, produced the following results for the year ended 31 March 2001.

|  | £ |
|---|---|
| *Income* | |
| Adjusted trading profit | 244,000 |
| Rental income | 15,000 |
| Bank deposit interest accrued (non-trading investment) | 4,000 |
| Capital gains:   25 September 2000 | 35,000 |
|                          28 March 2001 | 7,000 |
| (There were capital losses of £8,000 brought forward at 1 April 2000) | |
| Loan interest accrued (non-trading investment net of 20% tax) | 800 |
| Dividends from UK companies (including notional tax credits – June 2000) | 15,000 |
| | |
| *Charges paid* | |
| Patent royalties (gross) | 6,000 |
| Charitable covenant | 1,000 |
| | |
| *Dividend paid* | |
| 24 July 2000 | 48,800 |

There was no surplus ACT brought forward on 1 April 2000.

*Required*

(a)   Compute the mainstream corporation tax (MCT) payable by Abel Ltd for the above accounting period.

(b)   Advise the directors of the effect on the company's tax liability of their decision to sell the above asset on 28 March 2001.

**Approaching the question**

1    In working out a company's profits chargeable to corporation tax (PCTCT), we must bring together all taxable profits, including gains. You must therefore start by drawing up a working, and picking out from the question all relevant profit figures.

2    Once you have found the PCTCT, you can consider the rate of tax. You should find that small companies marginal relief applies. If you do not, look carefully to see whether you have missed anything.

3    You must then look for deductions from the tax after marginal relief. Are there any in this case?

4    Having completed your computation, you should move on to part (b). The answer will become clear if you remember that everyone would like to pay less tax, and to pay their tax later.

## 2   BERTIE LTD                                                                                                       *36 mins*

Bertie Ltd, a company resident in the United Kingdom, has owned 80% of the ordinary share capital of Wooster Ltd (also UK-resident) since 1992. Both companies make up accounts annually to 30 September.

The information listed below relates to Bertie Ltd's 12 month accounting period ended 30 September 2000.

3

|  | £'000 |
|---|---|
| *Income* | |
| Trading profit (adjusted for tax) | 480 |
| Rents receivable | 18 |
| Loan interest (gross; non-trading investment) | 20 |
| Building society interest (non-trading investment) | 8 |
| Capital gains | 99 |
| Dividends received from UK companies (cash amount received in September 2000) | 27.9* |
| *Charges paid (gross)* | |
| Patent royalties (paid May) | 12 |
| Charitable covenant (paid June under the gift aid scheme) | 3 |
| *Dividend paid* | |
| May 2000 | 221.6 |

* This does not include any dividend from Wooster Ltd

All loan interest accruing in the year was received in the year.

Surplus ACT of £80,000 was brought forward at the start of the year.

*Required*

Compute the mainstream corporation tax (MCT) payable by Bertie Ltd for the above accounting period, showing clearly your calculation and treatment of advance corporation tax (ACT). **20 Marks**

3   **TROG PLC**  *36 mins*

Trog plc had taxable profits of £510,000 for its year ended 31 March 2001. It has three wholly owned subsidiaries. Bilbo Limited is dormant, Baggins Inc is a trading company resident in Canada and Sylvester Limited is a trading company which was purchased during the current accounting period.

Trog plc paid corporation tax at the full rate in the year ended 31 March 2000.

*Required*

Prepare notes for a meeting with the company's finance director, explaining when Trog plc will have to pay its corporation tax liability for the year ended 31 March 2001, when the self assessment return must be filed and what penalties might be imposed if it is late. **20 Marks**

4   **PREPARATION QUESTION: QUARTERLY RETURNS**

H Ltd, a company with one subsidiary, commenced trading in 1985 and has the following results for the year ended 31 March 2001.

|  | £ |
|---|---|
| *Income* | |
| Adjusted trading profit (after deduction of debenture interest) | 214,000 |
| Debenture interest received on 30 June 2000 (non-trading investment) | 5,000 (gross sum) |
| Chargeable gains | 12,000 |
| Dividends received from UK companies on 30 November 2000 | 5,062 |
| *Outgoings* | |
| Debenture interest paid (trading loan relationship) | |
| 30 September 2000 | 3,000 (gross sum) |
| 31 March 2001 | 3,000 (gross sum) |

At 1 April 2000 there were unrelieved capital losses brought forward of £15,000.

None of the payments noted above were made to or by the subsidiary.

All debenture interest accruing during the year was either paid or received during the year.

*Required*

Compute the amounts of income tax and corporation tax payable or repayable for the year ended 31 March 2001, stating in all cases the dates of payment.

**Approaching the question**

1    Start by setting up the pro forma, with plenty of space for each return period.

2    Always put down all the amounts of *tax* on income, interest and charges first, then work out the payments and repayments.

3    An *adjusted* trading profit will take account of profits and losses on *trading* loan relationships.

4    Not all companies have to pay their corporation tax by quarterly instalments. Does this one?

5    **PREPARATION QUESTION: SUNDRY ADJUSTMENTS**

Advise the management of a limited company as to the consequences for corporation tax purposes of the following transactions which have occurred during its last accounting period.

(a)    Loan interest of £500 was received. The borrower advised that tax had been deducted from the interest. The loan was a non-trading investment.

(b)    £100,000 was received from the sale of a factory in respect of which capital allowances had been claimed. The factory was purchased new and first used in 1986. It had always been used as a factory.

(c)    Defalcations of cash by staff have been discovered in the sum of £8,000, of which £5,000 was attributable to junior staff and the balance to a member of the board of directors.

(d)    Additional retail premises were acquired for £40,000, which was well below normal market value due to the dilapidated state of these premises. Repairs and renewals expenditure of £60,000 had to be incurred.

(e)    Expenditure totalling £128,000 was incurred in entertaining the company's own staff, customers' staff and representatives from both UK and foreign business agencies.

**Approaching the question**

1    You can deal with each item separately, not worrying about the other items. The important thing is to state the treatment of each item clearly.

2    The tax deducted from the loan interest is income tax, but companies pay corporation tax instead. We need a treatment which will effectively substitute the latter tax for the former.

3    Capital allowances are not the only tax aspect of the sale of the factory to consider.

4    With the defalcations, the position of the guilty party is relevant. Directors run the business, and are therefore treated differently from junior staff.

5    With the retail premises, there is a legal case of particular relevance.

6    When entertaining expenditure is incurred, the tax treatment depends on who was entertained.

6   **PREPARATION QUESTION: CAPITAL AND REVENUE**

In taxation, the distinction between capital and revenue expenditure is crucial.

*Required*

Indicate how this distinction is applied when dealing with items appearing in a company's profit and loss account, supporting your answer by reference to relevant case law.

**Approaching the question**

1   Start by outlining the distinction. Why does it matter if expenditure is capital or if a profit is a capital gain?

2   Then explain what expenditure is likely to be treated as capital, giving some examples. A good area is repairs and improvements.

3   Cite cases by name if you can, but always make sure you outline the facts and show clearly why the case is relevant.

4   Finally, consider what makes a profit a capital gain.

7   **WOODCOCK PLC (11/94)**                                                              *36 mins*

The following items appeared in the profit and loss account of Woodcock plc for its accounting year ended 31 March 2001.

*Expenditure*

(a)   Included in the repairs figure was £5,900 spent on installing windows in a recently-acquired warehouse. Before being acquired by Woodcock plc, this building had been severely damaged in a fire and the previous owners had not been insured.

(b)   Included in wages was an amount of £40,000 paid to a manager who had been made redundant due to a contraction of the trade. His statutory redundancy entitlement was £8,000 and the remainder of the payment was gratuitous.

(c)   Included in the salaries figure was the salary of a marketing executive who, for the whole of the above year, had been seconded to work for a national charity.

(d)   A covenant of £3,000 was paid to Oxfam.

(e)   Included in the motor expenses were the following annual leasing costs.

   £8,000 in respect of a Jaguar car costing £24,000
   £9,400 in respect of a Mercedes car costing £28,000

   These cars were first leased in 1999.

(f)   A loss of £21,000 was sustained as a result of a fraud carried out by a stores manager.

*Income*

(g)   £8,000 was recovered from an insurance company in respect of the costs of repairing an office which had been damaged in a fire. The costs of repair had been incurred by the company during the year to 31 March 2000 and had been allowed as a deduction in that year's accounts.

(h)   An amount of £20,000 was received by Woodcock plc as a result of advice it gave to an overseas subsidiary. This advice involved instructing its staff in certain manufacturing processes which had been developed by the staff of Woodcock plc.

*Required*

Indicate how each of the above items would be treated in arriving at the adjusted Schedule D Case I profit of Woodcock plc for the above accounting period. For each item you should state whether the amount should be added to the reported profit (which is *not* given), or subtracted from the profit, or left unadjusted.

Quote the authority for each of your answers, including case law where appropriate.

**20 Marks**

8    **TRUNK LTD (11/95)**                                                *36 mins*

The profit and loss account of Trunk Ltd, a manufacturing company, for the year ended 31 March 2001 showed a loss of £42,000 after accounting for the under-noted items.

| Note | Expenditure | £ | £ | Income | £ |
|---|---|---|---|---|---|
| (1) | Premium on lease | | 2,000 | | |
| | Depreciation | | 9,500 | Discount received | 3,200 |
| | Patent fees (not royalties) | | 4,000 | Insurance recovery re flood | |
| | Debenture interest (gross: | | | damage to stock | 6,500 |
| |   trading relationship) | | 8,000 | Rents received | 10,000 |
| | Loss on sale of lorry | | 6,000 | Gain on sale of plant | 7,400 |
| | | | | | |
| | Bad debts: | | | | |
| | Amounts written off | 4,000 | | | |
| | Increase special provision | 2,000 | | | |
| | | 6,000 | | | |
| | *Less:* | | | | |
| | Reduction general provision | 1,000 | | | |
| | | | 5,000 | | |

| Note | Expenditure | £ |
|---|---|---|
| (2) | Entertainment expenses | 2,600 |
| | Legal fees: | |
| | Re new lease | 3,200 |
| | Re recovery of loan to former employee | 1,200 |
| | Re employees' service contracts | 600 |
| (3) | General expenses | 4,000 |
| (4) | Repairs and renewals | 6,400 |

Capital allowances for the accounting period were agreed at £7,160.

*Notes*

(1)   This represents the amount written off in respect of a premium of £20,000 paid by the company on being granted a ten-year lease on its premises on 1 April 2000.

(2)   Entertainment consists of expenditure on:

| | £ |
|---|---|
| Entertaining customers | 1,200 |
| Staff dance (40 people) | 800 |
| Gifts to customers of food hampers | 600 |

(3)   General expenses comprise:

| | £ |
|---|---|
| Penalty for late VAT return | 2,200 |
| Parking fines on company cars | 300 |
| Fees for employees attending courses | 1,500 |

(4) Included in this figure for repairs is an amount of £5,000 incurred in installing new windows in a recently-acquired second-hand warehouse. This building had suffered fire damage resulting in all of its windows being blown out shortly before being acquired by Trunk Ltd. Other repairs were of a routine nature.

*Required*

Compute the adjusted Schedule D Case I figure for the above period.

Your answer should show clearly your reasons for your treatment of each of the above items including those items not included in your computation.    **20 Marks**

9    **SCHEDULE D ADJUSTMENTS (5/97)**    *36 mins*

An examination of the draft accounts of your company for the year ended 31 March 2001 reveals the following details in respect of specific items of expenditure and income. The draft accounts showed a profit of £290,000.

EXPENDITURE

(a) Throughout the year, two of the directors were seconded to work elsewhere. One worked for Oxfam - a leading charity - and his salary , paid by your company, was £22,000. The other worked for a subsidiary company in the group and his salary, also paid by your company, was £24,000.

(b) Damages of £30,000 were paid to a customer who was injured by a falling crate while visiting your factory. Only £18,000 was recovered from your public liability insurers.

(c) During the year the company purchased freehold offices for £40,000. Your chief engineer estimated that it would cost £2,000 to get them ready for use. In the event it cost £12,000. The amount spent purchasing the offices was capitalised but the repair expenditure of £12,000 was deducted in the profit and loss account.

(d) Bad debts were written off amounting to £6,000. The appropriate ledger account for the year showed:

|  | £ |  | £ |
|---|---|---|---|
| Trade debts written off | 8,000 | Balances b/fwd: |  |
| Employee loans written off | 2,000 | Special provision | 10,000 |
| Balances c/fwd: |  | General provisions | 8,000 |
| Special provision | 12,000 | Bad debts recovered | 3,000 |
| General provision | 5,000 | Profit and loss account | 6,000 |
|  | 27,000 |  | 27,000 |

(e) Because of an overall contraction in trade, a supervisor was made redundant and given a severance payment of £18,000. His statutory redundancy entitlement was £11,000.

INCOME

(f) During the year the company obtained recoveries from its insurers amounting to £32,000. These related to damage caused and repairs completed in the year to 31 March 2000 and comprised:

|  | £ |
|---|---|
| In respect of repairs to the general office | 18,000 |
| In respect of repairs to property let by the company to another firm | 14,000 |
|  | 32,000 |

(g) Goods were sold to a subsidiary in the Caribbean for £80,000. Had they been sold to a UK customer the price would have been £120,000.

*Required*

Compute the adjusted Schedule D Case I profit starting with the profit of £290,000 shown by the accounts. Give reasons for your adjustments, quoting case law where appropriate.

**20 Marks**

10    **F LTD (11/00)**    *36 mins*

F Ltd is a large manufacturing company resident in the UK. It makes up accounts to 31 March each year.

(a)    Early in 2000, the directors of F Ltd were considering purchasing one of four possible second-hand industrial buildings, each of which had a purchase price of £200,000. The buildings would be purchased on 1 April 2000 and be brought into use immediately. Only ONE of these buildings would be purchased.

Information regarding the history of the four possible buildings is as follows:

|  | Bought by the original owner for £ | First brought into use for a qualifying purpose on |
|---|---|---|
| Building 1 | 180,000 | 1 April 1994 |
| Building 2 | 190,000 | 1 April 1975 |
| Building 3 | 160,000 | 1 April 1976 |
| Building 4 | 240,000 | 1 April 1997 |

(b)    The company had administration premises located in an enterprise zone and had purchased for £100,000 a factory in that zone during the year ended 31 March 2000. It claimed initial allowance of 60% of the cost. It intends claiming the maximum possible amount in future years.

(c)    During its accounting period to 31 March 2001, it sold for £70,000 a factory which had originally cost £80,000 on 1 April 1996, on which date it was brought into use for a qualifying purpose. The building continued to be used for such a purpose until 31 March 1999. On 1 April 1999 it started to be used for a non-qualifying purpose and that use remained until it was sold on 31 March 2001.

*Required*

Compute the maximum industrial buildings allowances (IBAs) which may be claimed by F Ltd for the year ended 31 March 2001, assuming the building generating the highest amount of IBAs in the year ended 31 March 2001 was purchased. The effect of the disposal of the building at (c) above should be reflected in your final answer.    **20 Marks**

11    **PREPARATION QUESTION: PLANT AND A FACTORY**

Freddie Ltd prepared accounts for the ten month period to 31 October 2001.

The following capital expenditure was incurred in this trading period.

(i)    30 April 2001        New computer equipment costing £2,500.

(ii)    1 June 2001         New motor car costing £16,000, secondhand motor car costing £5,000.

(iii)   2 September 2001    New plant costing £32,400, secondhand plant costing £33,442, secondhand factory and land costing £50,000 (including land £15,000) which had been purchased new by the original owner on 5 December 1986 for £10,000 (including land £2,500), and had always been used as a factory.

(iv) 31 October 2001     Extension to the factory built for £222,000.

Prior to 1 January 2001, all equipment was leased so there were no tax written down values brought forward on this date.

Freddie Ltd's business qualifies as a small enterprise for capital allowance purposes.

*Required*

(a) Calculate the maximum capital allowances which can be claimed by Freddie Ltd in the first accounting period.

(b) Set out the amount of tax benefit the reliefs calculated in (a) would yield and when this benefit would be obtained.

(c) Outline the relief available to Freddie Ltd in respect of expenditure on office accommodation.

Assume tax rates and allowances for FY 2000 throughout this period.

### Approaching the question

1   You should first read through the question, and note all the different types of asset involved.

2   You can then plan how your answer will look. Because there is only one accounting period, there is no real need for a multi-column computation.

3   Each type of asset should then be tackled separately. By breaking the question down into small pieces in this way, it becomes much more manageable.

4   Note the length of the accounting period. Will this affect WDAs or FYAs?

12   **R LTD (11/98)**                                          *36 mins*

R Ltd, a UK-resident manufacturing company, making up accounts each year to 31 March, provides the following information in respect of its various premises used in its trade.

FACTORY A

This was purchased new on 1 April 1975 for £80,000.

FACTORY B

This was acquired second-hand on 1 April 1991 for £60,000. The seller had bought it new on 1 April 1985 at a cost of £50,000.

FACTORY C

This was purchased new on 10 July 2000, the cost comprising:

|  | £ |
|---|---|
| Land | 25,000 |
| Preparing site | 10,000 |
| Factory building | 100,000 |
| Office facilities | 25,000 |

FACTORY D

This had been purchased on 1 April 1999 in an Enterprise Zone for £120,000. In the year to 31 March 2000, R Ltd had claimed allowances of £60,000: the company now wished to claim the maximum possible in the year to 31 March 2001.

FACTORY E

On 31 March 2001 R Ltd sold this factory for £90,000. It had been bought on 1 April 1993 for £70,000. The factory had been used for non-qualifying purposes from 1 April 1998 to 31 March 2000 but reverted to industrial use on 1 April 2000.

*Note.* This is a building on which there was a 20% initial allowance available at the date of purchase.

*Required*

(a)  Compute the Industrial Buildings Allowances (IBA) available to R Ltd for its year ended 31 March 2001 (net of any balancing charges arising).  **16 Marks**

(b)  Advise the directors of the IBA position in regard to factories which they are considering leasing rather than buying.  **4 Marks**

**Total Marks = 20**

13  **H LTD**  *36 mins*

H Ltd has owned 100% of the share capital of S Ltd for several years. Both companies are trading companies resident in the United Kingdom.

The following information relates to the ten-month accounting period to 30 September 2000 of H Ltd:

| | £ |
|---|---|
| INCOME | |
| Adjusted trading profit (before capital allowances) | 77,125 |
| Bank interest | 4,500 |
| Capital gains | 12,000 |
| Debenture interest (non-trading investment) | |
| - 25 February 2000 (gross) | 8,000 |
| Patent royalties received - 30 June 2000 (gross) | 6,000 |
| | |
| Charges paid | |
| Charitable covenant - 31 May 2000 | 2,000 |
| | |
| Dividend paid - 30 June 2000 | 40,000 |

H Ltd has surplus ACT brought forward on 1 December 1999 of £50,000.

H Ltd's balances brought forward at 1 December 1999 for capital allowances purposes were:

| *General pool* | *Car pool* | *Expensive car* |
|---|---|---|
| £38,000 | £16,000 | £14,000 |

Machinery was sold for £5,000 (original cost £9,000) on 31.12.99 and new desks were bought for £1,875 on 1 August 2000. On 1 August 2000 the expensive car was traded in for £10,000 against the cost of a new car costing £10,400.

All amounts accrued were paid or received in the year.

*Required*

(a)  Compute the maximum capital allowances which H Ltd may claim for the ten month accounting period to 30 September 2000.  **4 Marks**

(b)  Compute the tax payable by or repayable to H Ltd for the ten month accounting period to 30 September 2000, showing clearly your treatment of advance corporation tax (ACT) and income tax.  **16 Marks**

The company qualifies as a small or medium sized enterprise for capital allowance purposes.

**Total Marks = 20**

### 14   MAJOR LTD                                                   *36 mins*

Major Ltd, a trading company resident in the United Kingdom, acquired 80% of the ordinary shares of Minor Ltd, another UK trading company, during December 1999. Until 2000 Major Ltd made up accounts each year to 30 April, but decided to change its accounting date to 31 December. The information below relates to the eight month period to 31 December 2000:

|  | £ |
|---|---|
| INCOME | |
| Adjusted trading profit | 180,000 |
| Rents received *less* expenses | 30,000 |
| Loan interest received (gross figure) (see Note 1) | 24,000 |
| Capital gains | 40,000 |
| Franked investment income (FII) (received June 2000) | 20,000 |

|  | £ |
|---|---|
| PAYMENTS | |
| Patent royalties (gross figure – including £3,000 accrued) | 18,000 |
| Charitable covenant (paid September 2000) | 3,000 |
| Loan interest paid (see Note 2) | 30,000 |
| Dividend paid 30 July 2000 | 80,000 |

The company had surplus ACT b/f on 1 May 2000 of £34,000.

*Notes*

1   The loan interest was received in respect of a loan of £100,000 made by the company to Z Ltd, a main supplier of materials to Major Ltd. The directors of Major Ltd are concerned about the financial position of Z Ltd, but have decided to take no action at present.

2   The loan interest paid was to a UK bank in respect of funds raised to acquire the company's 80% interest in Minor Ltd in 1999.

*Required*

(a)   Compute the mainstream corporation tax (MCT) payable by Major Ltd in respect of the above accounting period.                                        **16 Marks**

(b)   Advise the directors of Major Ltd of the taxation implications of the loan to Z Ltd proving irrecoverable.                                               **4 Marks**

**Total Marks = 20**

### 15   FINANCING EXPANSION                                         *36 mins*

The directors of M Ltd, a medium-sized unquoted company engaged in manufacturing, have decided to embark on a major expansion of the business.

The company has a significant amount of unissued share capital and, to finance the expansion, the directors have been considering issuing further shares. They have also considered raising loan capital, using as security identified pieces of valuable property owned by the company.

M Ltd has always prepared accounts to 31 March each year and to date all returns have been filed on time. However, one of the directors is wondering what would happen if M Ltd was late in filing its corporation tax return.

*Required*

Draft a report dated 19 May 2000, to the board

 **12**

(a) Setting out the taxation implications for the company under each of the alternative methods of raising finance.

Your report should also identify any taxation implications for the providers of this finance.

**15 Marks**

(b) Advising the directors of the date by which M Ltd must file its corporation tax return for the year ended 31 March 2001 and of any penalties that may arise for late filing.

**5 Marks**

**Total Marks = 20**

## 16   PREPARATION QUESTION: CARRY-BACK CLAIMS

MA Ltd, a company with no associated companies, provides the following information in respect of the two 12 month accounting periods ended 30 September 2000.

|  | 12 months to 30.9.99 | 12 months to 30.9.00 |
|---|---|---|
| *Income* | £ | £ |
| Adjusted trading profits (losses) | 300,000 | (170,000) |
| Schedule A income | 4,000 | 2,000 |
| Bank deposit interest accrued (non-trading investment) | 5,000 | 4,000 |
| Chargeable gains (losses) | (6,000) | 12,000 |
| Dividends (including tax credits) | | |
| 30 June 1999 | 4,000 | |
| 30 June 2000 | | 8,000 |
| | | |
| *Charges paid* | | |
| Patent royalties (gross) | 9,000 | 4,000 |
| Donation under the gift aid scheme - 30 June 2000 | – | 1,000 |
| | | |
| *Dividends paid* | | |
| 30 April 1999 | 18,600 | |
| 30 April 2000 | | 16,000 |

There was no surplus ACT b/f on 1.10.98.

*Required*

(a) Compute the MCT payable by MA Ltd in respect of the year ended 30 September 1999, before any claims are made in respect of the loss incurred in the year ended 30 September 2000.

(b) Compute the amount of corporation tax repayable in respect of the year ended 30 September 1999, assuming all possible claims are made at the earliest opportunity in respect of the loss for the year ended 30 September 2000.

(c) Show any amounts available for carry forward at 30 September 2000.

**Approaching the question**

1    The first part of this question requires the computation of MCT for an accounting period that straddles two financial years. As tax rates change between the two financial years, it will be essential to split the accounting period for the purpose of computing corporation tax.

2    You must then consider loss relief. It is clear that s 393A(1) relief is at issue, but you cannot carry back all the loss. Remember that a carry back can only be done after a claim against current year profits.

3    Consider which amounts can be carried forward and which amounts will remain unrelieved.

17    **MACRO LTD (11/95)**                                                                  *36 mins*

Macro Ltd, a UK-resident company with no associated companies, has sustained a significant trading loss for its most recent year to 31 March 2001. The company ceased trading on 31 March 2001 and the directors wish to relieve as much of the loss as possible.

The results for the four most recent years are tabulated below.

|  | 31 March 1998 £'000 | 31 March 1999 £'000 | 31 March 2000 £'000 | 31 March 2001 £'000 |
|---|---|---|---|---|
| *Income:* | | | | |
| Schedule D Case I | 140 | 130 | 80 | (354) |
| Bank interest (non-trading investment) | 8 | 6 | 4 | 2 |
| Capital gain | 10 | | 40 | |
| Capital loss | | (20) | | |
| Dividends received from UK companies (cash amounts) (received June each year) | 6 | 3 | 6.975 | 4 |
| *Charges paid (gross):* | | | | |
| Patent royalties | 4 | 4 | 8 | 6 |
| Charitable covenants | 2 | 2 | 2 | |

*Required*

(a) Compute the amounts of MCT which were paid for each of the three accounting periods to 31 March 1998, 1999 and 2000.                                **6 Marks**

(b) Show the amounts of corporation tax which will be repayable as a result of claiming full relief in respect of the trading loss for the year ended 31 March 2001.    **9 Marks**

(c) Comment briefly on the overall effect of making the loss claim.          **5 Marks**

*Note.* Use FY 2000 tax rates for *all* years but gross up dividends received before 6.4.99 by 100/80.                                                              **Total Marks = 20**

18    **OBJECTIVE TEST QUESTIONS**                                                         *32 mins*

1    ABC Ltd prepares accounts for the 16 months to 30 June 2000. A notice requiring a return for the year ended 30 June 2000 was issued to ABC Ltd on 1 September 2000.

The accounting period(s) for which ABC Ltd must file a tax return is/are

A    12m to 29.2.00
      4m to 30.6.00

B    16m to 30.6.00

C    4m to 30.6.00

D    4m to 30.6.99
      12m to 30.6.00

2    Complete the following sentence

'A company has ___ days from the end of an enquiry to amend its self assessment in accordance with the Revenue's conclusions.'

A    7
B    21
C    30
D    60

3    Zeta Ltd has always made up accounts to 31 December each year. It is a 'large' company. For the year ended 31 December 2001 how much of its corporation tax liability must be paid by instalments?

A    60%
B    72%
C    88%
D    100%

4    If a company's CT liability does not exceed a certain de minimis limit it need not pay its CT tax by instalments.

For an accounting period ending on or after 1 July 2000, this de minimis limit is

A    £10,000
B    £100,000
C    £300,000
D    £1 million

5    Sed Ltd had always prepared accounts to 30 June each year but in 2001 it changed its accounting date to 31 March. Sed Ltd had a CT liability of £510,000 for the nine months to 31 March 2001. What should the first quarterly instalment of corporation tax have been in respect of this period?

A    £91,800
B    £112,200
C    £122,400
D    £149,600

6    Xera Ltd files the return for the year ended 31 December 2000 on 15 January 2002.

What penalty will be charged (if any)?

A    Nil
B    £50
C    £100
D    £200

7    Zil Ltd has a year ended 31 December 2000 during which it is a large company.

Instalments of corporation tax are due on which dates?

A    14.7.2000, 14.10.2000, 14.1.2001, 14.4.2001
B    14.7.2001, 14.10.2001, 14.1.2002, 14.4.2002
C    14.4.2000, 14.7.2000, 14.10.2000, 14.1.2001
D    31.3.2000, 30.6.2000, 30.9.2000, 31.12.2000

8    A company has a corporation tax liability for the eight month period to 30 November 2001 of £2,000,000. Previously 31 March was the accounting date.

How much corporation tax must be paid on 14 October 2001?

A    Nil (tax not due on this date)
B    £440,000
C    £540,000
D    £660,000

9   Chorly Ltd had profits chargeable to corporation tax of £300,000 for the year to 31.3.01.

On 14 March 2001 it paid a dividend of £90,000.

On 1.4.00 surplus ACT of £50,000 was brought forward.

How much ACT remains to carry forward at 1.4.01?

A    £nil
B    £12,500
C    £22,500
D    £10,250

**Total Marks = 18**

If you struggled with these objective test questions go back to your BPP Study Text for Paper 5 and revise Chapters 1 to 7 before you tackle the preparation and exam-standard questions in this part.

If you would like a bank of objective test questions which covers a range of syllabus topics, order our MCQ cards using the order form at the back of this Kit.

**Chargeable gains**

Questions 19 to 23 cover chargeable gains, the subject of Part B of the BPP study text for Paper 5.

## 19   PREPARATION QUESTION: A BUILDING AND SHARES

Jolly Cove Ltd, which commenced trading in 1981, makes up its accounts annually to 31 March, and has no associated companies.

During its accounting year ended 31 March 2001 Jolly Cove Ltd disposed of the following assets.

(a)   In June 2000, a non-industrial building was sold for £200,000. It had been purchased in July 1981 for £40,000. The value at 31 March 1982 was £65,000.

(b)   In July 2000, 5,000 shares in Z plc were sold for £27,500. The shares in Z plc had been acquired as follows.

| | |
|---|---|
| August 1980 | 2,000 shares for £3,000 |
| May 1982 | 2,000 shares for £4,000 |
| March 1986 | 2,000 shares for £5,000 |

The value at 31 March 1982 was £1.75 per share.

There were no capital losses brought forward.

Jolly Cove Ltd's taxable profits for the year ended 31 March 2001, excluding capital gains, were £2,000,000.

*Required*

(a)   Calculate the amount of corporation tax payable as a result of the above transactions, stating the due date of payment.

(b)   Advise Jolly Cove Ltd as to the consequences of its replacing the building referred to above with another building costing either £225,000 or alternatively £175,000.

*Indexation factors*

| | | | |
|---|---|---|---|
| March 1982 - June 2000 | 1.141 | April 1985 - March 1986 | 0.020 |
| March 1982 - July 2000 | 1.147 | March 1986 - July 2000 | 0.799 |
| May 1982 - April 1985 | 0.162 | | |

**Approaching the question**

1   The building requires a basic capital gains computation. Note that it was acquired before 31 March 1982, but only do two computations if you think it is worth it.

2   Some of the shares fall into the FA 1985 pool, and some into the 1982 holding. Two separate computations are therefore needed. The FA 1985 pool includes indexation within it, firstly up to its starting point April 1985 and then up to each purchase or sale. The 1982 holding computation deals with indexation separately on each sale, as indexation will always run from March 1982.

3   Part (b) is about rollover relief. Remember that the general rule is that a company which sells an asset and claims rollover relief will still be taxed on the gain immediately, to the extent of the cash it puts into its pocket instead of into the new asset.

**20    BD LIMITED** (5/98)                                                                         *36 mins*

BD Ltd is a UK resident company owning 100% of the shares of a French company, Mince SA. During its accounting period of twelve months to 31 March 2001, it made the following disposals, all during July 2000.

(i)    In July 1992, BD Ltd had acquired a thirty-five year lease at a cost of £48,000. In July 2000, it granted a sub-lease of six years to E Ltd for a premium of £12,000.

*In using this information in your answer, you should show the effect of any Schedule A assessment on the amount of any chargeable gain.*

(ii)   An office was sold in July 2000 for £42,000. This had been acquired in October 1987 as part of a block of six offices which had cost, at that date, a total amount of £100,000. The market value (MV) of the five remaining offices was agreed at £190,000.

(iii)  In May 1980, BD Ltd purchased 20,000 ordinary shares in X Ltd at a cost of £15,000. In July 1992, following a re-organisation of the share capital of X Ltd, BD Ltd received, for each ordinary share then held, one 50p ordinary share and one 50p 6% preference share. The value of these shares on the day following the re-organisation were:

| | |
|---|---|
| 50p ordinary share | £1.80 |
| 50p preference share | £0.80 |

The MV of the original shares at 31 March 1982 can be taken as £1.00 per share.

In July 2000, BD Ltd sold all of the ordinary shares for £75,000.

*Required*

(a)    In each of the above situations, compute the chargeable gain or allowable loss arising.

**16 Marks**

(b)    Assuming that BD Ltd had other chargeable income of £160,000 (but no FII) for the above period, compute the amount of corporation tax (CT) payable on the above gains.

**4 Marks**

Note that in part (b) you are NOT required to compute the total CT payable, only the CT on the chargeable gains.

*Indexation factors*

| | |
|---|---|
| July 1992 – July 2000 | 0.228 |
| October 1987 – July 2000 | 0.657 |
| March 1982 – July 2000 | 1.147 |

**Total Marks = 20**

**21    B LTD** (11/96)                                                                           *36 mins*

(a)    B Ltd, a UK-resident company with no associated companies, trades from several retail stores.

During its year ended 31 March 2001 it made the following disposals:

(i)     *30 September 2000*

A painting which had been hanging in the dining room was sold for £4,200. It had originally cost £7,100 in January 1990.

(ii)    *31 October 2000*

A lease for a retail unit was sold for £100,000. B Ltd had acquired this lease, which had a term of 35 years, in October 1995 at a cost of £45,000.

In addition, you are informed that a warehouse, which had cost £12,000 in October 1978 and which had a market value at 31 March 1982 of £7,000, was destroyed in a fire in December 2000. Unfortunately, the building had been under-insured and the insurers paid only £5,000.

In January 1995, the company had made an election under section 35 of the Taxation of Chargeable Gains Act 1992 (TCGA).

*Required*

Compute the amount to be included in respect of chargeable gains in the company's corporation tax computation for the above chargeable accounting period.

**13 Marks**

(b)  Z Ltd acquired 50,000 shares in X Ltd in June 1988 for £55,000. In January 2001 X Ltd made a rights issue of one share for every five held at £1 per share. Z Ltd did not take up the rights issue and instead sold the rights for £4,980. The market value of each X Ltd share on the first dealing day after the rights issue was £1.80.

*Required*

(i)    Compute the chargeable gain arising as a result of the sale of the rights.

**4 Marks**

(ii)   Show the capital gains tax treatment had the rights been sold for £4,000 rather than for £4,980.                                                      **3 Marks**

*Indexation factors*

| | | | |
|---|---|---|---|
| January 1990 - September 2000 | 0.435 | June 1988 - January 2001 | 0.628 |
| October 1995 - October 2000 | 0.148 | | |

**Total Marks = 20**

22   **V LTD**                                                        *36 mins*

The following information relates to transactions carried out by V Ltd, a UK resident company, during its accounting year ended 31 March 2001.

(a)  In March 1992, the company sold for £250,000 a building which had cost £120,000 in May 1984. Of the proceeds, £210,000 was used to purchase fixed plant and machinery and the maximum possible holdover relief was claimed.

In July 2000 a fire completely destroyed all of this plant, and compensation was received from the company's insurers.

(b)  A new office block was constructed during the year, and the directors decided to dispose of, during July 2000, some of the contents of the previous boardroom, as follows:

(i)    A painting, which had cost £2,000 in January 1980 and which had a market value (MV) at 31 March 1982 of £1,000, was sold at auction for £8,000 on which fees of £200 were paid. A global election for MV at 31 March 1982 had been made by V Ltd on the occasion of a previous disposal in 1991.

(ii)   A pair of matching sculptures were gifted, one to the general manager and the other to his wife who was also an employee. The market value of the pair of sculptures at July 2000 was agreed at £10,000 and they had been bought by the company for £4,000 in May 1992.

(iii)  A table was sold in July 2000 to an individual employee for £3,000, having cost the company £6,500 in June 1990.

19

(c) In July 2000, V Ltd sold 10,000 75p ordinary shares in X Ltd for £60,000. These had been acquired as part of a re-organisation of the share capital of X Ltd in March 1991. In March 1989, V Ltd had purchased 20,000 ordinary £1 shares in X Ltd for £30,000, and in March 1991, these were converted into the following holdings:

|  | *Market value immediately after re-organisation* |
|---|---|
| 15,000 75p ordinary shares | £1.40 per share |
| 8,000 7% £1 preference shares | £1.25 per share |
| £5,000 debentures | At par, ie £5,000 |

*Required*

(a) Compute the chargeable capital gains or allowable losses which will arise as a result of the above transactions. **16 Marks**

(b) Advise the board of any other tax implications arising from the transactions involving staff members, and suggest how these might be dealt with. **4 Marks**

**Total Marks = 20**

*Indexation factors*

| May 1984 | - | March 1992 | 0.536 |
|---|---|---|---|
| March 1982 | - | July 2000 | 1.147 |
| May 1992 | - | July 2000 | 0.224 |
| June 1990 | - | July 2000 | 0.346 |
| March 1989 | - | July 2000 | 0.518 |

**23    P LTD**                                                          *36 mins*

(a) On 25 July 2000, P Ltd sold 25,000 ordinary shares in T Ltd for £150,000. These shares were part of holding of 27,000 shares which had been acquired as follows:

| *Date* | *Shares* | *Cost* |
|---|---|---|
|  |  | £ |
| January 1980 | 3,000 | 3,000 |
| February 1982 | 4,000 | 6,000 |
| January 1984 | 5,000 | 10,000 |
| March 1990 | 10,000 | 50,000 |
| April 1996 | 5,000 | 20,000 |

You are advised that a global election is in place to have all assets owned at 31 March 1982 dealt with at their market value at that date. The market value of each share in T Ltd at 31 March 1982 was £1.20.

*Required*

Compute the chargeable gain arising as a result of this disposal **8 Marks**

(b) The managing director of G Ltd has decided that his company should acquire 80% of the share capital of H Ltd, a company in the same trade. On examining the latest balance sheet of H Ltd, he noted that its premises were valued at £60,000. He considers that this property will be surplus to the company's requirements and that it could be sold for £150,000 once his company has acquired H Ltd thus providing valuable working capital. On making further enquiries he establishes that the property had cost H Ltd £40,000 in March 1991 and that H Ltd had rolled over a previous gain of £10,000 against the cost.

*Required*

On the assumption that H Ltd is acquired in April 2000 and that the property is sold in July 2000, advise the managing director of the amount of additional funds that will be generated, after paying any corporation tax on the resulting gain. H Ltd's other taxable profits will be approximately £350,000 for the year ended 31 March 2001.

**6 Marks**

(c) R Ltd is about to make its first disposals for capital gains tax purposes. In July 2000, it sells two factories as follows:

|  | Date purchased | Cost | Market value at 31 March 1982 | Sold for |
|---|---|---|---|---|
|  |  | £ | £ | £ |
| Factory A | October 1979 | 80,000 | 100,000 | 70,000 |
| Factory B | March 1978 | 37,000 | 50,000 | 120,000 |

*Required*

Advise the board of R Ltd whether a global election for market value (MV) at 31 March 1982 should be made, supporting your advice with detailed computations.

**6 Marks**

*Indexation factors:*

| March 1982 | - | July 2000 | 1.147 | March 1990 | - | April 1996 | 0.257 |
|---|---|---|---|---|---|---|---|
| January 1984 | - | April 1985 | 0.092 | April 1996 | - | July 2000 | 0.117 |
| April 1985 | - | March 1990 | 0.281 | March 1991 | - | July 2000 | 0.298 |

**Total Marks = 20**

## 24 PREPARATION QUESTION: BENEFITS

You have been asked to assist in the completion of forms P11D in respect of the directors of your company for the year 2000/01.

The following benefits are enjoyed by various directors.

(a) A director has had the use of a private house bought by the company for £120,000 in 1996. The director paid all of the house expenses plus the agreed open market annual rental of £2,000. The annual value of the house is £2,000.

(b) A television video system, which had been provided at the start of 1996/97 for the use of a director and which had cost the company £3,500, was taken over by the director on 6 April 2000 for a payment of £600 (its market value at that date).

(c) A director has a loan of £4,000 at 4% interest to enable him to purchase his annual season ticket. This is the only loan he had taken out.

(d) Medical insurance premiums were paid for a director and his family, under a group scheme, at a cost to the company of £800. Had the director paid for this as an individual the cost would have been £1,400.

(e) On 6 September 2000 a director was given the use of a Mercedes car which had cost £24,000 when new in 1995. On the same day his mother, who has no connection with the company, was provided by the company with a brand new Ford car for her private use, costing £10,000. No fuel was provided for this car. The director used the Mercedes for both business and private purposes. He was required to make good the cost of any fuel used for private mileage. His business mileage up to 5 April 2001 is estimated to be 10,000.

(f) On 6 April 2000 the company lent a director a computer costing £3,900 for use at home. The director used the computer for both business and private purposes.

*Required*

Show how each of the above benefits would be quantified for inclusion in the forms P11D. Assume that the official rate of interest is 10%.

**Approaching the question**

1 Work through each benefit separately. Calculate its value before you move on to the next benefit. Watch out for exempt benefits.

2 Remember that any benefit that is only available for part of a year must be time apportioned. This is often the case in exam questions with car and fuel benefits. Is it relevant here?

## 25 MR K

*36 mins*

Mr K is the managing director of Q Ltd. The company provides him with a number of benefits in kind in addition to his salary of £60,000 per annum.

For 2000/01 these benefits comprise:

(a)  *Motor cars*

Mr K was given the use of a Mercedes car which had cost the company £24,000 in August 1999. On 5 August 2000, Mr K was involved in a serious accident in which the Mercedes was totally destroyed. Mr K was injured and did not drive or return to work until 5 October 2000.

Up to 5 August 2000 Mr K had covered 7,200 miles for business purposes.

On his return to work on 5 October 2000, he was provided with a Lexus motor car which cost the company £36,000 and, in the period from 5 October 2000 to 5 April 2001, he covered 8,000 miles for business purposes.

As a result of the car crash, Mr K was found guilty of dangerous driving and the company paid his legal costs and fine amounting to £1,200 with Mr K making a contribution of £300.

Mr K was provided with all fuel by the company, including that used for private mileage. The fuel benefits for 2000/01 for both the cars is £3,200 per annum.

(b)  *Suits*

Mr K was provided, for the whole of the tax year, with two suits of clothes, each costing £800.

(c)  *Housing*

Mr K lived in a house owned by the company, which bought it last year for £125,000. The annual rental value was £8,000 and Mr K paid rent of £5,000 to the company.

In addition to the above, the company provided other benefits to various members of staff, the total cost to the company in 2000/2001 being agreed with the Inland Revenue at £9,600 for the purpose of a PAYE Settlement Arrangement.

The company is currently considering, for the first time, paying annual cash bonuses to its directors.

*Required*

(a)  Compute the total value of the benefits assessable on Mr K for the year 2000/01. Assume the official rate of interest is 6.25%.                                                **12 Marks**

(b)  Compute any additional cost to be met by the company as a result of providing the above benefits.                                                                                    **3 Marks**

(c)  Draft a short memo to the board explaining the method of taxing bonuses paid to directors and indicating how the tax will be accounted for.                                        **5 Marks**

**Total Marks = 20**

26  **CONTRACTS FOR WORK ABROAD AND PAYMENT OF DIVIDENDS**   *36 mins*

(a)  Your company has a number of branches and subsidiaries trading outside the UK.

It is now November 2000 and the board is about to offer contracts to employees resident in the UK and working in UK locations, which will allow them to transfer to foreign locations on a temporary basis, with all of their duties being performed outside the UK.

There are two contracts being offered, one lasting nine months and one lasting 18 months.

**23**

*Required*

Draft a report to the board on the taxation implications, for the employees, of each of the two possible contracts.                                                                                    **15 Marks**

(b)  The board of a rapidly growing unquoted manufacturing company, which is not a close company, seeks your advice, in May 2001.

The taxation implications (for both the company and the employees) of paying by means of dividends those employees who are also shareholders in the company. The dividends would be paid during 2001.

*Required*

Prepare notes indicating the points you would raise in respect of each of the above areas at a preliminary meeting with the board.                                                    **5 Marks**

**Total Marks = 20**

27    **RW LTD**                                                                                          *36 mins*

The board of RW Ltd, a UK-resident company which has recently acquired a passenger railway operation, has decided to offer various benefits to staff members.

Some senior staff, none of whom are directors, will be offered interest-free personal loans. In addition, all members of staff will be offered reduced fares on all of the company's UK scheduled services and the board has indicated that, should the year prove successful for the company, all members of staff will be taken on a trip to Paris on one of the company's trains. No members of the public will be on this train.

The company has recently implemented a wide-ranging training programme for staff members and has agreed to meet the cost of most of the courses, which will be provided by external training firms. On some courses staff members will be required to meet their own costs. None of the courses last more than two weeks.

*Required*

Write a report to the board explaining the taxation implications for both the employees and the company of each of the above proposals.

**Total Marks = 20**

28    **SHARE OPTIONS, BENEFICIAL LOANS AND COMPANY CARS**                         *36 mins*

The directors of your company have decided to offer three forms of benefit to some members of staff. These are approved Share Option Schemes (not involving savings schemes), Beneficial Loans (some of which will be used to assist members of staff to purchases shares in a close company) and Company Cars. The directors seek your advice.

*Required*

(a)  Write a brief report to the board showing the various regulations surrounding share option plans.                                                                                            **5 Marks**

(b)  Prepare an information sheet which the directors can issue to staff. Setting out the various tax implications for staff members in receipt of share options and/or beneficial loans and/or company cars.                                                                                    **15 Marks**

**Total Marks = 20**

## 29   OBJECTIVE TEST QUESTIONS

1   Under Schedule E an expense is, in general, allowed as a deduction from earned income if it meets the definition 'wholly, _____ and _____ incurred in the performance of duties'.

The missing words are:
A   exceptionally and only
B   exclusively and only
C   exclusively and necessarily
D   exceptionally and normally

2   Tax relief is available for travel expenses incurred by an employee working at a temporary location.

What is the definition of 'temporary'?
A   Secondment of indefinite period but exceeding at least one week
B   Secondment expected not to last more than 12 months
C   Secondment expected not to last more than 24 months
D   Secondment expected not to last more than 36 months

3   What is the maximum amount a 40 year old employee earning £100,000 per annum can contribute to an approved occupational pension scheme in 2000/01 on which tax relief can be claimed?

A   £13,770
B   £15,000
C   £18,360
D   No maximum

4   Which of the following payments made on a termination of employment are entirely or partly exempt from tax?
A   Payment for doing extra work during the period of notice
B   Payment in lieu of notice as stated in contract of employment
C   Payment for work done to date
D   Payment on account of injury at work which has resulted in the termination of employment

5   John is the marketing director of Oz Ltd. He was granted an option over 3,000 company shares on 1 May 2001 when the market value of the shares was £5 per share. The option price is £1.50 per share on exercise and 50p per share to be granted the option. The scheme is unapproved and is available for as long as John remains an employee of Oz Ltd.

What is the taxable amount in May 2001 for John?
A   Nil, no tax on grant
B   £9,000
C   £10,500
D   £15,000

6   Which of the following conditions must be satisfied in respect of Company Share Option Plans (CSOP)?

(i)   Shares must be fully paid ordinary shares.

(ii)   The price of the shares must not be less than their market value at the time of the grant of the option.

(iii)   Options may only be granted to employees and full-time directors.

A    (i) only
B    (i) and (ii) only
C    (ii) and (iii) only
D    All of them

7    Edwardo is employed by the Spanish holding company of the Espan group. He is sent to the UK subsidiary on a 3 month assignment. During that 3 month period he has the following income:

(i)    3 months of salary from UK subsidiary paid in cash to Edwardo.

(ii)    3 months of salary from holding company paid into Spanish bank account.

(iii)    3 months of interest on his Spanish investments paid into his Bermudian bank account.

Edwardo is taxed in the UK on

A    None of these items
B    (i) only
C    (i) and (ii) only
D    All three items

8    Julia has recently taken up the post of Management Accountant for Cyma Ltd. Her remuneration package includes:

(i)    Payment of nursery fees for her two children of pre-school age at the Kiddiwinks Nursery which is 500 yards from Cyma's head office.

(ii)    Relocation expenses for her move from London to Manchester which total £6,920.

(iii)    A clothes allowance of £3,000 per annum - suits only allowed at work.

Julia's salary will be £50,000 per annum.

Of the benefits outlined above Julia will be taxed on

A    (i) only
B    (iii) only
C    (i) and (iii) only
D    All three items

9    Joe travels 10,200 business miles in his 2000cc V.W. Golf during 2000/01. His employer pays a business mileage allowance of 60p per mile for cars with engines up to and including 2000cc and 75p per mile for engine sizes in excess of this.

What taxable benefit will arise under the Inland Revenue Authorised Mileage Rate Scheme (ie FPCS) on Joe for income tax purposes?

A    Nil
B    £1,530
C    £2,770
D    £6,120

10    JoJo Ltd provides it's sales director with a brand new company car available for private use on his promotion on 1 June 2000. The car cost £35,000 plus VAT and is driven 2,100 business miles by the director during 2000/01.

The benefit in kind under Schedule E for the director is

A    £7,292
B    £8,568
C    £11,995
D    £14,394

11   Pete earns a salary of £18,000 pa. During 2000/01 he had two loans from his employer:

    (i)    £3,000 interest free to buy a season ticket to allow travel to work by train.

    (ii)    £40,000 loan at 3% to purchase a holiday home in France.

    The official rate of interest is 10%. What is the Schedule E benefit in kind in respect of the loans?

    A    Nil
    B    £2,800
    C    £3,100
    D    £4,300

12   Alice is aged 37 and single and earns £42,000 per annum as an accountant with Mega plc. She has benefits in kind totalling £720 in 2000/01. In 1999/00 she underpaid income tax by £300. Alice is entitled to a personal allowance of £4,385 in 2000/01 and the marginal rate of tax applies at 40%.

    What is Alice's PAYE code for 2000/01?

    A    183L
    B    291L
    C    336L
    D    438L

13   Which of the following non cash vouchers are exempt from NIC?

    (i)    Childcare vouchers.
    (ii)    Luncheon vouchers up to 15p per day.
    (iii)    Transport vouchers where the employee is 'lower paid'.

    A    (ii) only
    B    (ii) and (iii) only
    C    (iii) only
    D    All of them

14   Sarah travels 10,200 business miles in her 2000cc car during 2000/01. Her employers pays 60p per mile business mileage allowance for cars up to 2000cc.

    What taxable benefit will arise on Sarah for NIC purposes if the Inland Revenue Authorised Mileage Rate Scheme (FPCS) is applicable here?

    A    £Nil
    B    £1,530
    C    £2,770
    D    £6,120

**Total Marks = 28**

If you struggled with these objective test questions go back to your BPP Study Text for Paper 5 and revise Chapters 12 to 14 before you tackle the preparation and exam-standard questions in this part.

If you would like a bank of objective test questions which covers a range of syllabus topics, order our MCQ cards using the order form at the back of this Kit.

**Advanced corporate tax matters**

Questions 30 to 50 cover advanced corporate tax matters, the subject of Part D of the BPP study text for Paper 5.

30    **PREPARATION QUESTION: GROUP RELIEF**

P Ltd owns the following holdings in ordinary shares in other companies, which are all UK resident.

| | |
|---|---|
| Q Ltd | 83% |
| R Ltd | 77% |
| S Ltd | 67% |
| M Ltd | 80% |

The ordinary shares of P Ltd are owned to the extent of 62% by Mr C, who also owns 70% of the ordinary shares of T Ltd, another UK resident company. In each case, the other conditions for claiming group relief, where appropriate, are satisfied.

The following are the results of the above companies for the year ended 31 March 2001.

| | M Ltd | P Ltd | Q Ltd | R Ltd | S Ltd | T Ltd |
|---|---|---|---|---|---|---|
| | £ | £ | £ | £ | £ | £ |
| *Income* | | | | | | |
| Trading profit | 10,000 | 0 | 64,000 | 260,000 | 0 | 70,000 |
| Trading loss | 0 | 223,000 | 0 | 0 | 8,000 | 0 |
| Schedule A | 0 | 6,000 | 4,000 | 0 | 0 | 0 |
| | | | | | | |
| *Charges paid* | | | | | | |
| Patent royalties (gross) | 4,000 | 4,500 | 2,000 | 5,000 | 0 | 0 |

*Required*

(a)  Compute the MCT payable for the above accounting period by each of the above companies, assuming group relief is claimed, where appropriate, in the most efficient manner.

(b)  Advise the board of P Ltd of the advantages of increasing its holding in S Ltd, a company likely to sustain trading losses for the next two years before becoming profitable.

**Approaching the question**

1    Group relief questions nearly always require you to show the most efficient use of relief. You must work out the profits of each company involved, and consider the marginal tax rate of each company. Any company with small companies' marginal relief will have a marginal rate (for FY 2000) of 32.5%. Any company with starting rate marginal relief will have a marginal rate of 22.5% for FY 2000.

2    Before working out the rates of tax, you must find the lower and upper limits for small companies rate, the starting rate and marginal relief. These depend on the number of companies under common control.

3    You must also remember that eligibility for group relief depends not on common control, but on a 75% effective interest.

## 31   PREPARATION QUESTION: CORRESPONDING ACCOUNTING PERIODS

Harry Ltd owns 80% of the ordinary share capital of Sid Ltd. Neither company has any other associated companies and both companies have been trading since 1985.

The following information relates to the two most recent accounting periods of each company.

| *Harry Ltd* | *12 months to 31.12.99* | *9 months to 30.9.00* |
|---|---|---|
| | £ | £ |
| *Income* | | |
| Schedule D Case I/(loss) | 25,000 | (45,000) |
| Schedule A | 3,000 | 4,000 |
| *Charges paid* | | |
| Patent royalties (gross) | 2,000 | 2,000 |

| *Sid Ltd* | *12 months to 31.3.00* | *12 months to 31.3.01* |
|---|---|---|
| | £ | £ |
| *Income* | | |
| Schedule D Case I | 52,000 | 250,000 |
| Schedule D Case III | 8,000 | 10,000 |
| *Charges paid* | | |
| Patent royalties (gross) | 5,000 | 5,000 |

*Required*

Compute the MCT payable by each company for each of the above accounting periods and show any loss carried forward by Harry Ltd on the assumption that Harry Ltd surrenders as much of its loss to Sid Ltd as is permitted and Harry Ltd does not make any claim to set its loss against its own profits.

### Approaching the question

1   The general rule for group relief is that the profits and the losses which are to be matched up must have arisen at the same time.

2   To apply this rule where companies do not have matching accounting periods, time-apportionment must be used to work out the profits and losses of each period covered by accounting periods of the two companies. Time-apportionment is not, however, used when a company joins or leaves a group if the result would be unjust or unreasonable.

3   You may find the following table helpful.

| *Common period* | *Harry Ltd* | *Sid Ltd* |
|---|---|---|
| 1.1.00 - 31.3.00 | (1.1.00 - 30.9.00) × 3/9 | (1.4.99 - 31.3.00) × 3/12 |
| 1.4.00 - 30.9.00 | (1.1.00 - 30.9.00) × 6/9 | (1.4.00 - 31.3.01) × 6/12 |

4   The small companies rate was 21% for FY 98 and 20% for FY 99. The marginal relief fraction was 1/40 for both financial years.

5   Don't forget that there is a new starting rate of corporation tax that may apply in FY 2000.

## 32   GROUP RELIEF                                                  *36 mins*

HO Ltd, a UK resident company, owns holdings of ordinary shares in the following UK-resident companies.

| K Ltd | 90% |
|---|---|
| L Ltd | 80% |
| M Ltd | 80% |
| N Ltd | 100% |

The following is a summary of information relating to the year ended 31 March 2001:

| | HO Ltd £ | K Ltd £ | L Ltd £ | M Ltd £ | N Ltd £ |
|---|---|---|---|---|---|
| Chargeable profit | 110,000 | 18,000 | | 62,500 | 120,000 |
| Agreed trading loss | | | (75,000) | | |
| Dividend received from M Ltd | 8,000 | | | | |
| FII (including tax credit) | | | | 12,500 | |
| Dividend paid to HO Ltd (March 2001) | | | | 8,000 | |
| Other dividends paid (March 2001) | 60,000 | | | 2,000 | |

HO Ltd is about, for the first time, to engage in exporting its products. All of its customers will be situated in Northern America. The directors are aware that the VAT regulations governing export sales are somewhat different from those applying to UK sales but they are seeking your advice on the detail of the regulations.

*Required*

(a)  Compute the mainstream corporation tax (MCT) payable by each company for the year to 31.3.01, assuming group relief is claimed in the most effective manner.   **10 Marks**

(b)  State how the overall position would have changed had K Ltd been a non-resident controlled foreign company, giving reasons for your answer.   **5 Marks**

(c)  Write a brief report to the board setting out the main regulations covering VAT on export sales to North America.   **5 Marks**

**Total Marks = 20**

33   **M LTD**   *36 mins*

The share capital of M Ltd, a UK company, is held as follows:

| A Ltd | 15% |
|---|---|
| B Ltd | 60% |
| C Ltd | 5% |
| D Ltd | 4% |
| Individuals | 16% |

All of the shares in A Ltd, B Ltd, C Ltd and D Ltd are owned by individuals and none of these companies owns shares in any other company.

All of the companies make up accounts to 31 March. The trading results for the year ended 31 March 2001 were as follows:

| | £ |
|---|---|
| A Ltd | Loss (60,000) |
| B Ltd | Profit 160,000 |
| C Ltd | Loss (20,000) |
| D Ltd | Loss (40,000) |
| M Ltd | Profit 220,000 |

None of the companies had any other income.

*Required*

(a)  On the assumption that all possible claims for relief are made, compute the MCT payable by B Ltd and M Ltd.   **14 Marks**

(b)    Write brief notes on:

    (i)    VAT on surcharge liability notices;

    (ii)    Relief for VAT on bad debts.                              **6 Marks**

**Total Marks = 20**

34    **A LTD**                                                       *36 mins*

On 1 April 2000 A Ltd, a manufacturing company resident in the United Kingdom, acquired 100% of the share capital of B Ltd, also a manufacturing company. B Ltd makes up accounts each year to 31 March. For its year ended 31 March 2001, it sustained a trading loss of £130,000 and had no other chargeable income. A Ltd produced the following information in relation to its nine-month period of accounts to 30 September 2000.

| INCOME | £ |
|---|---|
| Adjusted trading profits | 42,000 |
| Rents receivable | 1,000 |
| Loan interest receivable (gross) | 8,000 |
| (including £2,000 accrued at 30 September 2000) | |
| Bank interest receivable | 5,000 |
| (including £3,000 accrued: £2,000 received 30 June 2000) | |
| Patent royalties receivable (gross) (including £3,000 accrued: £12,000 | |
| received June 2000) | 15,000 |
| Franked investment income (FII) | 1,000 |
| (including tax credit received August 2000) | |
| Charges Paid (gross figures): | |
| Patent royalties (paid August 2000) | 6,000 |
| Gift aid payment (paid September 2000) | 11,000 |

A dividend of £22,000 was paid in September 2000. You establish that there was no surplus ACT brought forward at 1 January 2000.

*Required*

Compute the final taxation position of A Ltd for the above accounting period, assuming maximum group relief is claimed by A Ltd in respect of B Ltd's trading loss.    **20 Marks**

35    **GROUP GAINS AND REBASING ELECTIONS**                          *36 mins*

A Ltd has owned 80% of the share capital of both B Ltd and C Ltd since their incorporation.

The following information relates to the accounting year to 31 March 2001.

(i)    A Ltd transferred a building to B Ltd under group arrangements on a no gain/no loss basis. The value of this building plus indexation for capital gains tax purposes to the date of transfer was £60,000 and the market value at the date of transfer was £100,000.

(ii)    B Ltd has unused capital losses brought forward of £80,000.

(iii)    C Ltd intends to dispose of two properties during the year. One will be sold for £150,000. The value of this property plus indexation for capital gains tax purposes to the date of sale is estimated at £70,000. The other will be sold for £70,000 giving rise to a chargeable gain of £45,000.

(iv)    A Ltd purchased a new building for £80,000.

*Required*

(a) Draft a report to:

(i) Advise the directors of the steps to be taken to ensure that no gains become chargeable to corporation tax for the year ended 31 March 2001. **10 Marks**

(ii) Advise the directors of the consequences of reducing their holding in B Ltd to 40% during the year ending 31 March 2002, and indicate how such consequences can be avoided. **5 Marks**

(b) N Ltd has been trading for many years and made, for the first time, during its year ended 31 March 2001, disposals which will come within the capital gains tax rules.

There were two disposals on 30 September 2000.

(i) A building bought in 1980 for £380,000 will be sold for £860,000. Its market value at 31 March 1982 was agreed at £360,000.

(ii) A building bought in 1971 for £220,000 will be sold for £200,000. Its market value at 31 March 1982 was agreed at £290,000.

*Required*

Compute the total chargeable gains arising assuming that:

(i) no global election for the market value at 31 March 1982 under S 35 TCGA 1992 is made; and

(ii) such an election is made;

and advise the directors whether the election should be made. **5 Marks**

*Indexation factors*
March 1982 - September 2000                   1.160

**Total Marks = 20**

**36    STD LTD** (5/96)                                                  *36 mins*

STD Ltd is a UK trading company whose whole share capital was acquired by D Ltd (also UK-resident) during 1996. During its 12-month accounting period to 31 March 2001, STD Ltd made the following disposals.

*10 October 2000*

Sold plant and machinery for £60,000. This had been acquired in August 1991 for £100,000, using part of the proceeds of the sale of an office block used to house the company's administration staff. The office block had been purchased in October 1987 for £70,000 and was sold in August 1991 for £120,000. The maximum possible rollover relief was claimed, in respect of the gain arising on the sale of the office block, against the purchase of the plant and machinery.

*30 December 2000*

Sold for £90,000, 20,000 shares in Z Ltd, being part of a holding of these shares acquired as follows.

|  |  | *Number of shares* | *Cost* |
| --- | --- | --- | --- |
| September 1985 | Bought | 10,000 | £23,000 |
| October 1988 | Bought | 15,000 | £40,000 |
| December 1992 | Bonus issue 2 for 5 |  |  |
| November 1994 | Sold for £18,000 | 5,000 |  |

*10 February 2001*

Sold one retail unit out of a block of five units which had been bought for a total price of £90,000 in August 1991. These had been let by the company to various businesses. The unit sold realised £28,000 and the market value of the remaining units was agreed at £100,000.

In addition to the above, you are informed that the whole share capital of STD Ltd was sold by D Ltd in March 2001 to H Ltd (a UK company).

*Required*

(a) Compute the chargeable gains or losses arising from each of the above transactions.

**15 Marks**

(b) Advise the board of STD Ltd of any other gains which may become chargeable for the above period as a result of the changes in the ownership of its shares.

**5 Marks**
**Total Marks = 20**

*Indexation factors*

| | | | |
|---|---|---|---|
| October 1987 - August 1991 | 0.303 | November 1994 - December 2000 | 0.191 |
| September 1985 - October 1988 | 0.148 | August 1991 - February 2001 | 0.298 |
| October 1988 - November 1994 | 0.327 | August 1991 - October 2000 | 0.283 |

37    **CLARISSA LTD**                                                    *36 mins*

Clarissa Ltd, a UK resident company, has been a member of a group of companies for capital gains tax purposes since 1980. The group had in place a global election to have all assets owned at 31 March 1982 dealt with for capital gains tax purposes at their market values at that date.

During the year ended 31 December 2000, Clarissa Ltd sold the following assets to third parties (ie non-group members). These assets were part of a property portfolio owned by Clarissa Ltd and none of them had been used for the purpose of Clarissa Ltd's trade.

10 May 2000          Sold a warehouse for £150,000. This had cost £50,000 in May 1978 and its market value at 31 March 1982 had been agreed at £38,000.

8 September 2000     Sold a shop unit for £180,000. This was part of a block of six shops bought in May 1983 for a total cost of £270,000. The value of the remaining five shops had been agreed at £720,000.

31 October 2000      Sold a property for £115,000. This had been acquired in June 1989 for £60,000 (its then market value) from D Ltd, another member of the same capital gains group. D Ltd had acquired it in 1980 for £45,000 and its market value at 31 March 1982 was agreed at £50,000.

*Required*

(a) Compute the chargeable gains arising from the above transactions.         **13 Marks**

(b) Explain, on the assumption that the above assets had been used for the purpose of Clarissa Ltd's trade, what action could have been taken to improve the taxation position of the group.                                          **7 Marks**

**Total Marks = 20**

*Indexation factors*

| | | | |
|---|---|---|---|
| March 1982 - June 1989 | 0.453 | May 1983 - September 2000 | 1.027 |
| March 1982 - May 2000 | 1.135 | June 1989 - October 2000 | 0.490 |
| March 1982 - October 2000 | 1.166 | | |

**38   S LTD (11/98)**                                              *36 mins*

The following information relates to the accounting year ended 31 March 2001 of S Ltd, a company whose whole share capital had been acquired by T Ltd during 1996. In addition, you establish that on 31 October 2000, T Ltd disposed of 40% of the shares in S Ltd to a third party.

(i)   In April 1989, S Ltd had acquired 20,000 ordinary shares in X Ltd (being 10% of the total share capital) at a cost of £120,000. During November 2000, X Ltd made a rights issue of one share for every four shares held, which S Ltd chose not to take, and the rights were sold for £18,000. The value of the shares in X Ltd at November 2000, immediately after the rights issue, was agreed with the Inland Revenue at £9 per share.

(ii)  On 1 April 1990, S Ltd sold for £175,000 a business property, which had cost £80,000 in January 1980. The MV of the property at 31 March 1982 was agreed at £90,000. The proceeds received in 1990 had been wholly invested in new plant and machinery, all of which was still in use at 31 March 2001. Holdover relief was claimed in respect of the gain arising in April 1990.

(iii) In May 1996, T Ltd had transferred a factory building to S Ltd under the group arrangements for capital gains purposes. The factory had cost T Ltd £80,000 in May 1991, and its agreed market value at May 1996 was £105,000. As stated above, T Ltd sold 40% of the shares in S Ltd during the year.

*Required*

(a)   Compute the chargeable gains or allowable losses for S Ltd arising during the accounting period to 31 March 2001 as a result of the above information.     **16 Marks**

(b)   Assuming that S Ltd had other chargeable income for the above period of £140,000 (but not FII), compute the corporation tax (CT) which will be attracted by any gains in your answer to part (a) above.

NB. You are not required to calculate the total corporation tax liability – only the tax on the gains.                                              **4 Marks**

*Indexation factors:*

| | |
|---|---|
| April 1989 - November 2000 | 0.509 |
| March 1982 - April 1990 | 0.576 |
| May 1991 - May 1996 | 0.145 |

**Total Marks = 20**

**39   AC AND DC LTD**                                              *36 mins*

On 1 April 2000 AC Ltd, a company engaged in the manufacture and wholesale distribution of electric plugs and switches, acquired a controlling interest in DC Ltd, a company involved in retail sales of household electrical appliances.

DC Ltd had a poor trading record in recent years but your board takes the view that, with improved systems and marketing, it can become profitable within a few years.

DC Ltd had the following balances brought forward at 31 March 2000:

|  | £ |
|---|---|
| Trading losses | 110,000 |
| Surplus ACT | 35,000 |
| Capital losses | 60,000 |

*Required*

(a)   Draft a report to the board of AC Ltd on the possible use of the above losses and ACT.

**15 Marks**

(b)   The directors of AC Ltd have advised you that in the next accounting period, they will dispose of an asset which is likely to give rise to a capital gain. They have also advised you that DC Ltd will dispose of an asset giving rise to a capital loss.

Advise the directors on the procedures which should be adopted in order to minimise the taxation liability of the group   **5 Marks**

**Total Marks = 20**

## 40   DIVERSIFY                                        *36 mins*

A diversified group of companies comprises a parent and several subsidiaries which had been acquired over a period from 1986 until 1996. The group is about to re-organise its business activities by focusing on one main trading activity which it hopes to expand over the next few years.

This will involve the disposal of a number of assets held by various companies in the group and the sale of some of the subsidiary companies themselves.

None of the companies in the group are currently registered as a group for VAT purposes. However, the directors would like to consider the possibility of a VAT group registration.

*Required*

Draft a report to the board on the potential taxation implications of the reorganisation and of a VAT group registration. Your report should concentrate mainly on the capital gains aspects of the reorganisation.   **20 Marks**

## 41   CONTROL                                        *36 mins*

A Ltd wishes to acquire control of B Ltd. There are two methods of achieving this commercial objective:

1.   For A Ltd to acquire a majority holding of the voting shares in B Ltd.

2.   For A Ltd to purchase the assets, trade and contracts of B Ltd, and offer continuing employment to its workforce. B Ltd would then be wound up.

*Required*

Draft a report to the directors of A Ltd that identifies and discusses the taxation implications of each of the above alternative courses of action.   **20 Marks**

**42    HGJL LTD (5/00)**                                                      *36 mins*

The following information relates to a UK-resident group of companies, the parent company being H Ltd, the shares of which are all held by individuals.

H Ltd has the following holdings of shares:

68% of G Ltd        80% of J Ltd        90% of L Ltd

J Ltd owns 80% of K Ltd, the other 20% of K Ltd being owned by G Ltd.

L Ltd owns 80% of M Ltd and X Ltd holds 24% of G Ltd.

All of the other shares in these companies are owned by individuals.

All of the companies make up accounts to 31 March each year and the results for the year ended 31 March 2001 are as follows:

|  | H Ltd £ | G Ltd £ | J Ltd £ | L Ltd £ | K Ltd £ | M Ltd £ | X Ltd £ |
|---|---|---|---|---|---|---|---|
| Trading losses |  |  | (64,000) |  |  | (42,000) | (24,000) |
| Trading profits | 48,000 | 60,000 |  | 30,000 | 90,000 |  |  |
| Schedule D Case III | 4,000 | 5,000 | 6,000 |  | 10,000 | 6,000 |  |
| Trade charges (paid) | 2,000 | 4,000 | 6,000 |  |  | 8,000 |  |

*Required*

(a)   Draw a diagram illustrating the above structure.                        **3 Marks**

(b)   Identify all of the associated companies and any group and/or consortia present in the structure.                                                              **5 Marks**

(c)   Compute the MCT payable by each company, assuming all possible reliefs are claimed in the most tax-efficient manner, with taxable profits after the deduction of reliefs.
                                                                         **12 Marks**

**Total Marks = 20**

**43    PREPARATION QUESTION: FOREIGN TAX**

Mumbo Ltd, a UK resident trading company, owns 6% of the share capital of Z Inc and 8% of the share capital of X SA. Neither of these companies is resident in the UK for tax purposes. In addition, Mumbo Ltd has a controlling interest in four UK resident companies.

The following information relates to Mumbo Ltd's 12 month accounting period ended 30 April 2001.

|  | £ | £ |
|---|---|---|
| *Income* |  |  |
| Schedule D Case I trading profits |  | 550,000 |
| | | |
| Schedule D Case V |  |  |
| Dividend from Z Inc - after deduction of withholding tax of 28% | 36,000 |  |
| Dividend from X SA - after deduction of withholding tax of 5% | 38,000 |  |
|  |  | 74,000 |
| *Charge paid* |  |  |
| Patent royalties (gross figure) |  | 60,000 |
| | | |
| *Dividend paid on (June 2000)* |  | 434,000 |

There was surplus ACT of £20,000 brought forward on 1.5.00.

*Required*

Compute the MCT payable for the above period by Mumbo Ltd, showing clearly your treatment of ACT and the relief for double taxation. Assume FY 2000 tax rates and allowances apply throughout.

**Approaching the question**

1    This question requires you to compute mainstream corporation tax on overseas income, taking account of double taxation relief.

2    Charges should be set first against UK profits and then against the overseas income which has borne the lowest rate of overseas tax.

3    The restriction of double taxation relief to the lower of the overseas tax and the UK tax on the overseas income must be applied to each source of income separately.

4    ACT is set off after DTR. The maximum set off applies to each source of income separately.

5    The maximum set off limit for ACT is reduced by the Shadow ACT deemed to have been paid in the period.

## 44    B AND W LTD

*36 mins*

B Ltd acquired 80% of the voting rights of W Ltd in December 2000. Both companies are resident in the United Kingdom. B Ltd has, for several years, owned 5% of the voting capital of P Inc, a company resident abroad.

The following information relates to B Ltd for its twelve-month accounting period ended 31 January 2002.

|  | £ |
|---|---|
| INCOME |  |
| Adjusted trading profits | 280,000 |
| Capital gains | 30,000 |
| Dividend from P Inc (net of 40% overseas tax) | 1,200 |
| Debenture interest received 30 November 2001 (gross - non trading investment) | 8,000 |
| Patent royalties received 31 October 2001 (gross) | 16,000 |
| FII (inclusive of tax credit) received in May 2001 | 32,000 |
|  |  |
| CHARGES PAID |  |
| Gift Aid to charity (May 2001) | 18,000 |
|  |  |
| DIVIDEND PAID (in May 2001) | 236,000 |

In addition, you establish that the following amounts are brought forward at 1 February 2001:

Surplus ACT                                                        £7,800

W Ltd also made up accounts for the twelve months to 31 January 2002 and its only taxable income consisted of trading profits of £6,000.

There were no accruals of debenture interest at the beginning or end of the year.

*Required*

Compute the mainstream corporation tax (MCT) payable by both B Ltd and W Ltd for the above accounting period, assuming all appropriate claims are made.

Show clearly your treatment of advance corporation tax (ACT), income tax and double tax relief. Assume FY 2000 rates apply throughout.                    **20 Marks**

**45  J LTD**                                                                *36 mins*

J Ltd is a UK-resident company which has three wholly-owned UK subsidiary companies. In addition, it holds 5% of the shares of P Inc and 6% of the shares of L Inc. Both these companies are non-UK resident companies.

The following information concerning J Ltd relates to the 12-month accounting period ended on 31 March 2001.

|  |  | £ | £ |
|---|---|---:|---:|
| UK trading profits |  |  | 600,000 |
| Schedule D Case V: | overseas dividends from P Inc (after withholding tax at 35%) | 32,500 |  |
|  | overseas dividends from L Inc (after withholding tax at 10%) | 36,000 | 68,500 |
| Patent royalties paid (gross figure) |  |  | 12,000 |

J Ltd will shortly become involved in the import of goods from the USA.

*Required*

(a)  Compute the MCT payable by J Ltd for the above period showing clearly your treatment of foreign tax.                                              **11 Marks**

(b)  Explain briefly how the computation would have differed had the holdings in the foreign companies been 10%. You are not required to re-calculate the figures.  **4 Marks**

*Required*

(c)  Draft a short memo to the board on the VAT treatment of the goods imported from the USA.                                                              **5 Marks**
                                                                   **Total Marks = 20**

**46  X LTD**                                                                *36 mins*

X Ltd, a company resident in the United Kingdom, makes up accounts each year to 30 April. It acquired a 55% interest in Z Ltd on 30 December 2000 and sold its 60% interest in Y Ltd on 30 November 2000.

During its year ended 30 April 2001, X Ltd had an adjusted trading profit (before capital allowances) of £220,000 after adding back £10,000 in respect of a loan to a customer which proved irrecoverable. The company let various properties to other businesses and, during the year to 30 April 2001, this activity resulted in a loss of £16,000 (before any interest paid on loans used to purchase one of these properties).

The other income and payments during the year ended 30 April 2001 were:

INCOME

| (Gross figures - including tax credits where relevant) | £ |
|---|---:|
| Debenture interest (including an accrual of £2,000) | 14,000 |
| Patent royalties received | 12,000 |
| Chargeable gain arising on the sale of shares in Y Ltd | 28,000 |
| Loan interest (on loan to customer)[received net of 20% tax] | 1,000 |
| Dividend from foreign company (withholding tax was 35%) | 4,000 |
| Franked Investment Income (FII) (received May 2000) | 15,000 |

| PAYMENTS (Gross figures): | £ |
|---|---:|
| Loan interest paid in year (purchase of let property) | 6,000 |
| Patent royalties (including £2,000 accrued) | 8,000 |
| Gift Aid payment to charity | 2,000 |

*Note.* A dividend of £180,000 was paid on 31 May 2000.

In addition, you establish that there is surplus advance corporation tax (ACT) of £24,000 brought forward at 1 May 2000.

The balances for capital allowances purposes at 1 May 2000 were:

| | |
|---|---|
| General pool | £102,000 |
| Expensive car | £18,000 |

During the year there were two items bought - plant, costing £12,000, on 30 May 2000, and a lorry, costing £23,750, on 31 July 2000.

*Note*: The company is a small enterprise for first year allowance purposes.

*Required*

(a) Compute the capital allowances claimable for the year ended 30 April 2001.  **3 Marks**

(b) Compute the mainstream corporation tax (MCT) payable for the year ended 30 April 2001, showing clearly your treatment of shadow ACT, income tax and interest paid and received under the loan relationship rules. Assume FY 2000 tax rates and allowances continue to apply.  **17 Marks**

**Total Marks = 20**

47  **CONTROLLED FOREIGN COMPANY**  *36 mins*

A Ltd, a company resident in the United Kingdom, owns 65% of the ordinary share capital of B Ltd, which is also UK resident. In addition, it owns all of the share capital of C Inc, a company which is resident for tax purposes in a country where the rate of corporation tax is 8%. C Inc has been deemed to be a controlled foreign company for the purposes of UK taxation.

A Ltd provides the following information in respect of its accounting period of 12 months ending 30 April 2001.

| | £'000 |
|---|---|
| *Income* | |
| Schedule D Case I profits | 340 |
| Bank interest (non-trading investment) | 50 |
| Capital gains | 150 |
| Rental income | 20 |
| Patent royalties (gross; October) | 35 |
| Dividends from UK companies (gross) (1 May) | 30 |
| | |
| *Charges* | |
| One-off payment to charity (June) | 10 |
| Patent royalties (gross; December) | 25 |
| | |
| *Dividends* | |
| Paid during period (30 May 2000) | 341 |
| Proposed (June 2001) | 54 |

In addition, you establish that the following amounts were brought forward at 1 May 2000.

| | £'000 |
|---|---|
| Surplus ACT | 42 |
| Surplus FII for shadow purposes | 10 |
| Capital losses | 40 |

C Inc's profit for the year to 30 April 2001 was £46,000 after deducting 8% local tax. No amounts were remitted to the UK.

*Required*

Compute the mainstream corporation tax (MCT) payable by A Ltd for the above accounting period, showing clearly your treatment of advance corporation tax (ACT).

**Total Marks = 20**

48    **ZEBEDEE INC**                                                                *36 mins*

Your company has acquired a 40% interest in the ordinary shares of Zebedee Inc, a profitable foreign resident manufacturing company which seems likely to be a Controlled Foreign Company (CFC).

Your company is also about to commence making exports to customers in other EU countries and the directors are concerned about the VAT implications.

Your directors have arranged a meeting on 1 April 2001 to discuss these matters.

Your company prepares accounts to 31 March each year.

*Required*

Draft notes in preparation for the board meeting on:

(a)    The taxation implications of the shareholding in Zebedee Inc.            **5 Marks**

(b)    The circumstances in which Zebedee Inc could escape being treated as a CFC.

**10 Marks**

(c)    The VAT implications of making sales to customers in other EU countries.    **5 Marks**

**Total Marks = 20**

49    **CL PLC**                                                                *36 mins*

The following is the distribution of the ordinary share capital of CL plc.

|  | *Number of shares* |
|---|---|
| Mr F | 10,000 |
| Mr G | 5,000 |
| Mrs G (his wife) | 5,000 |
| Mr H | 2,500 |
| Miss J | 2,500 |
| R Ltd - a non-close company | 10,000 |
| Members of the public - each owning fewer than 100 shares | 5,000 |
| Total shares in issue | 40,000 |

Mr F and Mr and Mrs G are the only directors of CL plc. None of them holds shares in R Ltd. None of the other shareholders work for either CL plc or R Ltd.

Mr H was provided with a brand new car by CL plc on 1 April 2000. The list price of the car when new was £12,000. Mr H did not drive any business miles and was not provided with any petrol by CL plc.

*Required*

(a)    Demonstrate whether CL plc is a close company.                        **8 Marks**

(b)    Show the effect on the company's status of R Ltd selling, 3,000 shares to members of the general public in lots of under 100 shares to each person.            **8 Marks**

(c)    Describe the tax implications for the company of providing Mr H with a car.    **4 Marks**

**Total Marks = 20**

## 50   OBJECTIVE TEST QUESTION

1   Family Co Ltd is a close company. It makes a loan of £100,000 to Fred who is the shareholding Managing Director on 2 January 2001. The company makes up accounts to 31 December. The company pays small companies rate tax.

How much tax must the company pay in respect of the loan and when?

A   £20,000 on 14.4.2001
B   £20,000 on 1.10.2002
C   £25,000 on 14.4.2001
D   £25,000 on 1.10.2002

---

If you struggled with this objective test question go back to your BPP Study Text for Paper 5 and revise Chapters 15 to 17 before you tackle the preparation and exam-standard questions in this part.

If you would like a bank of objective test questions which covers a range of syllabus topics, order our MCQ cards using the order form at the back of this Kit.

---

## 51    PREPARATION QUESTION: REGISTRATION AND ACCOUNTING

You have recently received a letter from the managing director of a new company (which will make no exempt supplies and will have no dealings outside the UK) requesting your help with matters concerning value added tax. The following is an extract from the letter.

(a)    We understand that some businesses are registered for VAT whilst others are not registered. We have only recently commenced trading and consider that it will take us about five years to reach full potential of sales, which we envisage will rise from £20,000 to £100,000 a year in that period. Could you please advise us of the position regarding registration?

(b)    Once we are registered, how should the VAT content of our income and expenditure be reflected in our budgets and final accounts at the year end?

(c)    When and how is the amount of VAT to be accounted for to HM Customs & Excise, and what is the position if we should pay out more VAT than we charge?

(d)    What records must be kept by us in order to satisfy the regulations?

*Required*

Prepare a letter in response to the above requests.

### Approaching the question

1    You are asked for a letter, so you should present your answer in letter format.

2    The company will clearly need to register at some stage. You should explain the rules on registration, but note that there will be no dealings outside the UK.

3    For part (b), it is relevant that there will be no exempt supplies. The partial exemption rules will not restrict the recovery of VAT. However, VAT on some items of expenditure is never recoverable.

4    You should consider the alternatives to quarterly accounting, both monthly and annual accounting. Also, might cash accounting be appropriate?

5    Several records must be kept. Most of these are records which a business would be likely to keep in any case, but you still need to list them because there are penalties for failure to keep the required records.

## 52    PREPARATION QUESTION: VAT COMPUTATIONS

A manufacturing business had the following transactions for the quarter ended 31 December 2000. The business started on 1 October 2000 and was VAT registered from that date.

|  | £ |
|---|---|
| Sales at standard rate | 172,500 |
| Sales at zero rate | 50,000 |
| Exempt sales | 75,000 |
| Purchases at standard rate * | 115,575 |
| Purchases at zero rate * | 7,200 |
| Exempt purchases * | 62,600 |
| Purchased new motor car (business use 75%) | 10,150 |

* These purchases are analysed as follows.

|  | Standard rated purchases £ | Zero rated purchases £ | Exempt purchases £ |
|---|---|---|---|
| Purchases attributable to standard rated sales | 66,500 | 4,000 | 18,000 |
| Purchases attributable to zero rated sales | 20,350 | 2,200 | 10,500 |
| Purchases attributable to exempt sales | 28,725 | 1,000 | 34,100 |
|  | 115,575 | 7,200 | 62,600 |

All the above amounts include VAT where this is applicable.

*Required*

Calculate the amount of VAT to be accounted for to HM Customs & Excise for the quarter.

**Approaching the question**

1   The output VAT is straightforward. It is simply the standard rated sales including VAT × the VAT fraction.

2   VAT will have been suffered on the standard rated purchases, but not all of this VAT will be recoverable. If the purchases were attributable to standard rated sales the VAT will be recoverable, whereas if they were attributable to exempt sales the VAT will not be recoverable. What about purchases attributable to zero rated sales?

3   There will also have been VAT on the car. You must decide whether all, some or none of this VAT is recoverable.

## 53   PREPARATION QUESTION: CASH ACCOUNTING AND LAND

(a)   In what circumstances may a trader register under the cash accounting scheme for VAT? What are the advantages of such a registration?

(b)   In relation to VAT, indicate the action which is open to a landlord who acquires an office building for letting. The building was constructed 10 years ago.

**Approaching the question**

1   Take care to distinguish between the VAT cash and annual accounting schemes. You are asked here about the cash accounting scheme.

2   It is important to read a question carefully and answer all parts of it. Make sure you cover the advantages of the cash accounting scheme.

3   In part (b) consider whether the supply is exempt. Could it be standard rated?

## 54   OBJECTIVE TEST QUESTIONS    *75 mins*

1   A VAT registered retail outlet sells a table to a customer for £705 (including VAT) which it had purchased from a manufacturer for £250 plus VAT.

   What is the net amount of VAT which the retail outlet will have to account for on this sale?

   A   £61.25
   B   £79.63
   C   £105.00
   D   £123.38

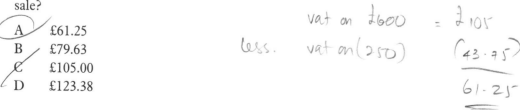

BPP
PUBLISHING

2    Which of the following is not a supply of goods?

    A    Gas for home use

    B    Chocolate covered biscuits

    C    Milk

    D    Repair of washing machine

3    Arun Ltd started to trade providing interior design services on 1 July 2000 with the following invoiced sales:

|  | £ |
|---|---|
| July 2000 | 10,000 |
| August 2000 | 11,800 |
| September 2000 | 7,600 |
| October 2000 | 14,900 |
| November 2000 | 13,000 |
| December 2000 | 17,500 |

By which date must the company notify Customs & Excise of a need to register for VAT?

    A    30 November 2000

    B    30 December 2000

    C    31 December 2000

    D    1 January 2001

4    Arun Ltd started to trade providing interior design services on 1 July 2000 with the following invoiced sales:

|  | £ |
|---|---|
| July 2000 | 10,000 |
| August 2000 | 11,800 |
| September 2000 | 7,600 |
| October 2000 | 14,900 |
| November 2000 | 13,000 |
| December 2000 | 17,500 |

From which date will Customs register Arun Ltd for VAT assuming it notifies them of a need to register by the required date?

    A    1 December 2000

    B    1 March 2001

    C    1 February 2001

    D    1 January 2001

5    ABC Ltd's turnover has just exceeded the registration limit for VAT. Which of the following ways of notifying Customs and Excise is acceptable to them?

    (i)    By telephoning the local VAT office.

    (ii)    By writing to the local VAT office.

    (iii)    By completing and sending Form VAT 1 to the local VAT office.

    A    (ii) and (iii)

    B    (iii) only

    C    All three ways

    D    (i) and (iii)

6   A Ltd is a UK holding company which owns shares in the following subsidiaries:

   80% of B Ltd (UK retailer)
   60% of C Ltd (UK wholesaler)
   55% of D Ltd (UK insurance company)
   55% of X Inc (overseas manufacturer with no UK business establishment)
   40% of E Ltd (UK retailer)

   Which companies could be included in a VAT group registration if the group wishes to include as many companies as possible?

   A    A, B, C, D, X and E
   B    A, B, C, D, X
   C    A, B, C, D
   D    A, B, C

7   Prospector Ltd started to trade on 1 January 2001 and registered for VAT on 1 March 2001. Prior to trading the company incurred the following expenses:

   |  |  | Gross cost |
   |---|---|---|
   |  |  | £ |
   | 1 March 2000 | Accounting advice on the impact of trading | 9,000 |
   | 1 May 2000 | Purchase of office equipment | 25,000 |
   | 21 September 2000 | Marketing advice on forthcoming adverts | 10,000 |
   | 1 December 2000 | Christmas Party for potential customers | 10,000 |

   How much VAT can Prospector Ltd recover as pre-registration input tax?

   A    £8,043
   B    £6,553
   C    £5,213
   D    £3,723

8   XYZ Ltd takes an order from Mr Smith to manufacture and deliver to him a cabinet made to his requirements on 1 March 2001. The cabinet is finished on 4 June 2001 and delivered to Mr Smith on 6 June 2001. An invoice is raised on 12 June 2001 which Mr Smith pays on 4 August 2001.

   What is the tax point of the supply?

   A    4 June 2001
   B    6 June 2001
   C    12 June 2001
   D    4 August 2001

9   A1 Plumbing Services repair a broken central heating boiler for Mrs Yamani on 1 April 2001. They send an invoice for the work on 17 April 2001 which Mrs Yamani pays in two instalments on 2 September 2001 and 2 October 2001.

   What date is the tax point of the supply?

   A    1 April 2001
   B    17 April 2001
   C    2 September 2001
   D    2 October 2001

10 Joe Wright orders a book on-line from eBooks Ltd on 21 May 2001. He pays for the books on 31 May 2001.

The book is dispatched on 20 June 2001. An invoice is also raised on 20 June 2001 and a receipt is issued two days later.

What date is the tax point of this supply?

A   21 May 2001
B   31 May 2001
C   20 June 2001
D   No tax point - books are a zero-rated supply

11 DDB Ltd offer a prompt payment discount of 10% to all customers who settle their accounts within 30 days. The company sells books with a net price of £3,000 and stationery with a net price of £5,000 to JJ Ltd.

JJ Ltd take 4 months to pay.

How much VAT is charged on this sale?

A   £787.50
B   £875.00
C   £1,260.00
D   £1,400.00

12 Y Ltd declares output tax of £100,000 and claims input tax of £32,000 for the quarter ended 30 June 2001. It is subsequently discovered that output tax was understated by £30,000.

How much misdeclaration penalty will be charged?

A   Nil
B   £50 minimum penalty
C   £4,500
D   £9,000

13 YZY Ltd fails to submit a VAT return for the quarter to 31 December 2001. Customs issue an assessment for £200,000 on 1 March 2002.

YZY Ltd submit the return late on 5 April 2002 showing the true liability for the quarter:

|  | £ |
| --- | --- |
| Output tax | 370,000 |
| Input tax | (80,000) |
|  | 290,000 |

How much misdeclaration penalty will be charged?

A   Nil
B   £50 minimum penalty
C   £13,500
D   £27,000

14   Due to a computer error Alpha Ltd's VAT return for the quarter ended 30 June 2001 showed VAT due of £120,000 when really £150,000 was due. The VAT return was submitted on 21 July 2001.

Customs discovered the error made on 5 December 2001 during a control visit.

Alpha Ltd paid the extra £30,000 due on 20 December 2001.

Interest will run on the £30,000 due from

A     30 June 2001
B     21 July 2001
C     1 August 2001
D     5 December 2001

15   J Jones and Son Ltd completed the construction of a 5 storey office block in March 2001. On 2 May 2001 they granted a 99 year lease of the building to ABC Ltd for £1.2 million.

Which statement best describes the VAT position regarding this transaction?

A     Standard-rated supply. VAT due at 17.5%
B     Exempt supply. No VAT to charge. Option to tax not available for leases
C     Exempt supply with option to tax available to charge VAT at 17.5%
D     Zero-rated supply of newly constructed building by the constructor

16   Alpha Ltd hired a new car for it's director of marketing for two weeks in June 2001 whilst his company car was being repaired following an accident. The car hire cost £500 plus £87.50 VAT and was used 75% on business travel and 25% on private travel by the director.

How much input tax may Alpha Ltd (a fully taxable VAT registered trader) obtain on this hire?

A     None
B     £43.75
C     £65.63
D     £87.50

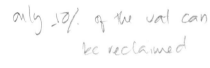 *only 50% of the vat can be reclaimed*

*87.50 × 50% = 43.75*

17   In the quarter to 31 March 2001 D Ltd makes the following supplies:

|                | £       |
|----------------|---------|
| Taxable        | 300,000 |
| Exempt         | 100,000 |

Input tax is analysed as attributable to:

|                        | £       |
|------------------------|---------|
| Taxable supplies only  | 2,500   |
| Exempt supplies only   | 750     |
| Both kinds of supplies | 2,800   |

How much input tax can D Ltd recover?

A    £2,500
B    £4,600
C    £5,300
D    £6,050

18   On 21 January 2001 A Ltd sells goods to Mr Jones for £10,000 plus £1,750 of VAT. An invoice is raised on 1 February 2001 requesting payment by 15 February. Mr Jones declares himself bankrupt on 1 May 2001 having not paid the invoice. A Ltd makes up VAT returns to calendar quarters.

On which date is the above debt eligible for VAT bad debt relief.

A    1 May 2001
B    1 August 2001
C    15 August 2001
D    1 November 2001

19   Xero Ltd is in the cash accounting scheme for VAT. It supplies £20,000 of building materials to Bens Builders on 29 January 2001. An invoice was raised on 10 February 2001. Payment was received on 2 May 2001. Xero Ltd makes up VAT returns to calendar quarters.

What is the date the above supply takes place for VAT accounting purposes?

A    29 January 2001
B    10 February 2001
C    31 March 2001
D    2 May 2001

20   D Ltd buys secondhand furniture from Mr Smith after seeing an advert in the local paper for £500. The company repairs the furniture at a cost of £200 for materials and £100 labour. The furniture is then sold by D Ltd for £1,100.

How much VAT must be accounted for on the above sale by D Ltd if D Ltd uses the secondhand goods scheme?

A    £59.57
B    £89.36
C    £163.83
D    £192.50

21  Which of the following are exempt supplies for VAT?

   (i)   Funeral services ✓
   (ii)  Insurance ✓
   (iii) Drugs and medicines on prescription ✗
   (iv)  Health services ✓

   A   All of them
   B   (i) and (ii) only
   C   (i), (ii) and (iii) only
   D   (i), (ii) and (iv) only

**Total Marks = 42**

If you struggled with these objective test questions go back to your BPP Study Text for Paper 5 and revise Chapters 18 to 19 before you tackle the preparation and exam-standard questions in this part.

If you would like a bank of objective test questions which covers a range of syllabus topics, order our MCQ cards using the order form at the back of this Kit.

55    **SELL FOR CASH**                                                                    *80 mins*

(a)    P Ltd is a UK resident retail company with two wholly owned UK resident subsidiaries, Q Ltd and R Ltd. A recent fall in trade has had an adverse effect on the group's cash position and the directors have realised that in the next accounting period (the year to 31.3.01) they must raise £520,000 in order to pay off a loan due to mature in December 2000.

They have in mind the sale, in October 2000, of one of three assets, all of which have recently increased in value. Each of these will realise £600,000 (after costs of selling) and the directors are hoping that, after any corporation tax due on the gain made, there will be sufficient cash remaining to meet their liability.

The three assets are as follows.

(i)    A plot of land, currently used for a car park for a warehouse and on which they had hoped to build a new retail unit. This had cost £300,000 in June 1984 and had been bought using the full proceeds of the sale of another plot of land (also used as a car park) sold in June 1984. This first plot had cost £20,000 in August 1972 and on its disposal in June 1984, full rollover relief had been claimed against the replacement plot which may now be sold in October 2000 for £600,000.

(ii)   A retail store which had been originally purchased in September 1979 for £80,000. Extensions were added as follows.

|                  | £      |
|------------------|--------|
| October 1980     | 20,000 |
| November 1983    | 20,000 |
| December 1990    | 25,000 |

The market value of the store at 31 March 1982 was £90,000.

(iii)  58,000 ordinary shares in X Ltd, a major supplier. These were part of a holding of 60,000 shares which had been acquired as follows.

| Date      |                       | Shares | Cost    |
|-----------|-----------------------|--------|---------|
|           |                       |        | £       |
| May 1985  | Purchased             | 60,000 | 180,000 |
| June 1986 | Rights issue 1 for 3 @ £4 | 20,000 | 80,000  |
| July 1990 | Sold for £240,000     | 30,000 |         |
| May 1991  | Purchased             | 10,000 | 50,000  |

The directors estimate that P Ltd's only profits apart from any of the above chargeable gains, will be Schedule D Case I profits of £600,000.

The directors have asked you, as chief accountant of the company, to advise them as to which assets should be sold in order to realise sufficient funds in order to meet their objective of repaying the loan due to mature in December 2000.

**Requirement**

Prepare a report to the directors of P Ltd dated 13 March 2000.

(i)   Producing your calculation of the estimated chargeable gains that would arise on the sale of each of the assets in October 2000.   **17 Marks**

(ii)  Advising the directors which asset should be sold for £600,000, so that after taking into account any corporation tax arising, there will be sufficient funds to meet their debt obligations.   **7 Marks**

Presentation and style   **3 Marks**

**Total Marks = 27**

*Note.* Your calculations, in arriving at the chargeable gains and the corporation tax liability thereon should be shown in appendices attached to your report.

*Indexation factors*

| | | | |
|---|---|---|---|
| March 1982 – June 1984 | 0.123 | May 1985 - June 1986 | 0.027 |
| June 1984 – October 2000 | 0.928 | June 1986 - July 1990 | 0.297 |
| March 1982 – October 2000 | 1.166 | July 1990 - May 1991 | 0.053 |
| November 1983 - October 2000 | 0.984 | May 1991 - October 2000 | 0.288 |
| December 1990 - October 2000 | 0.324 | | |

(b)   During July 2000  Z Ltd, an unconnected third party, approached P Ltd with a view to buying all of the share capital in Q Ltd. P Ltd agreed to this offer and in August 2000 all of the share capital in Q Ltd was sold for £500,000. The entire share capital in Q Ltd had been bought by P Ltd in April 1998 for £430,000.

The directors of  P Ltd would like to invest £485,000 of the proceeds from the sale of Q Ltd in acquiring a new and particularly attractive retail outlet in Swindon. They would still need to sell another asset to repay the loan of £520,000 due to mature in December and it is still estimated that the Schedule D profits will be £600,000 for the year to 31 March 2001.

**Requirement**

Prepare a report to the directors of P Ltd dated 31 August 2000:

(i)   Producing your calculation of the gain on the sale of the shares in Q Ltd and indicating whether there will be sufficient net proceeds to buy the new retail store.   **8 Marks**

(ii)  Explaining whether the sale of Q Ltd and the acquisition of the new retail unit alters the advise you gave in your report dated 13 March 2000 concerning the best asset to sell in order to fund the loan repayment.   **7 Marks**

Presentation and style   **4 Marks**

**Total Marks = 19**

Any detailed calculations should be shown in appendices attached to your report.

*Indexation factors*
April 1998 - August 2000          0.052

**Total Marks = 46**

---

56   **JAY AND CO**   *80 mins*

(a)   Jay and Co is a successful firm which had been run for many years as a partnership. Most of the work has been done by the three partners, helped by a small number of freelance people.

A company has now been formed to take over the business on 1 April 2000. The three partners will become directors. They have informed you that over the first twelve months they will be taking on twenty full-time employees who will be paid salaries, ranging from £5,000 to £20,000 per annum. Most of these employees will be given various benefits in kind.

The directors are aware that this will impose new fiscal responsibilities on them, and seek your advice.

**Requirement**

Prepare a report dated 1 March 2000 to the directors

(i)   Setting out the company's duties in relation to reporting benefits in kind provided to members of staff.   **12 Marks**

(ii)   Identifying the forms to be used, their broad content, the relevant time limits for submission and the penalties for late submission.   **5 Marks**

(iii)   Indicating what additional costs will arise on the company as a result of providing benefits in kind.   **5 Marks**

(iv)   Outlining the PAYE requirements with which the company must comply.

**5 Marks**

Presentation and style   **5 Marks**

**Total Marks = 32**

(b)   It is now March 2001.

The board has decided that all sales persons engaged from 1 April 2001 onwards will be required to provide their own motor car, with the company paying them a mileage allowance for any business use of the car.

**Requirement**

Prepare an information sheet to be given to all new recruits explaining the taxation implications of these arrangements. Assume the provision of the Finance Act 2000, continue to apply.

*Note.* You are not expected to quote the specific rates published by the Inland Revenue.

**11 Marks**

Presentation and style   **3 Marks**

**Total Marks = 14**

**Total Marks = 46**

57   **PGD LTD**   *80 mins*

(a)   PGD Ltd is a manufacturing company in the United Kingdom which has no associated companies. For the purposes of this scenario you are the chief accountant of PGD Ltd.

It is now December 1999 and the directors of PGD Ltd are very concerned about the company's cash flow position. They have asked you to prepare a report for the Board, estimating the company's tax liability for the year to 30 September 2000 and outlining when tax payments will need to be made over the next year. They would also like you to explain to them how loan interest payable/receivable is dealt with for tax purposes. Some of the directors are confused because sometimes loan interest is included in trading profits and sometimes it is not.

The directors have produced a budgeted profit and loss account for its accounting year ended 30 September 2000 showing a net profit before taxation of £231,300, *after* accounting for the following items:

|  | £ |  |
|---|---|---|
| *Expenditure* | | |
| Debenture interest payable (gross) | 12,000 | Note 1 |
| Loan interest (gross) | 8,000 | Note 2 |
| Patent royalties (gross) | 10,000 | Note 3 |
| Depreciation | 11,000 | |
| *Income* | | |
| Loan interest receivable (gross) | 6,000 | Note 4 |
| Rents from let property | 7,000 | Note 5 |
| Insurance recovery | 6,800 | Note 6 |
| Patent royalties to be received during year (September 2000) (gross amount) | 30,000 | |
| Franked investment income (FII) [including tax credits] | 8,000 | Note 7 |

*Notes*

1   This represents interest on debentures issued by PGD Ltd to provide funds for a factory extension. The amount is payable in two equal instalments 31.12.99 and 30.6.00.

2   This represents interest payable on a ten-year loan raised by PGD Ltd to purchase property which is currently let to another company. All the interest is payable on 30.9.00.

3   The figure for patent royalties includes an accrued amount of £2,000 (gross). The other £8,000 (gross) will be paid in August 2000.

4   The loan interest receivable is in respect of a loan made by PGD Ltd to a supplier. The full amount is receivable on 1.2.00.

5   The rents relate to the property let by PGD Ltd.

6   This represents an amount expected to be recovered from the company's insurers during the year in respect of goods destroyed in a fire in September 1999. The cost of these goods was written off and allowed as an expense in the year to 30 September 1999.

7   The dividend is expected to be received in January 2000.

PGD Ltd had the following balances for capital allowances purposes brought forward at 1 October 1999

|  | £ |
|---|---|
| General pool | 40,000 |
| Motor cars | 21,500 |
| SLA (computer) | 12,000 |
| Expensive car | 11,200 |

During the year the company expected to sell plant for £9,400 (inclusive of VAT) which had cost £18,500 (exclusive of VAT). It also expects to sell the computer for £4,700 (inclusive of VAT). Purchases during the year are expected to comprise electrical machinery costing £18,800 (inclusive of VAT), a motor car costing £10,500 and computer equipment costing £5,875 (including VAT). The purchases will all be made in April 2000.

PGD Ltd qualifies as a small enterprise for FYA purposes.

**Requirement**

Prepare a report for the directors of PGD Ltd dated 1 January 2000:

(i) Producing your calculation of the estimated maximum capital allowances which may be claimed by PGD Ltd for its chargeable accounting period to 30 September 2000. **7 Marks**

(ii) Producing your calculation of the estimated adjusted Schedule D Case I profit. **4 Marks**

(iii) Stating clearly your treatment of any interest paid or received. **4 Marks**

(iv) Producing your calculation of the estimated mainstream corporation tax (MCT) payable by PGD Ltd in respect of the above accounting period. **10 Marks**

(v) Illustrating when tax payments will be due. **7 Marks**

Presentation and style **5 Marks**

*Note.* Any detailed calculations should be shown in appendices attached to your report.

**Total Marks = 37**

(b) The results for the year to 30 September 2000 were exactly as estimated above. The only matter which differed from the directors' expectations was that two wholly owned UK resident subsidiaries were set up and began trading on 1 April 2000.

**Requirement**

Prepare a report to the directors of PGD dated 1 October 2000 setting out the actual corporation tax liability and explaining why this differs from your original estimate. **5 Marks**

Presentation and style **4 Marks**

**Total Marks = 9**

**Total Marks = 46**

**58  P LTD** *80 mins*

P Ltd is a large manufacturing company with one wholly owned UK resident subsidiary Q Ltd. The group of companies sell their manufactured goods to wholesalers and also large retail chains. The group is now experiencing rapid growth, after a short period of poor results, due to a change in several key management posts over the last 12 months.

You have recently been appointed as Chief Accountant of P Ltd.

The Board of Directors of P Ltd want to improve the remuneration package of employees and has been considering setting up an approved occupational pension scheme. Also suggested at the same recent board meeting was the idea of rewarding certain key employees by providing them with motor cars. The Board wants to consider these proposals further at its next meeting scheduled for 4 February 2001.

The Managing Director has sent you the following memo:

---

### MEMORANDUM

To:     P. Giles, Chief Accountant
From:   A. Waites, Managing Director
Date:    22 January 2001
Subject:  PAYE Codes

There has been a lot of press coverage lately concerning the level of errors occurring in Pay As You Earn (PAYE) code numbers.

Can you conduct an investigation to identify any errors present in the code numbers of our company employees with a view to reporting back to me by the end of February.


Signed


A. Waites

---

You propose to delegate the investigation to your assistant in the first instance with further investigation by you of any major points arising.

**Requirements**

(a) Prepare a report for the assistant indicating the areas in which PAYE errors are most likely to have occurred.    **6 Marks**

(b) Prepare a report for the board to be used at a preliminary meeting to discuss the taxation implications for both the company and the employees of

   (i)    Setting up an approved occupational pension scheme    **7 Marks**
   (ii)   Providing senior staff with motor cars for business and private use    **7 Marks**

Presentation and style    **5 Marks**

                                 **Total Marks = 25**

It is now June 2001.

The company's auditors have just provided draft accounts of P Ltd for the year to 31 March 2001. The accounts show a trading loss of £110,000 for the year and the finance director has briefly outlined below various items which have gone through the accounts but which he thinks are probably not deductible/taxable under Schedule D Case I.

*Expenditure:*

(i) A director of the company was temporarily seconded to a national charity. The company paid his salary and employers' national insurance contributions during this period, amounting to £32,000.

(ii) During the year, debenture interest of £18,000 (gross) was charged in the accounts. This included an accrued amount of £3,000. The debenture was raised to acquire new buildings for the trade.

(iii) During the year, loan interest of £6,000 (gross) was paid. The loan was raised to enable P Ltd to acquire a subsidiary company.

(iv) £15,000 was spent refurbishing a recently acquired office which, at the date of purchase, was capable of use but was in a poor condition.

(v)  The accounts showed a charge for bad debts amounting to £16,000. This had arisen as follows:

*Bad Debts Account*

| | £ | | | £ |
|---|---|---|---|---|
| Bad debts written off | 45,000 | Balances b/fwd: | | |
| Loan to customer written off | 10,000 | General provision | | 24,000 |
| Balances c/fwd: | | Specific provision | | 18,000 |
| General provision | 16,000 | Bad debts recovered | | 36,000 |
| Specific provision | 23,000 | Profit and loss | | 16,000 |
| | 94,000 | | | 94,000 |

(vi)  A branch of the business was closed and all ten employees were made redundant at a cost of £150,000. The statutory redundancy amount due was £3,000 for each employee.

*Income:*

(vii)  A sum of £42,000 was recovered from the company's insurers in respect of damage caused by a fire in the previous year, during which time the costs of repair were incurred. The £42,000 comprised:

| | £ |
|---|---|
| In respect of the business premises | 30,000 |
| In respect of premises let by the company | 12,000 |
| | 42,000 |

(viii) During the year, P Ltd sold goods to its subsidiary Q Ltd at a price of £120,000. The normal price would have been £80,000 and this policy was intended to reduce Q Ltd's tax liability since it was paying tax at the marginal rate.

**Requirement**

(c)  Prepare a report for the Finance Director

|   |   |   |   |
|---|---|---|---|
| (i) | Computing the adjusted profit/loss of P Ltd | **8 Marks** |
| (ii) | Explaining clearly your treatment of all the aforementioned items | **9 Marks** |
| | Presentation and style | **4 Marks** |

*Note.* Your computation in arriving at the adjusted profit/loss should be shown in an appendix attached to your report.

**Total Marks = 21**

**Total Marks = 46**

59   **WJ LTD**                                                              *80 mins*

(a)  WJ Ltd is a trading and manufacturing company in the United Kingdom with no associated companies. For many years, it has been making up accounts annually at 31 October. Shortly before October 2000, the directors decided to change the accounting date to the end of February and consequently made up one set of accounts for the sixteen month period from 1 November 1999 to 28 February 2001.

You are the Chief Accountant who reports directly to the Finance Director of WJ Ltd. After a review of the accounts for the period ending 28 February 2001 you have gathered the following information:

| INCOME: | £ |
|---|---|
| Trading profit (before capital allowances) | 602,000 |
| Capital gains: | |
|      31 August 2000 | 40,000 |
|      20 December 2000 | 360,000 |
| Rents accruing monthly: | |
|      To 31 October 2000 | 1,500 |
|      From 1 November 2000 | 5,000 |
| Debenture interest received (gross non-trading investment) – 30 June 2000 | 10,000 |
| Patent royalties received (gross) – 30 November 2000 | 24,000 |
| Dividend received [including tax credit] | 20,000 |
|      (received 15 January 2000) | |
| PAYMENTS: | |
| Gift aid donation – 31 October 2000 | 8,000 |
| Loan interest paid (gross) – 30 September 2000 | 15,000 |
|      (this interest was on a loan raised to buy an investment | |
|      property which was let to another company) | |
| Dividends paid: | |
|      31 January 2000 | 252,000 |
|      31 January 2001 | 424,000 |

In addition, you establish that there were capital losses brought forward at 1 November 1999 of £30,000 and surplus ACT of £50,000.

The written-down values at 1 November 1999, for capital allowances purposes, were as follows:

| | £ |
|---|---|
| General pool | 140,000 |
| Motor cars | 28,000 |
| Expensive car | 20,000 |
| Computer (short-life asset) | 8,000 |

The following transactions in assets took place during the above accounting period:

| Purchases | | | Disposals | | |
|---|---|---|---|---|---|
| | | £ | | | £ |
| 10 March 2000 | Plant | 10,000 | 8 July 2000 | Lorry sold for | 6,000 |
| 10 July 2000 | Lorry | 24,000 | 26 Sept 2000 | Expensive car | 11,000 |
| 10 October 2000 | Car | 14,000 | 20 Nov 2000 | Computer | 2,000 |

WJ Ltd qualifies for a First Year Allowance (FYA) where appropriate.

**Requirement**

Prepare a report to the Finance Director of WJ Ltd in which you

(i)    Compute the maximum amount of capital allowances which can be claimed by WJ Ltd in respect of the period involved.    **6 Marks**

(ii)    Compute the mainstream corporation tax (MCT) payable in respect of the period, showing clearly your treatment of ACT. Assume all interest accrued during the accounting period in which it was paid or received.    **20 Marks**

Presentation and style    **4 Marks**

*Note.* Your computations should be shown in appendices attached to your report.

**Total Marks = 30**

(b)    WJ Ltd has, up to the present time, produced only with goods which are standard-rated for VAT purposes.

In the near future it will begin to make, for the first time, supplies which are exempt from VAT. This will account for about one-quarter of the total turnover in a full year.

The directors wish to be advised of the effect this decision will have on the company's ability to claim a deduction for input VAT.

**Requirement**

Prepare a report for the Board on the VAT implications of this change in the sales mix.

**13 Marks**

Presentation and style **3 Marks**

**Total Marks = 16**

**Total Marks = 46**

**60   ZAD LTD**                                                     *80 mins*

(a)   ZAD Ltd is a UK resident manufacturing company with a 75% subsidiary company, JWD Ltd. Both companies prepare accounts to 31 March each year.

You are a management accountant working for ZAD Ltd.

Your assistant has prepared a draft corporation tax computation and has calculated that during its chargeable accounting period of twelve months to 31 March 2001, ZAD Ltd had profits chargeable to corporation tax of £84,000. However, your assistant was unsure of how to deal with a loan to a supplier and has included a deduction from Schedule D Case I profits of £65,000 in respect of a loan to the supplier which had gone into liquidation, as it was unable to pay any of its debts. Interest of £2,600 (gross) had been received on this loan during the early part of the above period, and this is also provisionally included within the computation of Schedule D Case I profits for the year ended 31 March 2001.

JWD Ltd had profits chargeable to corporation tax of £286,000, for the year to 31 March 2001.

ZAD Ltd occupies a factory which it bought on 1 June 1997, the cost comprising:

|                 | £       |
|-----------------|--------:|
| Land            | 90,000  |
| Preparing site  | 10,000  |
| Factory         | 138,000 |
| Office unit     | 52,000  |
|                 | 290,000 |

The company is considering buying two additional factories on 30 September 2001:

(1)   A secondhand factory which will cost £80,000.
      This had cost the original owner £150,000 on 1 October 1996.

(2)   A newly constructed factory.
      This will cost £200,000 (including £32,000 for office accommodation).

The Finance Director would like your advice on the allowances that will be available in the year to 31.3.02 if these factories are purchased.

**Requirements**

You are required to:

(i)   Write a report to your assistant dated 1 May 2001 advising him of the tax implications of the irrecoverable loan to the supplier. **8 Marks**

(ii)    Draw up a report for the Finance Director outlining

       (1)    The maximum industrial buildings allowance (IBA) which may be claimed by ZAD Ltd for its accounting period of 12 months to 31 March 2002 if the above factories are purchased.        **9 Marks**

            (Note that you are not required to compute the IBA for any other year.)

       (2)    State what the IBA will be if the newly constructed factory been located in an enterprise zone.        **2 Marks**

Presentation and style        **5 Marks**

Assume Finance Act 2000 tax rates and allowances continue to apply.

                                                  **Total Marks = 24**

(b)    You receive the following memo from the payroll clerk.

---

### MEMORANDUM

To:        Management Accountant
From:      Payroll Clerk
Date:       6 April 2001
Subject:   P11D Preparation

I have been asked to assist in the completion of forms P11D in respect of the directors of ZAD Ltd for the year 2000/01.

The following benefits are enjoyed by various directors, all of whom earn in excess of £30,000 per annum:

(a)    A director has the use of a private house bought by the company two years ago for £80,000. The annual value of the house is £2,000 and the director concerned pays rent to the company of £1,500 a year plus all running costs.

(b)    A video system, which had been provided at the start of 1997/98 for the use of a director and which had cost the company £1,500, was taken over by the director on 6 April 2000 for a payment of £400. The market value of the system was then £500.

(c)    A director has a loan of £20,000 at 4% interest to enable him to purchase his sole residence. This is the only loan he has taken out.

(d)    A dishwasher was purchased by the company for £280 and given to a director. The retail price was £350.

(e)    Medical insurance premiums were paid for a director and his family, under a group scheme, at a cost to the company of £1,200. Had the director paid for this as an individual the cost would have been £1,600.

I have not yet reached the Schedule E part of my study pack and should be most grateful for any help you could offer in quantifying the above benefits for completion of the forms P11D. I have been told that you will need to know that the official rate of interest is 10%.

I also understand that we may need to pay Class 1A NICs on certain benefits. Please could you tell me how to calculate this amount.

Signed

Payroll Clerk

---

**Requirements**

Write a report to the payroll clerk answering his memo.  **18 Marks**

Presentation and style  **4 Marks**

*Note*. Any calculations should be set out in appendices attached to your report.

**Total Marks = 22**

**Total Marks = 46**

**61  Z LTD**  *80 mins*

(a)  Z Ltd, a UK-resident company with two wholly-owned UK subsidiaries, also owns 7% of P Inc and 8% of Q SA, both of which are non-resident companies.

For its year to 31 December 2000, Z Ltd had a turnover of £1.5 million which resulted in UK trading profits of £500,000. The company also received the following income:

|  | £ |
|---|---|
| Overseas dividends – gross figures: | |
| P Inc (withholding tax £28,000) | 100,000 |
| Q SA (withholding tax £4,000) | 80,000 |

During the year to 31 December 2000, Z Ltd paid patent royalties of £10,000 (gross figure) in May 2000 and paid a dividend of £484,000 on 6 June 2000.

There was no surplus ACT b/f on 1 January 2000.

Z Ltd is a wholesale food retailer.

You are the recently appointed Chief Management Accountant of Z Ltd.

In June 2000 the previous Chief Management Accountant estimated that the corporation tax liability of Z Ltd would be £100,000 for the year to 31 December 2000. In January 2001, following your appointment, you revised this estimate to £120,000.

In July 2001 the Z Ltd return and self-assessment was submitted based on the figures given above.

It is now September 2001 and the accounts have only just been finalised.

**Requirement**

Write a report for the Board of Directors:

(i)  Computing the mainstream corporation tax payable by Z Ltd for the year ended 31 December 2000.  **10 Marks**

(ii)  Setting out the dates on which this corporation tax should have been paid.  **8 Marks**

(iii)  Explaining how much of this corporation tax Z Ltd paid has already paid (assuming all amounts due were paid on the correct due dates) and calculating the tax due to be paid at the date of the report.  **7 Marks**

*Note*. A discussion of interest or penalties is NOT required.

Presentation and style  **5 Marks**

**Total Marks = 30**

(b)  Following your meeting to discuss the above report you have been contacted by the acting Finance Director Jonas Tomelty:

**MEMORANDUM**

To:        Chief Management Accountant
From:      Acting Finance Director
Date:      22 September 2001
Subject:   VAT

As you know I an acting as Finance Director whilst Mr Jones is on sick leave. I have no accountancy experience (marketing is my field). However, after the last board meeting I have become confused. Why doesn't Z Ltd pay VAT by instalments?

The last firm I worked for paid VAT by instalments. Why not Z Ltd? I would be also be interested to know how the payments of VAT by instalments work.


Signed


Jonas Tomelty

**Requirement**

Write a memo in reply to Mr Tomelty.                                   **12 Marks**

Presentation and style                                                 **4 Marks**

                                                     **Total Marks = 16**

                                                     **Total Marks = 46**


62    **ABCD LTD**                                                      *80 mins*

(a)    You are the management accountant for A Ltd, B Ltd, C Ltd and D Ltd which are all companies in the same group for capital gains tax purposes. A Ltd had acquired its interest in C Ltd in 1995 when that company had unused capital losses of £40,000. All the companies are in manufacturing trades.

The directors advised you at a recent board meeting of their proposals to undertake the following transactions in assets in September 2000.

(i)     The transfer of a building from A Ltd to B Ltd. It had cost A Ltd £60,000 in August 1987 and its market value at the date of transfer will be £110,000.

(ii)    The following disposals to third parties by B Ltd:

(1)    A warehouse for £180,000 which had cost £92,000 in April 1989.

(2)    A factory unit for £140,000 which had cost £50,000 in 1979 and which had a market value at 31 March 1982 of £60,000.

(iii)   The purchase by D Ltd of a new bakery plant for £135,000.

You ascertain the following indexation allowance decimals:

| | |
|---|---|
| August 1987 to September 2000 | 0.680 |
| April 1989 to September 2000 | 0.500 |
| March 1982 to September 2000 | 1.160 |

All the companies prepare accounts to 31 March each year.

**Requirements**

Assuming today's date is 31 August 2000 draw up a report to the board

(i)     Giving advice in respect of each of the above proposals              **6 Marks**

(ii)    Assuming that all beneficial claims are made, computing the minimum amount of capital gains which will appear in the corporation tax computations of the various companies involved.              **7 Marks**

Presentation and style              **4 Marks**

*Note.* Your computation of capital gains should be included in an appendix to your report.

**Total Marks = 17**

(b)    Each of the companies, except B Ltd, is separately registered for VAT. B Ltd is not registered. At a recent board meeting the question of a VAT group registration was raised and the managing director now wishes to know whether there are any advantages or drawbacks in having a group registration. He has heard that it is not necessary to include all group companies in a VAT group registration and he would like to know what the reasons for excluding any particular company might be.

B Ltd currently makes exempt supplies totalling approximately £350,000 per annum.

C Ltd exports all of its production to the USA and Canada.

The management team of D Ltd were recently sacked for misconduct. A new team is being trained up. Unfortunately this has resulted in a few late VAT returns. The Board of Directors are also considering whether D Ltd is financially viable following several years of poor management.

Several of the companies make supplies to each other - prices are charged at the market rate.

C Ltd has been making up its accounts to 31 March for many years. During 2000, it decided to change its accounting date to 30 June. It made up accounts for the period from 1 April 1999 to 30 June 2000. C Ltd pays tax at the small companies rate and is expected to continue to do so.

**Requirement**

Write a report to the board outlining:

(i)     The impact of a VAT group registration, and              **18 Marks**

(ii)    Advising  the directors of their responsibilities under the corporation tax self assessment rules in terms of the filing requirements and of the payment dates involved in respect of C Ltd and the changed accounting period.              **6 Marks**

Presentation and style              **5 Marks**

**Total Marks = 29**

**Total Marks = 46**

63     **HAPPY MAIDS LTD**              *80 mins*

Happy Maids Ltd, a newly formed company, commenced trading on 1 June 2000. Happy Maids Ltd provides a custom cleaning service for domestic and commercial  premises. Happy Maids Ltd charges between £6 and £10 per hour for the services of its staff who in turn clean the premises to the customer's specifications using equipment and cleaning products supplied by Happy Maids Ltd. Happy Maids Ltd pays its staff between £4 and £6 per hour.

Happy Maids Ltd has already invested in the services of a leaflet mailing business to deliver brochures to premises in its target area. This service cost £1,000 in June 2000 but resulted in sufficient advance orders to justify the taking on of 10 staff members initially. In the four months since the business started, on 1 June 2000, Happy Maids Ltd has invoiced £25,250 for cleaning services and has paid staff wages of £18,000.

Happy Maids Ltd invoices at the end of each month for the services provided in the month then ending. It requires payment within 7 days. However, it is noticeable that only 50% of customers pay on time. One customer has not yet paid anything. As a result Happy Maids Ltd is considering offering a 5% discount on the invoice value for payment within the 7 day period.

Happy Maids Ltd's main expense is the wages bill for cleaners. The company has also incurred the costs of ten cleaning packages made up of industrial vacuum cleaners, brushes, attachments etc plus uniforms at a cost of £495 each. These will be written off through the profit and loss account on a replacement basis. It also purchases cloths, polishes, cleaning solutions etc and the costs of these are running at approximately £200 per month. Happy Maids Ltd's major outlay was for £5,000 in June 2000 on a new small van which is driven by one of its employees to transport cleaners who do not have their own cars. Cleaners who use their own cars are paid a mileage allowance by the company. The company also purchased a computer in July 2000 for £1,000 which is used to produce invoices, payslips and letters for the business.

There are minimal overhead costs at present as Beth, one of Happy Maids Ltd's directors, runs the business from her home.

Beth has no knowledge of financial matters but as an ex-home economics teacher feels she will be able to 'keep the books' herself. However she is completely ignorant of tax law and has contacted you to seek your advice with regard to the impact of tax on the business.

All the above amounts exclude VAT.

**Requirements**

(a)  Write a letter to Beth to explain

  •    The impact of VAT on the business
  •    The tax implications of taking on 10 members of staff
  •    The treatment of the mileage allowances paid to staff using their own cars

**17 Marks**

(b)  Assuming that Happy Maids Ltd registered for VAT on the 1 June 2000 prepare a draft of the first quarters VAT return if turnover in that period was £20,000.     **6 Marks**

(c)  Prepare a computation of the taxable profit if Happy Maids Ltd makes up the first set of accounts for the four months to 30 September 2000.     **8 Marks**

(d)  Outline the treatment of bad debts for Schedule D Case I purposes.     **2 Marks**

(e)  Discuss the effect on VAT if Happy Maids Ltd goes ahead with its plan to offer a 5% discount for prompt payment of its invoices     **4 Marks**

Presentation and style     **9 Marks**

**Total Marks = 46**

# Answers

**1** **PREPARATION QUESTION: CORPORATION TAX COMPUTATION**

> **Pass marks**. This was a straightforward corporation tax computation, but you had to think carefully about the point of part (b). Not only has the disposal put the company into the marginal rate band; it was also very close to the end of the period.

(a) CORPORATION TAX COMPUTATION

|  | £ | £ |
|---|---|---|
| Schedule D Case I |  | 244,000 |
| Schedule A |  | 15,000 |
| Schedule D Case III (£4,000 + £800 × 100/80) |  | 5,000 |
| Capital gains £(35,000 + 7,000) | 42,000 |  |
| Less losses brought forward | (8,000) |  |
|  |  | 34,000 |
|  |  | 298,000 |
| Less charges £(6,000 + 1,000) |  | (7,000) |
| PCTCT |  | 291,000 |
| Dividends plus notional tax credits |  | 15,000 |
| 'Profits' |  | 306,000 |

|  | £ |
|---|---|
| Corporation tax £291,000 × 30% | 87,300 |
| Less marginal relief 1/40 × £(1,500,000 − 306,000) × $\frac{291,000}{306,000}$ | (28,387) |
| Mainstream corporation tax | 58,913 |

(b) The disposal on 28 March 2001 increased the profits for small companies rate purposes from £299,000 to £306,000, thus leading to the application of the full rate less marginal relief. If the disposal had not been made, the mainstream corporation tax would have been only £284,000 × 20% = £56,800, a saving of £2,113. It might be that had the disposal taken place in the next accounting period, starting only four days later, the gain would only have been taxed at 20% (assuming FY 2000 rates continue to apply), giving rise to tax of £1,400. Thus the company might have been able to save tax of £2,113 − £1,400 = £713 (and this ignores the benefit of an extra month's indexation allowance). Payment of tax on the gain would also have been deferred by 12 months.

**2** **BERTIE LTD**

> **Pass marks**. Surplus ACT b/f must be dealt with under the shadow ACT rules.

BERTIE LIMITED
CORPORATION TAX COMPUTATION

|  | £ |
|---|---|
| Schedule D Case I | 480,000 |
| Schedule D Case III £(20,000 + 8,000) | 28,000 |
| Schedule A | 18,000 |
| Capital gains | 99,000 |
|  | 625,000 |
| Less charges £(12,000 + 3,000) | (15,000) |
| Profits chargeable to corporation tax | 610,000 |
| Dividends plus tax credits £27,900 × 100/90 | 31,000 |
| Profits for small companies rate purposes | 641,000 |

As the small companies limits and tax rates are the same for both FY 1999 and FY 2000, the two years can be dealt with together.

Small companies marginal relief applies in both FY 1999 and FY 2000.

| | £ |
|---|---|
| *Corporation tax* | |
| *FY 1999 and FY 2000* | |
| £610,000 × 30% | 183,000 |
| *Less small companies marginal relief* | |
| $£(750,000 - 641,000) \times \dfrac{610,000}{641,000} \times 1/40$ | (2,593) |
| | 180,407 |
| Less ACT (W) | (73,575) |
| Less income tax suffered (£20,000 × 20% – £12,000 × 22%) | |
| | (1,360) |
| Mainstream corporation tax | 105,472 |

| | £ |
|---|---|
| *Working* | |
| 1   ACT | |
| Notional franked payment (£221,600 × 100/80) | 277,000 |
| FII for shadow purposes (£27,900 × 100/80) | (34,875) |
| FP for shadow purposes | 242,125 |
| Shadow ACT @ 20% | £48,425 |

| | £ |
|---|---|
| Maximum ACT set-off (£610,000 × 20%) | 122,000 |
| Less: shadow ACT | (48,425) |
| Set off | 73,575 |
| Surplus ACT c/f (£80,000 – £73,575) | 6,425 |

## 3   TROG PLC

> **Pass marks.** Large companies are determined by their level of profits. They must normally make payments on account of their corporation tax liability for a year.

**Notes for meeting with finance director**

**Payment of corporation tax**

(i)   With effect from the first accounting period ending on or after 1 July 1999, **'large' companies have to pay their actual corporation tax liability by quarterly instalments. The instalments are based on the estimated current year's corporation tax charge**.

(ii)   **A large company is any company that has to pay corporation tax at the full rate.**

Four equal instalments are due, in months 7, 10, 13 and 16 following the start of the accounting period.

(iii)   Trog plc had taxable profits of £510,000 for its year ended 31 March 2001. It had three wholly owned subsidiaries. Bilbo Limited is dormant, Baggins Inc is a trading company resident in Canada and Sylvester Limited was purchased during the current accounting period. The upper and lower limits for small companies rate purposes are divided by three. The only company which is ignored is Bilbo Limited. This is because it is dormant. Overseas companies must be included, as must any other companies which have been group members during any part of the year. The upper limit for Trog is £500,000 and it must therefore pay corporation tax at the full rate.

(iv)   We are currently in a four-year transition during which the proportion of a company's corporation tax liability that has to be paid by quarterly instalments is gradually increasing.

(v) For the accounting period to 31 March 2000 Trog plc had to pay 60% of its tax by instalments. The balance was payable nine months after the end of the accounting period on 1 January 2001.

(vi) In the year to 31 March 2001, 72% of our CT liability will be payable by instalments, rising to 88% in the following year and finally 100% in the year to 31 March 2003.

(vii) For the year to 31 March 2001 Trog plc will need to make payments as follows:

*Quarterly instalments*

|  |  | £ |
|---|---|---|
| 14 October 2000 | 1/4 × 72% × 30% × £510,000 | 27,540 |
| 14 January 2001 | 1/4 × 72% × 30% × £510,000 | 27,540 |
| 14 April 2001 | 1/4 × 72% × 30% × £510,000 | 27,540 |
| 14 July 2001 | 1/4 × 72% × 30% × £510,000 | 27,540 |

*Balance*

|  |  | £ |
|---|---|---|
| 1 January 2002 | 28% × 30% × £510,000 | 42,840 |
| Total tax paid |  | 153,000 |

(viii) Where the actual instalments due for a period exceeds the instalments paid, the additional amount due will attract an interest charge. If a company deliberately under-estimates its liability or fails to pay an instalment altogether, a penalty will also apply.

(ix) Similarly, an overpayment will attract repayment interest.

**Filing**

The self assessment return must be filed by **the later of 31 March 2002 and three months after a notice requiring a return is made**.

**Penalties**

There is a **£100 penalty for failure to deliver a return by the filing date, increasing to £200 where the failure extends to three months**.

(i) The above **penalties increase to £500 and £1,000 respectively for the third successive failure**.

(ii) There are also **tax-related penalties of 10% of the tax unpaid six months after the return was due where failure extends to 6 months after the filing date, and 20% of this tax if the failure extends to 12 months after the filing date**.

4   **PREPARATION QUESTION: QUARTERLY RETURNS**

> **Pass marks**. If you are required to prepare quarterly returns, remember:
>
> (a)   A neat and carefully planned layout is essential.
>
> (b)   To check whether the amounts given in the question are net or gross.
>
> (c)   To find the tax element in each receipt or payment first, then work out the payments and repayments.

CORPORATION TAX COMPUTATION

|  | £ |
|---|---|
| Schedule D Case I | 214,000 |
| Schedule D Case III | 5,000 |
| Chargeable gains £(12,000 – 12,000): £3,000 loss carried forward | 0 |
| Profits chargeable to corporation tax | 219,000 |
| Dividends plus tax credits £5,062 × 100/90 | 5,624 |
| 'Profits' | 224,624 |

Small companies rate:   lower limit = £300,000/2 = £150,000
upper limit = £1,500,000/2 = £750,000

*Corporation tax payable*

|  | £ |
|---|---|
| Corporation tax on chargeable profits £219,000 × 30% | 65,700 |
| Less: small companies' marginal relief | |
| $1/40 \times £(750,000 - 224,624) \times \dfrac{219,000}{224,624}$ | (12,806) |
| MCT payable 1 January 2002 | 52,894 |

**Tutorial note.** Companies whose profits fall within the small companies' marginal relief band do not have to pay quarterly instalments of corporation tax.

INCOME TAX

| Return period | Tax on payments £ | Tax on income £ | Income tax Due £ | Income tax Repayable £ | Due date |
|---|---|---|---|---|---|
| 1.4.00 - 30.6.00 | | 1,000 | | | 14.7.00* |
| 1.7.00 - 30.9.00 | 600 | | | | 14.10.00* |
| 1.10.00 - 31.12.00 | no return | | | | |
| 1.1.01 - 31.3.01 | 600 | | 200 | | 14.4.01 |
| | 1,200 | 1,000 | | | |

* These are the due dates for the return

5   **PREPARATION QUESTION: SUNDRY ADJUSTMENTS**

> **Pass marks**. The factory had always been used as a factory, so you should not have discussed the effect of non-qualifying use.

(a)  It will be necessary for the company to gross up the interest to take account of the tax deducted at source. Using Finance Act 2000 rates this means multiplying the interest received by 100/80. The gross interest will then be included in the company's profits chargeable to corporation tax and charged to tax at the appropriate rate. **The gross interest is taxed under schedule D case III on an accruals basis. The company will be entitled to a credit for the income tax suffered**. In the first instance, this is set against tax deducted from interest and charges paid net. If, however, income tax suffered exceeds the tax deducted from such payments, the excess is deducted from the company's corporation tax liability. If it exceeds the liability to corporation tax the excess is repaid to the company.

(b)  **There will be a charge to corporation tax on any capital gain**. In addition, the residue before sale must be calculated, being the cost less any industrial buildings allowances to date. **If the proceeds exceed the residue before sale a balancing charge will arise** (restricted to the amount of the allowances claimed) and will be chargeable to corporation tax. **If the proceeds are less than the residue before sale, the difference will give rise to a balancing allowance which will be added to the company's other capital allowances.**

(c)  The **defalcations by the junior members of staff will be deductible** in arriving at the company's Schedule D Case I profits, provided that they are not covered by insurance. **Sums stolen by a director are not deductible** as a trading expense (*Bamford v ATA Advertising 1972*).

(d)  **Expenditure on repairs to a newly-acquired asset which cannot be used by the purchaser in its unaltered state is regarded as capital expenditure and is therefore**

**not deductible in arriving at the company's Schedule D Case I profit** *(Law Shipping Co Ltd v CIR 1923)*. Furthermore, as the expenditure was on retail premises it will not qualify for industrial buildings allowances either, unless the building is in an enterprise zone.

(e) **The cost of business entertainment is not deductible** for tax purposes. **The cost of staff entertainment, on the other hand, is deductible.**

## 6  PREPARATION QUESTION: CAPITAL AND REVENUE

> **Pass marks**. The topic of this question is a basic principle of UK taxation. It would be very easy simply to write everything you know about the distinction between capital and revenue items. This would, however, be a mistake. It is important to read this sort of question carefully. You are asked how the distinction is applied to items in a company's profit and loss account, so you should consider profits as well as deductions from them, and you are specifically required to refer to relevant case law.

The distinction between capital and revenue is an essential one in the application of UK corporation tax. **Capital expenditure is not deductible in the computation of trading profits, except to the extent that it gives rise to capital allowances. Capital profits are taxed as capital gains:** although the rate of corporation tax is the same as for income, an indexation allowance is available in the computation of capital gains, and **capital losses may only be relieved against capital gains.**

Capital expenditure

**Expenditure on an asset which is for the enduring benefit of the trade is capital.** Thus the cost of a machine which will be used to generate profits is capital, but the cost of stock bought for resale is a revenue expense.

**Legal and professional expenses associated with capital expenditure are themselves treated as capital.** However, **the cost of registration of patents and trade marks, the cost of legal advice on employment contracts and the cost of legal work on the renewal of a lease for less than 50 years are all deductible** in computing trading profits. The incidental costs of loan finance are deductible in that they are taken into account in computing profits and losses on loan relationships.

The most contentious items of expenditure will often be repairs (revenue expenditure) and improvements (capital expenditure). The distinction between the two is based on a number of important legal cases.

(a) **Restoration of an asset by, for instance, replacing a subsidiary part of the asset will be deductible expenditure.** It was held that expenditure on a replacement factory chimney was deductible since the chimney was a subsidiary part of the factory *(Samuel Jones & Co (Devondale) Ltd v CIR 1951)*. However, in another case a football club demolished a spectators' stand and replaced it with a modern equivalent. This was held not to be repair, since repair is the restoration by renewal or replacement of subsidiary parts of a larger entity, and the stand formed a distinct and *separate* part of the club (and was thus not a *subsidiary* part of the club) *(Brown v Burnley Football and Athletic Co Ltd 1980)*.

(b) **Initial repairs to improve a recently acquired asset to make it fit to earn profits will be treated as capital expenditure.** In *Law Shipping Co Ltd v CIR 1923* the taxpayer failed to obtain relief for expenditure on making a newly bought ship seaworthy prior to using it.

71

(c) **Initial repairs to remedy normal wear and tear of recently acquired assets will be deductible**. *Odeon Associated Theatres Ltd v Jones 1971* can be contrasted with the *Law Shipping* judgement. Odeon were allowed to deduct expenditure incurred on improving the state of recently acquired cinemas.

Where an asset is bought on hire purchase the cash cost is treated as capital, and the finance charges are treated as revenue expenditure, normally spread over the period of the hire purchase agreement. Where assets are leased, the lease payments are treated as revenue expenditure.

### Capital profits

Where an asset is held to be used in the business (for example machinery) and is then sold, any profit is a capital gain. The same would apply to investments. Sales of stock in the course of trade, on the other hand, give rise to revenue profits.

## 7 WOODCOCK PLC

> **Pass marks**. In a question of this type the important thing is to reach a clear conclusion on every item. You will get more marks for eight clear conclusions, three of which are wrong, than for eight vague answers, all of which might be either right or wrong.

(a) **The work on the warehouse appears to have been needed to put the warehouse in a fit state to be used at all. The expenditure is therefore capital in nature, and should be added back in finding the Schedule D Case I profit** *(Law Shipping Co Ltd v CIR 1923)*. However, a deduction in computing that profit may arise, if capital allowances are available in respect of the expenditure on the windows. Eligibility depends on the exact use of the warehouse.

(b) No adjustment is needed in respect of the £40,000 payment. **There is no limit on the deductible amount when the trade continues** (as here). **If the trade had ceased, the limit on the deductible payment would have been the statutory amount plus three times the statutory amount**. The amount given in the question exceeds this limit, so the excess of £8,000 would have had to be added back.

(c) **No adjustment is required in respect of the salary of the marketing executive seconded to a charity**. Such salaries are deductible by statute.

(d) The covenanted payment must, by statute, be added back in the computation of Schedule D Case I profit. **The amount paid will then be deducted as a charge in arriving at the profits chargeable to corporation tax**. The amount paid is treated as a donation made under the gift aid scheme.

(e) Under statutory rules, only a proportion of the leasing costs of cars costing over £12,000 may be deducted. The non-deductible amount, which must be added back in computing the Schedule D Case I profit, is £4,686, computed as follows.

|  | £ | £ |
|---|---|---|
| *Jaguar* | | |
| Total payment | | 8,000 |
| Deductible £8,000 × (12 + 24)/(2 × 24) | | 6,000 |
| Non-deductible | | 2,000 |
| | | |
| *Mercedes* | | |
| Total payment | 9,400 | |
| Deductible £9,400 × (12 + 28)/(2 × 28) | 6,714 | |
| Non-deductible | | 2,686 |
| | | 4,686 |

(f)  The loss of £21,000 need not be adjusted for in computing the Schedule D Case I profit, **because fraud by an employee (as opposed to a director) is an incident of the company's trading activities** *(Bamford v ATA Advertising Ltd 1972).*

(g)  **No adjustment is required for the insurance receipt in respect of revenue expenditure. The receipt is treated as a normal trading receipt.**

(h)  **The receipt for advice will probably be treated as trading income, in which case no adjustment will be needed.**

## 8  TRUNK LTD

> **Pass marks**. In a question such as this, it is a good idea to tick each item on the question paper as you deal with it, so that you do not miss anything.

TRUNK LIMITED
COMPUTATION OF ADJUSTED PROFIT OR LOSS

|  | £ | £ | Note |
|---|---|---|---|
| Loss per accounts | | (42,000) | |
| *Additions to profit* | | | |
| Lease premium amortisation | 2,000 | | (a) |
| Depreciation | 9,500 | | (a) |
| Loss on sale of lorry | 6,000 | | (a) |
| Entertaining | 1,800 | | (b) |
| Legal fees | 4,400 | | (c) |
| General expenses | 2,500 | | (d) |
| Repairs and renewals | 5,000 | | (e) |
| | | 31,200 | |
| | | (10,800) | |
| *Deductions from profit* | | | |
| Reduction in general provision | 1,000 | | (f) |
| Deemed extra rent | 1,640 | | (g) |
| Rents received | 10,000 | | (h) |
| Gain on sale of plant | 7,400 | | (a) |
| Capital allowances | 7,160 | | (i) |
| | | (27,200) | |
| Adjusted loss | | (38,000) | |

*Notes*

(a)  **Depreciation and amortisation are not deductible, being capital. Losses and gains on the sale of fixed assets** are essentially catching-up for inadequate or excessive depreciation, and **are similarly not deductible (losses) or taxable (gains).**

(b)  **The cost of entertaining customers, and the cost of gifts of food to customers, are by statute not deductible.** Entertaining staff is not caught by this rule.

(c)  The **legal fees in relation to the new lease are not deductible** because they are capital in nature. The **legal fees in relation to the recovery of the employee loan are not deductible** because they are not for trade purposes: the trade is manufacturing, not moneylending. **Legal fees in relation to service contracts, are, however, deductible.**

(d)  **Penalties and fines are not deductible.** Course fees for trade-related training of employees, on the other hand, are deductible.

(e)  **The cost of the new windows is not deductible because it is of a capital nature,** being needed to put the recently-acquired warehouse in a usable condition. Routine repairs, on the other hand, are deductible.

(f) **General provisions are not deductible, so reductions in them are not taxable.** Specific provisions, on the other hand, and actual bad debts, are deductible.

(g) **When a trader pays a lease premium, the part treated as income for the landlord is treated as extra rent payable by the trader, spread over the term of the lease.** The extra rent per year is:

£20,000 × [50 − (10 − 1)] × 2% × 1/10 = £1,640

(h) **Rents are taxed under Schedule A, not Schedule D Case I.**

(i) **Capital allowances are the statutory substitute for depreciation.**

(j) The following items require no adjustment.

(i) **Patent fees**, which **are deductible** by statute.

(ii) **Debenture interest on a trading loan relationship**, which is **deductible** by statute.

(iii) **Discounts received, which simply affect the cost of purchases.**

(iv) **The insurance recovery for damage to stock, which simply replaces some or all of the revenue which would have been earned had the stock not been damaged.**

## 9    SCHEDULE D ADJUSTMENTS

> **Pass marks**. It was important to answer this question by giving reasons for the adjustments you made and quoting case law where appropriate.

(a)

|  | £ | Notes | £ |
|---|---|---|---|
| Profits per accounts | | | 290,000 |
| Add: | | | |
| Director's salary | 24,000 | (ii) | |
| Damages | 12,000 | (iii) | |
| Repairs | 12,000 | (iv) | |
| Employee loan | 2,000 | (v) | |
| Goods sold abroad | 40,000 | (viii) | |
| | | | 90,000 |
| Deduct: | | | |
| Decrease in general bad debt provision | 3,000 | (vi) | |
| Insurance recoveries | 14,000 | (ix) | |
| | | | (17,000) |
| | | | 363,000 |

*Notes*

(i) **The costs of seconding employees to charities are deductible,** so no adjustment needs to be made in respect of the £22,000 paid to the director seconded to Oxfam.

(ii) **The salary paid to a director seconded to a group company** was not paid wholly and exclusively for the purpose of the company's trade so it is **not deductible** and an adjustment is needed.

(iii) **In *Strong and Co v Woodifield 1906* damages paid were held to be non-deductible because they were too remote from the trade.** In this case disallow the net costs after insurance recoveries.

(iv) **The cost of getting the office ready for use is non-deductible capital expenditure** (*Law Shipping Co Ltd v CIR 1923*).

(v)   **Employee loans are not made for the purposes of the company's trade so these are non-deductible.**

(vi)   **A decrease in the general bad debt provision is not taxable** so an adjustment must be made to the accounts figure. No adjustments are required in respect of specific provisions for bad debts, or in respect of bad debts written off.

(vii)   **Redundancy payments in a continuing trade are deductible provided they are paid wholly and exclusively for trade purposes.**

(viii)   **The company must make a transfer pricing adjustment to adjust the price of goods sold abroad to their market value.**

(ix)   **Insurance recoveries in respect of the let properties are taxable under Schedule A.** This means that you need to make an adjustment to ensure the recoveries are not also included in the Schedule D profits.

(x)   **Insurance recoveries in respect of repairs to the general office are taxable under Schedule D so no adjustment is needed.**

10   **F LTD**

> **Pass marks**. A building in an enterprise zone that is not written off in full in the first year is written off in subsequent years at the rate of 25% of cost.

(a)

*Building 1*

**When a secondhand factory which was previously used for industrial purposes is acquired the 'cost' that is written off for industrial purposes is the lower of**

(i)   **Price paid, £200,000**
(ii)   **Original cost, £180,000**

Thus £180,000 **is written off by F Ltd over the remaining tax life of the building.** £9,474 (£180,000/19) of writing down allowance is due if the building is in industrial use on 31 March 2001.

*Building 2*

The 25 year life of building 2 expired on 1 April 2000 thus no allowance is available in the year ended 31 March 2001 for this factory.

*Building 3*

Qualifying cost is lower of

(i)   Original cost, £160,000
(ii)   Purchase price, £200,000

Therefore £160,000 is written off over the remaining tax life of 1 year. £160,000 is written off in the year to 31.3.01.

*Building 4*

Qualifying cost is lower of

(i)   Original cost, £240,000
(ii)   Purchase price, £200,000

Therefore £200,000 is written off over the remaining 22 year tax life. £9,091 of writing down allowance is available in the year to 31.3.01.

**Summary - year to 31.3.01**

| Building | £ |
|---|---|
| 1 | 9,474 |
| 2 | – |
| 3 | 160,000 |
| 4 | 9,091 |

Therefore, building 3 would generate the highest amount of IBAs in the year 31.3.01.

(b)

| | £ |
|---|---|
| Factory in enterprise zone | 100,000 |
| Claimed y/e 31.3.00 | (60,000) |
| TWDV c/f | 40,000 |
| Y/e 31.3.01 | (25,000) |
| TWDV c/f | 15,000 |

**A building in an enterprise zone which is not completely written off in the first year is given allowances equal to 25% of cost in subsequent years.**

(c)

| | | £ |
|---|---|---|
| Cost | y/e 31.3.97 | 80,000 |
| | y/e 31.3.97 (4%) | (3,200) |
| | y/e 31.3.98 (4%) | (3,200) |
| | y/e 31.3.99 (4%) | (3,200) |
| | y/e 31.3.00 (4%) | (3,200) notional |
| | | 67,200 |

Adjusted net cost

£10,000 × 36/60 = £6,000

Allowances actually given £9,600

Balancing charge = £3,600 (£9,600 – £6,000)

**Conclusion**

The maximum IBAs that may be claimed by F Ltd in the year to 31.3.01 are

| | £ |
|---|---|
| (i) | 160,000 |
| (ii) | 25,000 |
| (iii) | (3,600) |
| | 181,400 |

## 11    PREPARATION QUESTION: PLANT AND A FACTORY

**Pass marks**. The tax benefit of capital allowances depends on the applicable rate of corporation tax, as set out in part (b). This fact may influence the timing of capital expenditure, if a company's tax rate fluctuates.

As the company is a small enterprise for first year allowances purposes, 100% first year allowances are available on the computer equipment. 40% first year allowances are available on other plant. FYAs are not pro-rated in short periods.

(a)  **Capital allowances**

**Computer equipment**

|  |  | £ | Total £ |
|---|---|---:|---:|
| (i) | *Plant £2,500: FYA @ 100%* |  | 2,500 |
| (iii) | *Cars* |  |  |
|  | General pool: 25% × 10/12 × £5,000 | 1,042 |  |
|  | Expensive: allowance restricted to £3,000 × 10/12 | 2,500 |  |
|  |  |  | 3,542 |
| (iii) | *Plant £65,842  FYA @ 40%* |  | 26,337 |

*Industrial building*

The original owner would have received IBAs but since the building was sold less than 25 years after 5 December 1986 a balancing charge would have been applied on sale. Freddie Ltd is given WDAs on the 'residue after sale' which is, generally, the lower of proceeds or original cost. Thus allowances will be given on £7,500 (£10,000 – £2,500). The building was 14 years 9 months old when Freddie acquired it. Of the 25 years tax life, 10 years 3 months (123 months) remain. Allowances of £7,500 × 12/123 are given each full year, but only 10/123 in this first, short period. Thus: £7,500 × 10/123                                                        610

| (iv) | *Extension to factory* |  |  |
|---|---|---:|---:|
|  | WDA 4% × 10/12 × £222,000 |  | 7,400 |
|  | Total allowances |  | 40,389 |

(b)  **The tax benefit of capital allowances**

**For corporation tax purposes capital allowances are treated as a trading expense.** They therefore reduce the taxable profit of the accounting period to which they relate. If Freddie Ltd makes profits exceeding £1,500,000 × 10/12 = £1,250,000, its profits will be taxed at 30%. The tax saved by virtue of the capital allowances will therefore be £40,389 × 30% = £12,117. If profits are less than £300,000 × 10/12 = £250,000 but above £50,000 × 10/12 = £41,667, the small companies rate of 20% will apply. The value of the allowances will then be £8,078. If profits are below £10,000 × 10/12 = £8,333, the starting rate of corporation tax applies and the value of allowances is then £40,389 × 10% = £4,039.

If profits fall between the limits of £1,250,000 and £250,000 the marginal rate of tax will be 32.5%, giving a tax saving of £13,126. If profits fall between the limits of £41,667 and £8,333, the marginal rate of tax will be 22.5% giving a tax saving of £9,087.

The cash flow benefit of the capital allowances will not be felt until the due date for payment of the mainstream corporation tax: provided the company does not pay tax at the full rate this will be 1 August 2002. If the company pays tax at the full rate it will normally have to make quarterly payments on account of its corporation tax liability.

**If capital allowances create or increase a loss the benefit will be enjoyed only under the loss relief provisions.**

(c)  **Expenditure on office accommodation**

**Rent payable is allowable** as a trading expense. **A lease premium, to the extent that it is taxable income of the landlord, will be divided into yearly deductions depending**

on the length of the lease. No industrial buildings allowance is given on the purchase of office accommodation except for expenditure of not more than 25% of the cost of an industrial building or where the office building is in an enterprise zone. Office equipment, including certain fixtures such as carpets, does attract capital allowances as plant. Repairs are deductible expenses unless disallowed as capital expenditure.

## 12  R LTD

> **Pass marks**. IBAs are not available on land but they are available on offices if the total cost of offices is less than 25% of the qualifying expenditure.

(a)  **Factory A**

The 25 year life of factory A expired on 1 April 2000 thus no allowance is available in the year ending 31.3.2001 for this factory.

**Factory B**

When a second hand factory which was previously used for industrial purposes is acquired the 'cost' that is written off for industrial buildings purposes is the lower of

(i)   price paid £60,000
(ii)  original cost £50,000

Thus £50,000 is written off by R Ltd over the remaining 19 year life of the building.

$£2,632 \left( \dfrac{£50,000}{19} \right)$ of writing down allowance is due if the building is in industrial use on the last day of the accounting period.

**Factory C**

Qualifying cost

|  | £ |
|---|---|
| Land | – |
| Site preparation | 10,000 |
| Factory | 100,000 |
| Offices | 25,000 |
|  | 135,000 |

Since the offices cost less than 25% of the total cost the full cost of £135,000 qualifies for IBAs.

A writing down allowance (WDA) of 4% × £135,000 = £5,400 is available.

**Factory D**

Commercial buildings in an enterprise zone qualify for an initial allowance in the first year of up to 100% of cost. If the full allowance is not taken allowances of 25% × cost are available in future years.

IBAs available on Factory D in the year to 31.3.01 are, therefore, £120,000 × 25% = £30,000.

**Factory E**

|  |  | *Allowances* |
|---|---|---|
| Y/e 31.3.94 | £ | £ |
| Cost | 70,000 |  |
| IA @ 20% | (14,000) | 14,000 |
| WDA @ 4% | (2,800) | 2,800 |
|  | 53,200 |  |
| Y/e 31.3.95 @ 4% | (2,800) | 2,800 |
| Y/e 31.3.96 @ 4% | (2,800) | 2,800 |
| Y/e 31.3.97 @ 4% | (2,800) | 2,800 |
| Y/e 31.3.98 @ 4% | (2,800) | 2,800 |
| Y/e 31.3.99 Notional WDA @ 4% | (2,800) | – |
| Y/e 31.3.00 Notional WDA @ 4% | (2,800) | – |
|  |  | 28,000 |
| TWDV at 31.3.01 | 36,400 |  |

As the factory is sold for more than its original cost a balancing charge equal to the allowances given of £28,000 will arise in the year to 31.3.01.

**Summary**

| Factory |  | £ |
|---|---|---|
| A | No allowance due | – |
| B | WDA | 2,632 |
| C | WDA | 5,400 |
| D | WDA | 30,000 |
| E | Balancing charge | (28,000) |
| Total |  | 10,032 |

(b)

REPORT

To:      Directors of R Ltd
From:    A N Accountant
Date:    21 January 2001
Subject: IBA position if factories are leased rather than purchased.

**IBAs are given to the person with a relevant interest** in the industrial building. The grant of a lease does not normally entitle the lessee to industrial buildings allowances. However, **where a lease of more than 50 years is granted an election may be made to treat the grant of the lease as the sale of the relevant interest thereby allowing the lessee to claim industrial buildings allowances.** The premium paid is treated as though it is the purchase price and the allowances that would normally be available on a secondhand building are given.

Signed: Management Accountant

13    **H LTD**

> **Pass marks**. Writing down allowances are pro-rated for short accounting periods. First year allowances are not.

(a)  CAPITAL ALLOWANCES

| | £ | Pool £ | Car pool £ | Expensive car (1) £ | Allowances £ |
|---|---|---|---|---|---|
| TWDV b/f | | 38,000 | 16,000 | 14,000 | |
| Transfer | | 16,000 | (16,000) | | |
| Additions | | 10,400 | | | |
| Less: Disposals | | (5,000) | | (10,000) | |
| | | 59,400 | | 4,000 | |
| WDA at 25% × 10/12 | | (12,375) | | | 12,375 |
| Additions qualifying for FYA | 1,875 | | | | |
| FYA @ 40% | (750) | | | | 750 |
| | | 1,125 | | | |
| Balancing allowance | | | | (4,000) | 4,000 |
| TWDV c/f | | 48,150 | | 0 | |
| | | | | | 17,125 |

(b)  MAINSTREAM CORPORATION TAX

| | £ |
|---|---|
| Schedule D Case I (£77,125 – £17,125) | 60,000 |
| Schedule D Case III (4,500 + 8,000) | 12,500 |
| Capital gain | 12,000 |
| Taxed income | 6,000 |
| | 90,500 |
| Less: Charge on income | (2,000) |
| PCTCT | 88,500 |

| | £ | £ |
|---|---|---|
| *FY 99 and FY 2000* | | |
| £88,500 × 20% | | 17,700 |
| Maximum set off of ACT (£88,500 × 20%) | 17,700 | |
| Less shadow ACT (£40,000 × 20/80) | (10,000) | |
| Set off surplus ACT brought forward | 7,700 | (7,700) |
| Less:  Income tax suffered | | |
|     Debenture interest (20%) | 1,600 | |
|     Patent royalty (22%) | 1,320 | |
| | | (2,920) |
| | | 7,080 |

Surplus ACT of £42,300 (£50,000 – £7,700) remains to be carried forward at 1.10.00.

*Note*. The charitable deed of covenant would be paid gross under the gift aid scheme.

## 14  MAJOR LTD

> **Passmarks**. Surplus ACT brought forward can only be set off after the set off of shadow ACT.

(a)  *Mainstream corporation tax*

|  | £ |
|---|---|
| Trading profit per question | 180,000 |
| Schedule A | 30,000 |
| Capital gains | 40,000 |
|  | 250,000 |
| Less charges |  |
| Patent royalties | (15,000) |
| Deed of covenant | (3,000) |
| Less non-trade deficit (£24,000 – £30,000) | (6,000) |
| PCTCT | 226,000 |
| Add Franked investment income | 20,000 |
| 'Profits' | 246,000 |

The eight month accounting period all falls to be taxed using rates for the financial year 2000.

| Small companies lower limit | £300,000 × 8/12 × ½ | £100,000 |
|---|---|---|
| Small companies upper limit | £1,500,000 × 8/12 × ½ | £500,000 |

Small companies marginal relief applies

*Corporation tax*

|  | £ |
|---|---|
| £226,000 × 30% | 67,800 |
| Less marginal relief (1/40 × (£500,000 – £246,000) × 226,000/246,000) | (5,834) |
|  | 61,966 |
| Less: ACT (W1) | (29,700) |
| Less: income tax suffered (W2) | (1,500) |
| Mainstream corporation tax | 30,766 |

*Working*

1   ACT

|  | £ |
|---|---|
| Notional franked payment (£80,000 × 100/80) | 100,000 |
| FII for shadow purposes (£20,000 × 90/80) | 22,500 |
| FP for shadow purposes | 77,500 |
| Shadow ACT @ 20% | £15,500 |

|  | £ |
|---|---|
| Maximum set off (£226,000 × 20%) | 45,200 |
| Reduction for shadow ACT | (15,500) |
| Set off limit | 29,700 |

Therefore surplus ACT to carry forward at 1 January 2001 (£34,000 – £29,700) = £4,300.

2   Income tax

|  | £ |
|---|---|
| Income tax suffered (£24,000 × 20%) | 4,800 |
| Less: income tax withheld on |  |
| Patent royalty (£15,000 × 22%) | (3,300) |
|  | 1,500 |

Interest on the bank loan is paid gross.

Charitable covenants are paid gross under the gift aid scheme.

(b) To:    The Directors of Major Ltd

     From:    Management Accountant

     Date:    1 December 2000

     Re:    Tax implications of the loan to Z Ltd becoming irrecoverable

It will not be possible for any amount of the loan written off to be deducted in computing Major Ltd's Schedule D Case I profits. This means that if the loan is written off in the company's profit and loss account, the amount written off must be added back to compute Schedule D Case I profits. Instead **any amount written off will be treated as a deficit on a non-trading loan relationship**. This means that **it will initially be deducted from income arising on non-trading loan relationships in the same accounting period. Any overall net deficit can be:**

(i) **Set against the company's total profits in the same accounting period,** or

(ii) **Set against income from non trading loan relationships arising in the previous twelve months,** or

(iii) **Set off against non-trading profits in the following period,** or

(iv) **Surrendered to set against Minority Ltd's total profits arising in the corresponding accounting period.**

Signed: Management Accountant

## 15   FINANCING EXPANSION

> **Pass marks**. The two main ways of raising finance are either through issuing share or through raising loan capital. You should have discussed both.

### REPORT

To:    The Board of M Ltd

From:    Management Accountant

Date:    19 May 2000

Re:    Taxation consequences of alternative methods of raising finance and of late filing of CT return

The purpose of this report is to set out the tax consequences of the alternative methods of finance that we are considering using to finance our expansion. The report will also set out the date by which we must file M Ltd's CT return for the year to 31 March 2001 and the penalties that will arise for the late filing of the return.

### Methods of financing expansion

The choice of raising additional funds to finance a major expansion of the business can be summarised as being between **loan capital or equity**. A major distinction between the two forms of financing **is that interest payable on borrowings is deductible** for corporation tax purposes **whereas dividends payable to shareholders are not.**

*Loan capital*

**Interest is tax deductible on an accruals basis under either Schedule D Case I (if put to a trading use) or Schedule D Case III.**

If the **loan interest being paid represents an annual payment other than to a UK bank, income tax should be deducted at source** and accounted for to the Collector of Taxes under the CT61 quarterly accounting procedure.

**Costs of obtaining loan finance will be treated as tax-deductible** in the same manner as interest payable on the loan. In contrast, costs in respect of issuing share capital are not deductible for CT purposes.

Interest income received by the providers of loan finance is taxable. It will be Schedule D Case III income of a company and subject to tax at normal corporation tax rates. Individuals in receipt of interest income will be subject to tax on the gross amount at either 20% or 40%.

*Equity finance*

**Dividends represent appropriations of profit after tax. They are not tax deductible and any costs associated with the raising of share capital are not tax deductible.**

With regard to providers of equity finance, there are tax benefits available to investors who invest in Enterprise Investment Scheme (EIS) shares:

(1) An individual subscribing for new ordinary shares in an unquoted trading company can claim income tax relief at 20% for an investment of up to £150,000 per tax year. If the EIS shares are held for three years, there is exemption from capital gains tax on a disposal of the shares. A capital loss may arise on a disposal before or after expiry of the three year period but it is restricted by reducing the acquisition cost by the amount of relief obtained.

(2) Chargeable gains realised by individuals may be deferred provided that those gains are reinvested in new ordinary shares of a qualifying EIS unquoted trading company. The reinvestment of gains must be made in the period twelve months before to three years after the relevant disposal. The gain is deferred and does not therefore usually crystallise before a subsequent disposal of the new EIS shares.

**CT return**

M Ltd's corporation tax return for the year to 31 March 2001 must be filed by the later of:

   (i)    31 March 2002
   (iii)   Three months after a notice requiring the return is issued

The **initial penalty** for the late filing of the return **will be £100. This will rise to £200 if the return is over three months late**. There will also be a tax related penalty of **10% of the tax unpaid six months after the filing date where the return is not filed within 6 months of the filing date and of 20% of this tax where the return is not filed within 12 months of the filing date.**

If you wish to discuss further any of the above points do not hesitate to contact me.

Signed: Management Accountant

## 16   PREPARATION QUESTION: CARRY-BACK CLAIMS

> **Pass marks**. The unrelieved trade charge in the second year must be carried forward. Such charges can only be carried back if they arise in the final accounting period of a trade.

(a) **Mainstream corporation tax computation for the accounting period ended 30 September 1999**

|  | £ |
|---|---|
| Schedule D Case I | 300,000 |
| Schedule A | 4,000 |
| Schedule D Case III | 5,000 |
|  | 309,000 |
| Less charges on income | (9,000) |
| Profits chargeable to corporation tax | 300,000 |
| Dividends plus tax credits | 4,000 |
| 'Profits' | 304,000 |

|  | *FY98* | *FY99* |
|---|---|---|
|  | *6/12* | *6/12* |
| PCTCT | 150,000 | 150,000 |
| Profits | 152,000 | 152,000 |
| Upper limit for small companies rate | 750,000 | 750,000 |
| Lower limit for small companies rate | 150,000 | 150,000 |

|  | £ |
|---|---|
| *FY 1998* |  |
| *Corporation tax* |  |
| £150,000 × 31% | 46,500 |
| (£750,000 – £152,000) × 1/40 × 150/152 | (14,753) |
|  |  |
| *FY 1999* |  |
| £150,000 × 30% | 45,000 |
| (£750,000 – £152,000) × 150/152 × 1/40 | (14,753) |
| Mainstream corporation tax | 61,994 |

(b) **The repayment of corporation tax**

|  | £ |
|---|---|
| Schedule D Case I | 300,000 |
| Schedule A | 4,000 |
| Schedule D Case III | 5,000 |
|  | 309,000 |
| Less trade charges | (9,000) |
|  | 300,000 |
| Less: s393A relief (W2) | (158,000) |
| Profits chargeable to corporation tax | 142,000 |
| Dividends plus tax credits | 4,000 |
| 'Profits' | 146,000 |

*Corporation tax payable*

|  | £ |
|---|---|
| *FY 1998* |  |
| £142,000 × 21% × 6/12 | 14,910 |
| *FY 1999* |  |
| £142,000 × 20% × 6/12 | 14,200 |
| Revised mainstream corporation tax | 29,110 |

*Repayment due*

|  | £ |
|---|---|
| Original MCT (part (a) above) | 61,994 |
| Less revised MCT (above) | (29,110) |
| Repayment due | 32,884 |

*Workings*

1    **Calculation of total chargeable profits for y/e 30.9.00**

|  | £ | £ |
|---|---:|---:|
| Schedule D Case I |  | 0 |
| Schedule A |  | 2,000 |
| Schedule D Case III |  | 4,000 |
| Chargeable gains | 12,000 |  |
| Less allowable losses brought forward | (6,000) |  |
|  |  | 6,000 |
| Chargeable profits before loss relief |  | 12,000 |

2    **Available loss relief in y/e 30.9.00**

|  | £ |
|---|---:|
| Trading loss for y/e 30.9.00 | 170,000 |
| Less   s 393A(1) relief against total profits of |  |
| y/e 30.9.00 (W1) | (12,000) |
| Available for carry back | (158,000) |

(c)  **Amounts carried forward**

|  | £ |
|---|---:|
| Trading loss of 12 month period to 30.9.00 | 170,000 |
| Less current year loss relief | (12,000) |
|  | 158,000 |
| Less loss carried back | (158,000) |
|  | 0 |
| Unrelieved trade charges of y/e 30.9.00 | 4,000 |
| Loss carried forward | 4,000 |

The donation under the gift aid scheme will be unrelieved. Non-trade charges cannot be carried forward.

17    **MACRO LTD**

> **Pass marks**. There was a capital loss in the second year. Such losses go *only* against capital gains of the same or future accounting periods, *not* against other profits.

(a)

|  | *Year ended 31 March* | | |
|---|---:|---:|---:|
|  | *1998* | *1999* | *2000* |
|  | £ | £ | £ |
| Schedule D Case I | 140,000 | 130,000 | 80,000 |
| Schedule D Case III | 8,000 | 6,000 | 4,000 |
| Capital gain £(40,000 – 20,000) | 10,000 | 0 | 20,000 |
|  | 158,000 | 136,000 | 104,000 |
| Less trade charges | (4,000) | (4,000) | (8,000) |
|  | 154,000 | 132,000 | 96,000 |
| Less non-trade charges | (2,000) | (2,000) | (2,000) |
| Profits chargeable to corporation tax | 152,000 | 130,000 | 94,000 |
| Dividends received plus tax credits | 7,500 | 3,750 | 7,750 |
| Profits for small companies rate purposes | 159,500 | 133,750 | 101,750 |
| Mainstream corporation tax at 20% | 30,400 | 26,000 | 18,800 |

(b)  Unrelieved trade charges in the final period of trading can be added to a loss carried back, this means the amount to carry back is £(354,000 – 2,000 + 6,000) = £358,000.

|  | | *Year ended 31 March* | |
|---|---|---|---|
|  | 1998 | 1999 | 2000 |
|  | £ | £ | £ |
| Profits after trade charges | 154,000 | 132,000 | 96,000 |
| Less loss relief | (130,000) | (132,000) | (96,000) |
|  | 24,000 | 0 | 0 |
| Less non-trade charges | (2,000) | 0 | 0 |
| Profits chargeable to corporation tax | 22,000 | 0 | 0 |
| Revised mainstream corporation tax at 20% | 4,400 | 0 | 0 |
| Less: starting rate marginal relief ($^1/_{40}$ (£50,000 | | | |
| $-£29,500) \times \dfrac{22,000}{29,500}$ | (382) | 0 | 0 |
|  | 4,018 | 0 | 0 |
| Original mainstream corporation tax | 30,400 | 26,000 | 18,800 |
| Repayment | 26,382 | 26,000 | 18,800 |
| Wasted non-trade charges | 0 | 2,000 | 2,000 |

(c)  The effects of the claim for loss relief are:

   (i)    To generate tax repayments of £71,182.
   (ii)   To waste non-trade charges of £4,000.

## 18   OBJECTIVE TEST QUESTIONS

1  A  The company must file a return for the two accounting periods ending in the period specified in the notice requiring a return.

2  C

3  C

4  A

5  C  $£510,000 \times 72\% \times ^3/_9 = £122,400$

6  C  Return less than 3 months late.

7  A

8  D  $88\% \times £2,000,000 = £1,760,000$

$$\frac{3}{8} \times £1,760,000 = £660,000$$

9  B  

| | £ |
|---|---|
| Maximum ACT set off: | |
| £300,000 × 20% | 60,000 |
| Less: Shadow ACT (£90,000 × 20/80) | (22,500) |
| | 37,500 |

ACT c/f £12,500 (£50,000 – £37,500)

## 19   PREPARATION QUESTION: A BUILDING AND SHARES

> **Pass marks**. Rollover relief is not automatically available on the facts given: conditions relating to trade use and the time of acquisition must be satisfied.

**(a) The building**

| | £ |
|---|---:|
| Proceeds | 200,000 |
| Less 31.3.82 value | (65,000) |
| Unindexed gain | 135,000 |
| Less indexation allowance on 31.3.82 value | |
| £65,000 × 1.141 | (74,165) |
| Chargeable gain | 60,835 |

A computation based on cost would clearly produce a higher gain.

**The Z plc shares**

| | Shares | Cost £ | Indexed cost £ |
|---|---:|---:|---:|
| *The FA 1985 pool* | | | |
| May 1982 acquisition | 2,000 | 4,000 | 4,000 |
| Indexation to April 1985: £4,000 × 0.162 | | | 648 |
| | | | 4,648 |
| Indexed rise to March 1986: £4,648 × 0.020 | | | 93 |
| March 1986 acquisition | 2,000 | 5,000 | 5,000 |
| | 4,000 | 9,000 | 9,741 |
| Indexed rise to July 2000: £9,741 × 0.799 | | | 7,783 |
| | | | 17,524 |
| July 2000 disposal | (4,000) | (9,000) | (17,524) |
| | 0 | 0 | 0 |

| | £ | £ |
|---|---:|---:|
| Sale proceeds £27,500 × 4,000/5,000 | | 22,000 |
| Less cost | | (9,000) |
| | | 13,000 |
| Less indexation allowance £(17,524 – 9,000) | | (8,524) |
| Indexed gain | | 4,476 |
| *The 1982 holding* | | |
| Sale proceeds £27,500 × 1,000/5,000 | 5,500 | |
| Less 31.3.82 value | (1,750) | |
| Unindexed gain | 3,750 | |
| Less indexation allowance | | |
| £1,750 × 1.147 | (2,007) | |
| Chargeable gain | | 1,743 |
| Total chargeable gain | | 6,219 |

A computation for the 1982 holding using cost would clearly give a higher gain.

Total chargeable gains for the year are £60,835 + £6,219 = £67,054.

Corporation tax payable thereon is £67,054 × 30% = £20,116.

As Jolly Cove Ltd pays corporation tax at the full rate it must pay its CT liability on the gains (together with the rest of its CT) in quarterly instalments. For the year to 31.3.01 72% of its total liability is due in instalments on 14 October 2000, 14 January 2001, 14 April 2001 and 14 July 2001. The balancing 28% is due on 1 January 2002.

(b) If the non-industrial building was occupied and used for trading purposes and the sale **proceeds are reinvested in another building (or other qualifying asset) for use in the company's trade, within 12 months before or 36 months after the disposal, capital gains rollover relief will be available**.

If the new qualifying building costs £225,000, full rollover relief will be available with the chargeable gain arising on the disposal (£60,835) being deducted from the acquisition cost of the new building, to give the revised base cost of that asset.

When not all of the sale proceeds of a qualifying asset are reinvested, the gain which becomes immediately chargeable is the lower of:

(i) The **gain on disposal of the old asset**.

(ii) The **proceeds not reinvested** in the new asset.

Thus, if the new building costs £175,000, a gain of £25,000 becomes chargeable immediately, with the balance of £60,835 − £25,000 = £35,835 being rolled over.

## 20 BD LTD

> **Pass marks**. Part (b) is very straightforward if you realise that all of the gains will fall within the small companies' marginal relief band.

(a) (i) **The lease**

|  | £ |
|---|---|
| Proceeds | 12,000 |
| Less: Cost adjusted for 'lease wasting' factors | |
| $£48,000 \times \dfrac{83.816 - 74.635}{91.981}$ | (4,791) |
|  | 7,209 |
| Less: Indexation allowance | |
| $£4,791 \times 0.228$ | (1,092) |
| Capital gain | 6,117 |
| Less: Schedule A assessment (W1) | (10,800) |
| Chargeable gain | Nil |

*Note*. **The Schedule A deduction reduces the chargeable gain to nil. It does not turn a chargeable gain into an allowable loss.**

(ii) **The office**

|  | £ |
|---|---|
| Proceeds | 42,000 |
| Less: Attributable cost | |
| $£100,000 \times \dfrac{42,000}{42,000 + 190,000}$ | (18,103) |
|  | 23,897 |
| Less: Indexation allowance | |
| $£18,103 \times 0.657$ | (11,894) |
| Chargeable gain | 12,003 |

(iii) **The shares**

|  | £ |
|---|---|
| Proceeds | 75,000 |
| Less: Attributable March 1982 value (W2) | (13,846) |
|  | 61,154 |
| Less: Indexation allowance | |
| $£13,846 \times 1.147$ | (15,881) |
| Chargeable gain | 45,273 |

Using the March 1982 value clearly gives an lower gain than cost.

**Summary of chargeable gains**

|  | £ |
|---|---|
| (i) | Nil |
| (ii) | 12,003 |
| (iii) | 45,273 |
| Total | 57,276 |

*Workings*

1    **Schedule A**

|  | £ |
|---|---|
| Premium | 12,000 |
| Less: 2% × £12,000 × (6 – 1) | (1,200) |
| Schedule A | 10,800 |

2    **Attributable cost/M82 value of shares**

Original holding: 20,000 ordinary shares

| Original cost | £15,000 |
|---|---|
| March 1982 value | £20,000 |

Reorganisation:

|  | *MV* |
|---|---|
|  | £ |
| 20,000 ordinary shares @ £1.80 | 36,000 |
| 20,000 preference shares @ 80p | 16,000 |
|  | 52,000 |

Split original cost/M82 value between new holding based on above values:

|  | *Cost* | *M82 value* |
|---|---|---|
|  | £ | £ |
| **New ordinary shares** | 10,385 | 13,846 |
| £15,000/£20,000 × $\dfrac{36,000}{52,000}$ |  |  |
| **New preference shares** | 4,615 |  |
| £15,000/£20,000 × $\dfrac{16,000}{52,000}$ |  | 6,154 |
|  | 15,000 | 20,000 |

(b)    As BD Ltd has one associated company for CT rate purposes, the upper and lower thresholds for small companies' rate purposes are divided by two, giving £750,000 and £150,000 respectively. The CT payable on the £57,276 chargeable gains at BD Ltd's marginal rate of 32.5% is therefore £18,615.

---

21    **B LTD**

> **Pass marks**. In part (b) it was important to think about the significance of being given two different values for proceeds by the examiner. This was a clue which should have lead you to the right answer.

(a)    Chargeable gains

**Painting**

|  | £ |
|---|---|
| Deemed proceeds | 6,000 |
| Less: cost | (7,100) |
| Allowable loss | (1,100) |

**Lease**

|  | £ |
|---|---|
| Disposal proceeds | 100,000 |

Less: Cost    $£45,000 \times \dfrac{P30}{P35}$

$£45,000 \times \dfrac{87.33}{91.981}$ ................................ (42,725)

|  | £ |
|---|---|
|  | 57,275 |
| Less: Indexation £42,725 × 0.148 | (6,323) |
| Chargeable gain | 50,952 |

**Warehouse**

|  | £ |
|---|---|
| Proceeds | 5,000 |
| Less: March 1982 value | (7,000) |
| Allowable loss | (2,000) |

The March 1982 value only is deducted in this computation as a s 35 TCGA 1992 election had been made.

Net chargeable gain to be included in CT computation.

|  | £ |
|---|---|
| Painting | (1,100) |
| Lease | 50,952 |
| Warehouse | (2,000) |
| Chargeable gain | 47,852 |

(b)  (i)

|  | £ |
|---|---|
| Proceeds | 4,980 |

Less: $\dfrac{4,980}{4,980 + (50,000 \times 1.80)} \times 55,000$ ............ (2,884)

|  | £ |
|---|---|
|  | 2,096 |
| Less: Indexation £2,884 × 0.628 | (1,811) |
| Chargeable gain | 285 |

(ii) **As the amount received for the rights is less than 5% of the value of the shares, no chargeable gains computation is required.** Instead, the value of the rights sold is deducted from the base cost of the shares for future disposal which, therefore, becomes £51,000 (£55,000 – £4,000).

**22    V LTD**

> **Pass marks.** A 'heldover' gain is deferred and eventually becomes chargeable in full.

(a)  (i)    **Plant and machinery**

**Gain arising in March 1992**

|  | £ |
|---|---|
| Proceeds | 250,000 |
| Less: cost | (120,000) |
|  | 130,000 |
| Less: indexation |  |
| £120,000 × 0.536 | (64,320) |
|  | 65,680 |
| Less: holdover relief | (25,680) |
| Chargeable gain (proceeds not reinvested) | 40,000 |

On the destruction of the plant and machinery in July 2000, the heldover gain of £25,680 crystallises.

No gain arises in respect of the plant and machinery as this is a chattel which qualified for capital allowances

(ii)   **Painting**

|  | £ |
|---|---|
| Net proceeds (£8,000 - £200) | 7,800 |
| Less: March 82 value | (1,000) |
|  | 6,800 |
| Less: indexation £1,000 × 1.147 | (1,147) |
| Chargeable gain | 5,653 |

The maximum gain chargeable cannot exceed:

5/3 (£8,000 – 6,000) = £3,333

∴ The chargeable gain is £3,333.

(iii)   **Sculptures**

|  | £ |
|---|---|
| Disposal value | 10,000 |
| Less: cost | (4,000) |
|  | 6,000 |
| Less: indexation £4,000 × 0.224 | (896) |
| Chargeable gain | 5,104 |

The maximum chargeable gain cannot exceed:

5/3 (£10,000 - £6,000) = £6,667

∴ The gain chargeable is £5,104.

(iv)   **Table**

|  | £ |
|---|---|
| Deemed proceeds | 6,000 |
| Less: cost | (6,500) |
| Allowable loss | (500) |

There is no indexation as indexation cannot increase an allowable loss.

(v)   **Sale of shares**

|  | Market value £ |
|---|---|
| 15,000 ordinary shares | 21,000 |
| 8,000 preference shares | 10,000 |
| £5,000 debentures | 5,000 |
|  | 36,000 |

Deemed cost of ordinary shares

$$£30,000 \times \frac{21,000}{36,000} = £17,500$$

|  | £ |
|---|---|
| Proceeds | 60,000 |
| Deemed cost £17,500 × 10/15 | (11,667) |
|  | 48,333 |
| Less: £11,667 × 0.518 | (6,044) |
| Chargeable gain | 42,289 |

The chargeable gain on the sale of shares is £42,289.

(b)

REPORT

To:       The Directors of V Ltd
From:   Management Accountant
Date:    6 June 2001
Subject: Tax advice on benefits implications

**If an asset is gifted to either an employee earning at the rate of £8,500 per annum or more, or a director, a taxable benefit in kind arises equal to the market value of the asset** at the date of the gift. **For other employees, there is a taxable benefit equal to the 'cash equivalent' of the gift.** The cash equivalent of the gift is the amount the employee could obtain if he sold the gift to a third party.

These rules will apply to both the sculptures and the tables gifted to employees during the year.

Any amount paid by the employees will reduce the value of the taxable benefit.

Signed: Management Accountant

23   **P LTD**

> **Pass marks.** This was a straightforward computation of gains on the disposal of shares and assets subject to rollover relief. Where a rebasing election has been made, details of costs incurred before 31 March 1982 are irrelevant.

(a)   P Ltd

|  | £ |
|---|---|
| *Total gains* | |
| 1985 pool | 9,422 |
| 1982 pool | 17,340 |
| Total gains | 26,762 |

**The FA 1985 pool**

|  | No. £ | Cost £ | Indexed Cost |
|---|---|---|---|
| *January 1984* | | | |
| Acquisition | 5,000 | 10,000 | 10,000 |
| *April 1985* | | | |
| Indexation | | | |
| 0.092 × £10,000 | | | 920 |
| Pool at 5.4.85 | 5,000 | 10,000 | 10,920 |
| *March 1990* | | | |
| Indexation | | | |
| 0.281 × £10,920 | | | 3,069 |
| Acquisition | 10,000 | 50,000 | 50,000 |
| | 15,000 | 60,000 | 63,989 |
| *April 1996* | | | |
| Indexation | | | |
| 0.257 × £63,989 | | | 16,445 |
| Acquisition | 5,000 | 20,000 | 20,000 |
| c/f | 20,000 | 80,000 | 100,434 |

*July 2000*

Indexation

|  |  |  |  |
|---|---|---|---|
| $0.117 \times £100,434$ |  |  | 11,751 |
|  |  |  | 112,185 |
| Sale | (20,000) | (80,000) | (112,185) |
| c/f | Nil | Nil | Nil |

*Gain on 1985 pool*

|  | £ |
|---|---|
| Proceeds $\dfrac{20,000}{25,000} \times £150,000$ | 120,000 |
| Less: cost | (80,000) |
| Unindexed gain | 40,000 |
| Less: indexation allowance £(112,185 - 80,000) | (32,185) |
| Indexed gain | 7,815 |

*Gain on 1982 pool*

|  | £ |
|---|---|
| Proceeds $\dfrac{5,000}{25,000} \times £150,000$ |  |
|  | 30,000 |
| Less: 31.3.82 MV ($£5,000 \times 1.20$) | (6,000) |
| Unindexed gain | 24,000 |
| Less: indexation allowance |  |
| $1.147 \times £6,000$ | (6,882) |
| Indexed gain | 17,118 |

As there is a global rebasing election in force, it is not necessary to consider the cost of the shares.

(b)  G Ltd

The gain on the sale in July 2000 will be:

|  | £ | £ |
|---|---|---|
| Proceeds |  | 150,000 |
| Less:   cost | 40,000 |  |
|         Less: rolled over gain | (10,000) | (30,000) |
| Unindexed gain |  | 120,000 |
| Less:   indexation allowance |  |  |
|         $0.298 \times £30,000$ |  | (8,940) |
| Indexed gain chargeable on H Ltd |  | 111,060 |

As G Ltd and H Ltd are associated companies for the purposes of the small companies rate of corporation tax, the limits are divided by two. The small companies lower limit is therefore £150,000 and the upper limit is £750,000. The capital gain will therefore be in the small companies marginal relief band and suffer 32.5% tax.

|  |  |
|---|---|
| Tax @ 32.5% | 36,095 |
| Net proceeds of sale £(150,000 - 36,095) | 113,905 |

(c)  R Ltd

If no election is made, the gains/losses will be as follows:

| Factory A | *Cost* | *31.3.82 MV* |
|---|---|---|
|  | £ | £ |
| Proceeds | 70,000 | 70,000 |
| Less:   cost/31.3.82MV | (80,000) | (100,000) |
| Losses | (10,000) | (30,000) |

No indexation allowance available to increase loss.

Smaller loss applies, ie £(10,000)

| Factory B | *Cost* | *31.3.82 MV* |
|---|---|---|
| | £ | £ |
| Proceeds | 120,000 | 120,000 |
| Less: cost/31.3.82MV | (37,000) | (50,000) |
| Unindexed gain | 83,000 | 70,000 |
| Less: indexation allowance | | |
| 1.147 × £50,000 | (57,350) | (57,350) |
| Indexed gain | 25,650 | 12,650 |

Smaller gain applies, ie £12,650

Therefore the net gains if no election is made would be £(12,650 – 10,000) = £2,650.

If a global 31.3.82 MV election is made, only the 31.3.82 MV computations would apply. This would give a loss of £(30,000) on factory A and an overall loss of £(12,650 – 30,000) = £(17,350).

Therefore, it would be more advantageous to make the election, provided that there are no other assets for which this would not be beneficial (ie those which would give a higher gain based on 31.3.82 MV instead of cost).

## 24    PREPARATION QUESTION: BENEFITS

> **Pass marks**. It was important to note that the cars were acquired part way through the year and to time apportion the benefits accordingly.

(a)  **The use of a private house which cost £120,000**

Two calculations are required.

(i)    The living accommodation benefit

| | £ |
|---|---|
| Annual value | 2,000 |
| Less contribution by director | (2,000) |
| | 0 |

(ii)   The additional charge for expensive accommodation

£(120,000 – 75,000) × 10%                                      £4,500

The total benefit is £4,500.

(b)  **The purchase of a company asset at an undervalue**

The **benefit is the greater** of:

(i)    The **asset's current market value**, and

(ii)   The **asset's market value when first provided, less the total benefits taxed during the period of use.**

The acquisition price paid by the director is deducted from whichever of (i) and (ii) is used.

| | £ | £ |
|---|---|---|
| Market value when first provided | | 3,500 |
| Less: taxed in 1996/97 (20% of market value) | 700 | |
| taxed in 1997/98 (20% of market value) | 700 | |
| taxed in 1998/99 (20%) | 700 | |
| taxed in 1999/00 (20%) | 700 | |
| | | (2,800) |
| | | 700 |

The figure of £700 is taken (as greater than the current market value of £600).

Benefit taxed in 2000/01

| | £ |
|---|---|
| Initial market value minus benefits already taxed | 700 |
| Less amount paid by director | (600) |
| Benefit | 100 |

(c) **A low-interest loan to a director to purchase a season ticket**

**This non qualifying loan is exempt as the total of all non qualifying loans to this director does not exceed £5,000.**

(d) **The provision of medical insurance**

**The general measure of a benefit for an employee earning £8,500 or more a year or a director is the cost to the employer of providing it**. The benefit is thus £800.

(e) (i) **Mercedes car**

The car was available for only seven months of the year so the benefit must be on a time basis. As the car was over four years old at the end of the year the benefit must be multiplied by ¾.

£24,000 × 25% × 3/4 (age) × 7/12        £2,625

(ii) **Ford car**

£10,000 × 35% × 7/12        £2,042

(f) **Computer**

| | £ |
|---|---|
| £3,900 × 20% | 780 |
| Less: de minimis | (500) |
| | 280 |

25   **MR K**

**Pass marks**. It was important to spot that each of the motor cars was only available for part of the tax year and to time apportion the benefit accordingly.

(a) (i) **Mercedes car**

| | £ | £ |
|---|---|---|
| Car benefit £24,000 × 4/12 × 15% | 1,200 | |
| Fuel benefit £3,200 × 4/12 | 1,067 | |
| | | 2,267 |
| **Lexus car** | | |
| Car benefit £36,000 × 6/12 × 25% | 4,500 | |
| Fuel benefit £3,200 × 6/12 | 1,600 | |
| | | 6,100 |
| **Legal costs and fine** | | |
| Amount paid by company | 1,200 | |
| Less: contribution | (300) | |
| | | 900 |

(ii) **Suits**

2 × £800 × 20%        320

(iii) **Housing**

| | | |
|---|--:|--:|
| Annual rate | 8,000 | |
| Less: rent | (5,000) | |
| | | 3,000 |
| Additional benefit | | |
| (£125,000 - £75,000) × 6.25% | | 3,125 |
| Total benefits in kind | | 15,712 |

(b) **The company must pay Class 1A NICS at 12.2% in respect of all of the benefits provided to Mr K:**

$$12.2\% \times £15,712 = £1,917$$

In addition **the company must pay Class IB NICs at 12.2% on the total cost of amounts provided under a PAYE settlement agreement:**

$$12.2\% \times £9,600 = £1,171$$

(c)                                                       MEMO

To:        Board of Q Ltd
From:      Management accountant
Date:      31 March 2001
Subject:   Annual cash bonuses to directors

**The payment of cash bonuses to the directors will result in a Class 1 NIC charge for the company.**

**The director will be liable to income tax under PAYE on the bonus paid plus if the director's other cash remuneration is below the Class 1 NIC earnings upper limit then he/she will be liable for Class 1 NIC until that limit is reached.**

Q Ltd will be responsible for collecting the director's PAYE and NIC due as well as accounting for its own NIC liability to the Inland Revenue.

Any amounts of tax and national insurance contributions that Q Ltd is liable to deduct during each tax month ending on the 5th are due for payment to the Collector of Taxes not later than 14 days after the month ends, ie by the 19th of each month.

**Schedule E is taxed on the receipts basis.** Thus the PAYE due will be collected on the date the bonus is deemed to be received by the director.

The time emoluments are received is the earliest of:

(i)    The date of the actual payment of, or on account of, emoluments, or

(ii)   The date an individual becomes entitled to such a payment.

However, in the case of directors, they are deemed to have received emoluments on the earliest of potentially five dates which are the two dates already outlined plus the following three dates.

(iii)  The date when sums on account of emoluments are credited in the accounts

(iv)   The end of a period of account, where emoluments are determined before the end of the period, and

(v)    The date when the amount of emoluments for a period are determined if that is after the end of that period.

Signed: Management Accountant

## 26    CONTRACTS FOR WORK ABROAD AND PAYMENT OF DIVIDENDS

> **Pass marks**. An employee working abroad on an 18 month contract may or may not remain UK resident. It depends on the dates.

REPORT

(a)    To:        The Board of Directors
       From:      Management Accountant
       Date:      28 November 2000
       Subject:   The tax position of employees working abroad

### Employees on nine month contracts

Such employees will remain UK resident and will therefore be subject to UK taxation on all of their income, including their salaries for work abroad. The tax position of travelling and subsistence expenses is covered below.

### Employees on 18 month contracts who are absent from the UK for a complete tax year (6 April to 5 April)

Such employees will be non-UK resident for the whole of the time they are employed abroad, and will not be subject to UK taxation on their salaries for work abroad or on any other overseas income. They will, however, remain subject to UK taxation on their income from UK sources (such as interest on a building society account), and will be entitled to the personal allowance.

### Employees on 18 month contracts who are not absent from the UK for a complete tax year

Such employees will remain UK resident, and will therefore be subject to UK taxation on all of their income, including salaries for work abroad. The tax position of travelling and subsistence expenses is covered below.

### Travelling and subsistence expenses: all employees

Employees working abroad but who remain resident and ordinarily resident in the UK will be able to deduct the cost of certain items from their emoluments for tax purposes. If the company pays for these items, the employees will be able to obtain deductions equal to the Schedule E benefits on the amounts involved. The items are:

(i)     Travel from any place in the UK to take up the overseas employment, and travel back to any place in the UK on its termination.

(ii)    Board and lodging outside the UK provided for the purpose of enabling the employee to perform the duties of the overseas employment.

Similarly, if the employee is absent from the UK for a continuous period of 60 days or more a deduction is available for the cost of up to two return journeys per tax year by the employees' spouse and any children under 18 (at the start of the visit).

Signed: Management Accountant

(b)    **Payment in dividends**

(i)     There is no ACT payable on dividends paid after 5 April 1999, although shadow ACT will be relevant if the company has surplus real ACT that it wishes to utilise.

(ii)    Dividends are not a tax-deductible expense for the company, unlike wages.

(iii) An individual who receives a dividend after 5 April 1999 has taxable income of the dividend × 100/90, with a non-repayable tax credit of 10% of this income. If the taxpayer's taxable income is below £28,400 there will be no further tax to pay.

(iv) There are no national insurance contributions on dividends.

(v) Dividends are not earnings for pension contribution purposes.

(vi) In order to pay the right amount to each employee, it may be necessary to issue new shares to some employees. Unless the shares are issued under an approved profit-sharing scheme (which seems unlikely), the employees will have taxable benefits of the values of the shares issued less the amounts they pay for the shares. Class 1A NICs will be payable by the company on the taxable value of any benefits in kind.

## 27 RW LTD

> **Pass marks**. Ensure you answer all parts of a question like this as concisely as possible.

To:       The Board of Directors
From:     Management Accountant
Date:     1 September 2000
Subject:  Tax implications of various benefits

This report sets out the tax implications of various proposed benefits for both employees and the company.

### Interest free personal loans

Assuming that all senior staff to be provided with an interest free loan earn at the rate of £8,500 per annum or more, the tax implications for the staff concerned are:

(a) No taxable benefit arises when any non-qualifying loans do not exceed £5,000.

(b) No taxable benefit arises if a loan is used for a qualifying purpose (e.g. a loan to buy shares in an employee controlled company).

(c) In other cases a taxable benefit arises. There are two alternative methods of calculating the amount of the benefit. The first method is to multiply the average balance of the loan outstanding during the year by the Revenue's official rate of interest. This method is applied automatically unless the taxpayer or the Revenue elect for the second method. The second method involves multiplying the actual loan outstanding on each day by the official rate of interest.

No corporation tax implications arise as a result of making the loan for the company. However, the company must pay Class 1A NICs at 12.2% on the taxable value of any benefits arising.

### Reduced cost rail fares

No taxable benefit will arise in respect of reduced price rail fares offered to staff earning less than £8,500 per annum provided that neither vouchers nor credit tokens are used to provide the benefit. Directors and other employees will be taxed, but only on the marginal cost to the company of providing the reduced fares. This means that if the company does not incur any additional cost in providing the reduced price rail tickets, there will again be no taxable benefit.

A corporation tax deduction will be available for all costs incurred by the company in connection with providing the concessionary fares. If there is a taxable benefit in respect of any of the reduced price fares, the company will have to pay Class IA NICs at 12.2% on the taxable value of any benefit.

**Trip to Paris**

Directors and employees earning at the rate of £8,500 per annum or more will be taxed on the cost to the company of providing the trip to Paris. There will not be a taxable benefit for other employees.

A corporation tax deduction will be available for all costs incurred by the company in connection with providing the trip. Class IA NICs at 12.2% will be payable on the taxable value of benefits in kind.

**Training**

No taxable benefit will arise in respect of work related training provided to employees. Work related training is training that is likely to be useful to an employee in performing his duties or training that better qualifies him for the employment or a charitable or voluntary act associated with the employment.

The cost to the company of other training will be a taxable benefit for directors and employees earning at the rate of £8,500 per annum or more although the benefit is reduced by any amount met by the employee.

A corporation tax deduction will be available for all costs incurred by the company in connection with providing training, if the training is provided wholly and exclusively for trade purposes. Where a taxable benefit arises the company will have to pay Class IA NICs at 12.2% on the value of the benefit arising.

Signed: Management Accountant

## 28  SHARE OPTIONS, BENEFICIAL LOANS AND COMPANY CARS

> **Pass marks**. It was important to produce both a report to the Board and an information sheet for staff.

REPORT

(a)  To:          Board of Directors
     From:       Management Accountant
     Date:       31 March 2001
     Subject:    Staff benefits: Share Option Scheme, Beneficial Loans and Company Cars

Enclosed, as requested, is an information sheet which can be issued to staff setting out the tax implications of the above benefits.

**Share option plans.**

To obtain the income tax advantages outlined in the enclosed staff information sheet, the employee must be granted and subsequently exercise options under an 'approved' scheme.

To obtain approval a scheme must fulfil the following conditions:

(a)   The shares must be **fully paid ordinary shares**.

(b)   The **price of the shares must not be less than their market value at the time of the grant** of the option.

(c)   **Participation in the scheme must be limited to employees and full-time directors**. Options must not be transferable. However, ex-employees and the personal representatives of deceased employees may exercise options; personal representatives must do so within one year after the death. The scheme need not be open to all employees and full-time directors.

(d)     **No options may be granted which take the total market value of shares for which an employee holds options above £30,000.** Shares are valued as at the times when the options on them are granted.

(e)     If the issuing company has more than one class of shares, the majority of shares in the class for which the scheme operates must be held other than by:

  (i)     persons acquiring them through their positions as directors or employees (unless the company is an employee controlled company);

  (ii)    a holding company (unless the scheme shares are quoted).

Signed: Management Accountant

(b)   INFORMATION SHEET FOR EMPLOYEES

*Approved share option schemes*

Members of staff may be offered the opportunity to participate in the company's approved share option scheme.

**If you are granted options on shares under the scheme, there is no income tax on the grant** of the option **nor on the profit arising from the exercise of the option between three and ten years after its grant.**

**Capital gains tax will, however, arise on the gain made when you eventually sell your shares.**

The tax exemption is lost in respect of an option if it is exercised earlier than three years or later than ten years after grant, or within three years after you last exercised an option on which the tax exemption was obtained. However, neither of these three year waiting periods need be observed when personal representatives exercise the options of a deceased employee (but the ten year rule still applies).

*Beneficial loans*

Staff members may be offered an opportunity to take out a loan from the company at a favourably 'cheap' interest rate, but please note that a taxable benefit may arise for those earning at least £8,500 pa. The value of the taxable benefit will be calculated by applying the Revenue's official interest rate to the average loan balance (using an annual or daily basis) in the tax year and deducting interest actually paid.

**No taxable benefit arises if the loan balance does not exceed £5,000 at any time in the tax year. In addition no benefit arises on such loans used for a qualifying purpose. An example of such a loan is a loan taken out to buy an interest in a close company.**

If circumstances arise in which loan accounts are written off, these are taxable benefits.

*Company cars*

A taxable benefit may arise on a company car for those earning at the rate of £8,500 per annum or more. **The taxable benefit will be based on the list price of the car and will depend on the number of business miles travelled in the car per annum. If the car is only available for part of the tax year, the taxable benefit is time apportioned. If the car is over four years old at the end of a tax year the taxable benefit is multiplied by ¾. If fuel is provided for private purposes (and the cost of this is not fully reimbursed) a taxable benefit will arise in respect of the fuel.**

**29  OBJECTIVE TEST QUESTIONS**

1  C

2  C

3  A   15% × earning cap of £91,800 = £13,770.

4  D   Payment on injury is fully exempt. All the other payments are fully taxable since the employee is contractually entitled to receive them.

5  B

|  |  £ |
|---|---|
| Market value at grant (3,000 × £5) | 15,000 |
| Cost |  |
|  Share price (3,000 × £1.50) | (4,500) |
|  Option price (3,000 × 50p) | (1,500) |
|  | 9,000 |

As the option could be exercised more than ten years after its grant, a Schedule E charge will arise on the grant of the option.

6  D

7  B   Edwardo is not resident in the UK. He is only taxed on his UK source income.

8  C   Relocation expenses not exceeding £8,000 are tax free.

The nursery is not employer run so therefore not tax free.

The clothing allowance is taxable.

9  C

|  |  £ |
|---|---|
| Paid 10,200 @ 60p | 6,120 |
| Less FPCS |  |
|  4,000 @ 45p | (1,800) |
|  6,200 @ 25p | (1,550) |
|  | 2,770 |

10  B

|  |  £ |
|---|---|
| Cost | 35,000 |
| Irrecoverable VAT | 6,125 |
|  | 41,125 |

£41,125 × 25% × 10/12 = £8,568

2,100 miles over 10 months is equivalent to > 2,500 miles over 12 months hence 25%.

Available only 10 months hence 10/12ths.

11  C

|  |  £ |
|---|---|
| Loans @ official rate |  |
| £43,000 @ 10% | 4,300 |
| Less: interest paid |  |
| £40,000 @ 3% | (1,200) |
|  | 3,100 |

The total of non-qualifying loans exceeds £5,000 so a taxable benefit arises in respect of both of the loans.

12  B

|  | £ |
|---|---|
| Personal allowance | 4,385 |
| Less: BIK | (720) |
| Unpaid tax | |
| £300 × 100/40 | (750) |
| | 2,915 |

= 291L

13  D

14  B

|  | £ |
|---|---|
| Paid 10,200 @ 60p | 6,120 |
| Less: 10,200 @ 45p | (4,590) |
| | 1,530 |

The excess allowance paid above the FPCS 'up to 4,000' business rate is used for calculating NIC earnings even if mileage exceeds 4,000.

## 30  PREPARATION QUESTION: GROUP RELIEF

> **Pass marks**. You are asked to use group relief in the most efficient manner. This means giving it first to companies in the small companies' marginal relief band, then to companies paying tax at the full rate and then to companies in the starting rate marginal relief band. You must recognise that T Ltd is an associated company, being under common control with the P Ltd group.

(a)  There are six associated companies, so the lower and upper limits for small companies' rate purposes are £50,000 and £250,000 respectively. The upper and lower limits for starting rate purposes are £8,333 and £1,667 respectively.

S Ltd and T Ltd are outside the P Ltd group for group relief purposes. P Ltd's loss should be surrendered first to Q Ltd, to bring its taxable profits down to £50,000, then to R Ltd to bring its taxable profits down to £50,000 and finally to M Ltd.

|  | M Ltd £ | P Ltd £ | Q Ltd £ | R Ltd £ | S Ltd £ | T Ltd £ |
|---|---|---|---|---|---|---|
| Schedule D Case I | 10,000 | 0 | 64,000 | 260,000 | 0 | 70,000 |
| Schedule A | 0 | 6,000 | 4,000 | 0 | 0 | 0 |
| | 10,000 | 6,000 | 68,000 | 260,000 | 0 | 70,000 |
| Less charges | (4,000) | (4,500) | (2,000) | (5,000) | 0 | 0 |
| | 6,000 | 1,500 | 66,000 | 255,000 | 0 | 70,000 |
| Less group relief | (2,000) | 0 | (16,000) | (205,000) | 0 | 0 |
| PCTCT | 4,000 | 1,500 | 50,000 | 50,000 | 0 | 70,000 |
| | | | | | | |
| Corporation tax: at 10% | | 150 | | | | |
| at 20% | 800 | | 10,000 | 10,000 | 0 | |
| at 30% | | | | | | 21,000 |
| Less starting rate marginal relief | | | | | | |
| 1/40 × £(8,333 – 4,000) | (108) | | | | | |
| Less: small companies rate marginal relief | | | | | | |
| 1/40 (£250,000 – 70,000) | | | | | | (4,500) |
| MCT payable | 692 | 150 | 10,000 | 10,000 | 0 | 16,500 |

(b) If P Ltd were to acquire another 8% of the share capital of S Ltd, bringing the total holding to 75%, S Ltd's losses could be surrendered to P Ltd, Q Ltd, R Ltd or M Ltd.

## 31 PREPARATION QUESTION: CORRESPONDING ACCOUNTING PERIODS

> **Pass marks**. The maximum group relief in each corresponding period is the lower of the time-apportioned profits and the time-apportioned losses.

*Harry Ltd*

|  | 12 months to 31.12.99 | 9 months to 30.9.00 |
|---|---|---|
|  | £ | £ |
| Schedule D Case I | 25,000 | 0 |
| Schedule A | 3,000 | 4,000 |
|  | 28,000 | 4,000 |
| Less charges on income | (2,000) | (2,000) |
| Profits chargeable to corporation tax | 26,000 | 2,000 |
| | | |
| *Corporation tax payable* | | |
| £26,000 × 21% × 3/12 | 1,365 | |
| £26,000 × 20% × 9/12 | 3,900 | |
| £2,000 × 20% × 3/9 | | 133 |
| £2,000 × 10% × 6/9 | | 133 |
| Mainstream corporation tax | 5,265 | 266 |

*Sid Ltd*

|  | 12 months to 31.3.00 | 12 months to 31.3.01 |
|---|---|---|
|  | £ | £ |
| Schedule D Case I | 52,000 | 250,000 |
| Schedule D Case III | 8,000 | 10,000 |
|  | 60,000 | 260,000 |
| Less charges on income | (5,000) | (5,000) |
|  | 55,000 | 255,000 |
| Less group relief (W) | (13,750) | (30,000) |
| Profits chargeable to corporation tax | 41,250 | 225,000 |
| | | |
| *Corporation tax payable* | £ | £ |
| £41,250 × 20% | 8,250 | |
| £225,000 × 30% | | 67,500 |
| Less small companies marginal relief | | |
| 1/40 × £(750,000 – 225,000) | | (13,125) |
| Mainstream corporation tax | 8,250 | 54,375 |

*Working: group relief*

|  | £ |
|---|---|
| Loss in 9 month accounting period to 30.9.00 | 45,000 |
| Less surrender to Sid Ltd (y/e 31.3.00), restricted to lower of: | |

(i) £45,000 × 3/9 =    £15,000
(ii) £55,000 × 3/12 =    £13,750

|  | £ |
|---|---|
| | (13,750) |
| | 31,250 |

Less surrender to Sid Ltd (y/e 31.3.01), restricted to lower of:

(i)   £45,000 × 6/9  =    £30,000                                    (30,000)
(ii)  £255,000 × 6/12 =   £127,500

Unrelieved loss carried forward                                      1,250

## 32    GROUP RELIEF

> **Pass marks.** It was important to use a columnar layout to answer part (a) of this question. Dealing with each company on a separate page would makes your answer hard to follow.

(a)    YEAR ENDED 31 MARCH 2001

|  | HO Ltd | K Ltd | L Ltd | M Ltd | N Ltd |
|---|---|---|---|---|---|
|  | £ | £ | £ | £ | £ |
| Schedule D Case I | 110,000 | 18,000 | 0 | 62,500 | 120,000 |
| Less: group relief (W1) | (15,000) | 0 | 0 | 0 | (60,000) |
| PCTCT | 95,000 | 18,000 | Nil | 62,500 | 60,000 |
| FII | - | - | - | 12,500 | - |
| Profits | 95,000 | 18,000 | Nil | 75,000 | 60,000 |
| Corporation tax at 20% | 0 | 3,600 | 0 | 0 | 12,000 |
| Corporation tax at 30% | 28,500 | 0 | 0 | 18,750 |  |
| Less: marginal relief |  |  |  |  |  |
| 1/40 (£300,000 – £75,000) |  |  |  |  |  |
| $\times \dfrac{62,500}{75,000}$ |  |  |  | (4,688) |  |
| 1/40 (£300,000 – £95,000) | (5,125) |  |  |  |  |
|  | 23,375 | 3,600 | 0 | 14,062 | 12,000 |

*Working*

*Associated companies*

There are five associated companies

Upper limit for small companies rate $\dfrac{1,500,000}{5}$ = £300,000

Lower limit for small companies rate $\dfrac{300,000}{5}$ = £60,000

Upper limit for starting rate $\dfrac{50,000}{5}$ = £10,000

The loss should be surrendered to reduce profits otherwise taxed at the small companies' marginal rate. In this case there are several alternative answers and it did not matter which one you chose.

(b)  **Controlled foreign company**

If K Ltd was a controlled foreign company (CFC) then under the CFC provisions 90% of its profits (ie the interest held by HO Ltd in K Ltd) should be apportioned to HO Ltd. HO Ltd must decide whether the rules apply, and if so fill in the additional page for CFCs and file it with its CT600.

However, these provisions will not apply if for an accounting period K Ltd;

(i)     has profits not exceeding £50,000 (as is the case here); or

(ii)    pursues an acceptable distribution policy (generally being that at least 90% of its taxable profits ignoring capital gains and foreign tax are distributed).

This means that for the year to 31 March 2001 no apportionment would be made, and there would have been no effect on the overall position, if K Ltd had been a non-resident CFC.

Clearly, if K Ltd was a non-resident company it would not itself be subject to UK tax. However, it would still count as an 'associated' company for the purposes of the group's limits for the starting rate and small companies rate of tax.

(c)                                    REPORT

To:             Board of Directors
From:          Management Accountant
Date:          1 March 2001
Subject:       VAT on exports

I note that we are shortly to engage in exporting activities for the first time and are anticipating making sales to customers in North America. I therefore set out below for your information a summary of the main VAT regulations on exporting to the American market.

**Non-EU exports**

(i)    There is a general zero-rating of goods exported to a customer outside the EU. This is irrespective of how the goods would be treated if sold in the UK.

(ii)   The zero-rating will only apply if Customs can be satisfied that we did export the goods concerned. This means that we will have to retain suitable evidence of export such as commercial shipping documentation.

If you need further information, please contact me.

Signed: Management Accountant

## 33    M LTD

> **Pass marks.** A consortium member can only surrender a loss to eliminate its share of the consortium company's profits.

(a)    M Ltd

In general terms **a company is owned by a consortium** (and is known as a consortium-owned company) **if 75% or more of its ordinary share capital is owned by UK resident companies** (the members of the consortium), **none of which has a holding of less than 5%.**

In this case, therefore, M Ltd is a consortium-owned company. The consortium members are A Ltd, B Ltd and C Ltd. D Ltd is not a member of the consortium because it does not have a 5% or more holding.

**A member of a consortium may surrender its losses to set against its share of the consortium-owned company's profits.** Therefore A Ltd can surrender 15% × £220,000 = £33,000 of losses to M Ltd and C Ltd 5%× £220,000 = £11,000 of losses to M Ltd. It is not possible for consortium members to surrender losses between themselves eg to reduce B Ltd's chargeable profits.

M Ltd and B Ltd are also associated companies for the purposes of the small companies and starting rate of tax. The small companies rate limits are therefore £150,000 and £750,000. The marginal rate of tax in the band between these limits is 32.5%. Therefore, the best use of losses is to reduce the chargeable profits in this band and so the full amounts of the losses from A Ltd and C Ltd should be surrendered.

The MCT payable by the companies is therefore as follows:

*B Ltd*

|  | £ |
|---|---|
| PCTCT | 160,000 |
|  |  |
| Tax payable @ 30% | 48,000 |
| Less: small companies' marginal relief |  |
| £(750,000 – 160,000) × 1/40 | (14,750) |
| MCT | 33,250 |

*M Ltd*

|  | £ |
|---|---|
| PCTCT before loss relief | 220,000 |
| Less:  from A Ltd | (33,000) |
| from C Ltd | (11,000) |
|  | 176,000 |
|  |  |
| Tax payable @ 30% | 52,800 |
| Less: small companies' marginal relief |  |
| £(750,000 – 176,000) × 1/40 | (14,350) |
| MCT | 38,450 |

(b) (i) **Surcharge liability notices**

The default surcharge regime is triggered when **a VAT return or payment is submitted late, leading to the issue of a surcharge liability notice.** The notice specifies **a surcharge period which starts on the day of the notice and ends one year after the end of the period of default. A surcharge is charged if a further default involving the late payment of VAT occurs during the surcharge period.** Furthermore, **the surcharge period is extended to the anniversary of the end of the period of any further default** (whether or not it involves the late payment of VAT).

The surcharge is 2% of the VAT not paid on time for the first default involving the late payment of VAT, 5% for the second such default, 10% for the third and 15% for the fourth and later defaults. The minimum surcharge per default involving late payment is £30. However, surcharges at 2% and 5% are not normally collected unless they are at least £200.

(ii) **Relief for VAT on bad debts**

**Relief is available for VAT on bad debts if the debt is over six months old** (measured from when payment is due) **and has been written off in the creditor's accounts.** Where a supplier of goods or services has accounted for VAT on the supply and the customer does not pay, the supplier may claim a refund of VAT on the amount unpaid. Where payments on account have been received, later debts are regarded as bad before earlier ones. When the debtor later pays VAT is accounted for at that time in the usual way to HM Customs & Excise.

**Claims for relief must be made within three years,** the creditor must have a copy of the tax invoice, and records to show that the VAT in question has been accounted for and that the debt has been written off. The VAT is reclaimed on the creditor's VAT return, and must be recorded in a 'refunds for bad debts' account.

**Creditors must notify debtors that a VAT bad debt relief claim has been made within 7 days of the claim.** Debtors must repay any VAT reclaimed which has not been paid and on which the supplier has claimed bad debt relief.

## 34   A LTD

> **Pass marks**. B Ltd's loss could be set only against the available profits of the corresponding accounting period.

### Corporation Tax computation

| | £ | £ |
|---|---:|---:|
| Schedule D Case I | | 42,000 |
| Schedule A | | 1,000 |
| Schedule D Case III | | |
| Bank interest accrued | 5,000 | |
| Loan interest accrued | 8,000 | |
| | | 13,000 |
| Patent royalties received (gross) | | 12,000 |
| | | 68,000 |
| Less: charges on income: | | |
| Patent royalties (gross) | 6,000 | |
| Gift aid (gross) | 11,000 | |
| | | (17,000) |
| | | 51,000 |
| Less: group relief (W1) | | (34,000) |
| PCTCT. | | 17,000 |
| Add: Franked Investment Income | | 1,000 |
| 'Profits' | | 18,000 |

| | £ |
|---|---:|
| Corporation tax | |
| FY1999 | |
| £17,000 × 3/9 × 20% | 1,133 |
| FY2000 | |
| £17,000 × 6/9 × 20% | 2,267 |
| Less: starting rate marginal relief | |
| $1/40 \, (\pounds18,750 - 18,000) \times \dfrac{17,000}{18,000} \times 6/9$ | (12) |
| Less: income tax (W3) | (2,920) |
| Mainstream corporation tax | 468 |

*Notes*

It is assumed that the loan interest and the bank interest arose on non-trading loans and is therefore taxable under Schedule D Case III.

*Workings*

1   B Ltd joined the group with A Ltd on 1.4.00 so for A Ltd's profit making accounting period to 30.9.00 there are 6 months in common with B Ltd's loss making period.

*Thus*

| | | |
|---|---|---|
| A Ltd | 6/9 × £51,000 | = £34,000 |
| B Ltd | 6/12 × (£130,000) | = £65,000 |

Maximum group relief available is lower of two, ie £34,000.

2   The 9 months to 30.9.00 falls 3 months into FY99 and 6 months into FY2000.

In FY99 'profits' are below the small companies' lower limit of £300,000 × 9/12 ÷ 2 = £112,500 so the small companies' rate applies.

In FY2000 'profits' are between the starting rate upper and lower limits of £50,000 × 9/12 ÷ 2 = £18,750 and £10,000 × 9/12 ÷ 2 = £3,750, so the starting rate marginal relief applies.

3    Income tax suffered

|  | £ |
|---|---|
| Loan interest accrued (£8,000 × 20%) | 1,600 |
| Patent royalty received (£12,000 × 22%) | 2,640 |
| Less: patent royalty paid (£6,000 × 22%) | (1,320) |
|  | 2,920 |

Gift aid payments are paid gross.

## 35    GROUP GAINS AND REBASING ELECTIONS

> **Pass marks**. This question required some tax planning. You were given the goal to aim at: the avoidance of any corporation tax on chargeable gains. There are obviously several steps to be taken, but you should have started by working out in rough what the steps were individually, and then checked at the end in case any step impinged on other steps.
>
> The measure required in part (b) was quite simple: transfer the building back to A Ltd, or to C Ltd, before the shareholding is reduced. This shows that while tax planning questions require some thought, complicated schemes are not required. Do not be afraid to state the obvious, because if you do not state it the examiner will have to assume that you do not know it.

(a)                                            REPORT

| | |
|---|---|
| To: | The Board of Directors |
| From: | Management Accountant |
| Date: | 28 November 2000 |
| Subject: | Group chargeable gains |

The purpose of this report is to advise on the steps that need to be taken by the group to ensure that no capital gains become chargeable in the year to 31 March 2001. It will also advise on the implications of reducing A Ltd's holding in B Ltd to 40%.

**Avoiding chargeable gains**

Because A Ltd has owned 80% of the share capital of B Ltd and C Ltd since their incorporation the anti-avoidance legislation preventing the use for group capital losses against transferred assets standing at a gain does not apply to this group. The following steps should be taken to ensure that group companies do not suffer corporation tax on gains.

(i)     In relation to the transfer of the building from A Ltd to B Ltd, no action is needed. This transfer will be deemed to be at a price giving rise to no gain and no loss.

(ii)    An election should be made for the property which C Ltd sells for £150,000 to be treated as though it was disposed of by B Ltd. This election must be made within two years of the end of the accounting period in which the sale of the property takes place. B Ltd will then be able to set its capital loss brought forward against the gain arising.

(iii)   The gain on C Ltd's other property should be rolled over against the acquisition of the new building by A Ltd (assuming that the building will be occupied and used solely for the purposes of a trade carried on by a group member). All group members can be treated as one company for the purposes of rollover relief.

**Reduction of holding in B Ltd**

**If A Ltd's holding in B Ltd is reduced to below 75%, B Ltd will leave the group for the purposes of corporation tax on capital gains.** Because **it will have acquired an asset intra-group** (the building transferred from A Ltd) **in the preceding six years, a chargeable gain will arise in B Ltd.** The amount of the gain will be £40,000, and the gain will accrue in the year ending 31 March 2002.

This gain may be avoided by B Ltd's transferring the building back to A Ltd, or to C Ltd, before the shareholding is reduced to below 75%. Such a transfer would give rise to neither a gain nor a loss, regardless of any amount paid to B Ltd for the building.

Signed: Management Accountant

(b)  **Chargeable gains**

(i)    **No global election**

| Building 1 | Cost | M82 value |
|---|---|---|
| | £ | £ |
| Proceeds | 860,000 | 860,000 |
| Less: Cost/M82 value | (380,000) | (360,000) |
| | 480,000 | 5500,000 |
| Less: Indexation 1.160 × £380,000 | (440,800) | (440,800) |
| | 39,200 | 59,200 |

With no election the lower gain of £39,200 is taken.

| Building 2 | Cost | M82 value |
|---|---|---|
| | £ | £ |
| Proceeds | 200,000 | 200,000 |
| Less: Cost/M82 value | (220,000) | (290,000) |
| Allowable loss | (20,000) | (90,000) |

With no election the lower loss of £20,000 is taken.

(ii)   **Global election**

If a global election is made the gain on building 1 will be computed using the March 1982 value and an indexation allowance based on the March 1982 value.

| | £ |
|---|---|
| Proceeds | 860,000 |
| Less M82 value | (360,000) |
| | 500,000 |
| Less indexation (£360,000 × 1.160) | (417,600) |
| | 82,400 |

The allowable loss on building 2 will be based on the March 1982 value, ie it will be £90,000.

**Summary**

| | No election | Election |
|---|---|---|
| | £ | £ |
| Building 1 – gain | 39,200 | 82,400 |
| Building 2 – loss | (20,000) | (90,000) |
| Net gain/(loss) | 19,200 | (7,600) |

The directors should make an election as this will result in a net allowable loss of £7,600.

## 36 STD LTD

> **Pass marks**. When a gain is held over against a depreciating asset, the base cost of the depreciating asset is *not* reduced. Instead, the gain is noted down separately and crystallises in due course.

(a) (i) **The plant and machinery**

The gain held over crystallises on the sale. This gain is £8,790, as follows.

|  | £ |
|---|---|
| Proceeds | 120,000 |
| Less cost | (70,000) |
|  | 50,000 |
| Less indexation allowance £70,000 × 0.303 | (21,210) |
|  | 28,790 |
| Less proceeds not reinvested | (20,000) |
| Gain held over | 8,790 |

The loss on the plant and machinery itself is zero as follows.

|  | £ |
|---|---|
| Proceeds | 60,000 |
| Less cost less net capital allowances £(100,000 – 40,000) | 60,000 |
| Loss | 0 |

(ii) **The shares in Z Ltd**

The FA 1985 pool is as follows.

|  | Shares £ | Cost £ | Indexed cost £ |
|---|---|---|---|
| September 1985 purchase | 10,000 | 23,000 | 23,000 |
| Indexed rise to October 1988 | | | |
| £23,000 × 0.148 | | | 3,404 |
| October 1988 purchase | 15,000 | 40,000 | 40,000 |
|  | 25,000 | 63,000 | 66,404 |
| December 1992 bonus | 10,000 | | |
|  | 35,000 | | |
| Indexed rise to November 1994 | | | |
| £66,404 × 0.327 | | | 21,714 |
|  | | | 88,118 |
| November 1994 sale | (5,000) | (9,000) | (12,588) |
|  | 30,000 | 54,000 | 75,530 |
| Indexed rise to December 2000 | | | |
| £75,530 × 0.191 | | | 14,426 |
|  | | | 89,956 |
| December 2000 sale | (20,000) | (36,000) | (59,971) |
|  | 10,000 | 18,000 | 29,985 |

The gain on the December 2000 sale is as follows.

|  | £ |
|---|---|
| Proceeds | 90,000 |
| Less cost | (36,000) |
|  | 54,000 |
| Less indexation allowance £(59,971 – 36,000) | (23,971) |
|  | 30,029 |

(iii)  *The retail unit*

|  | £ |
|---|---|
| Proceeds | 28,000 |
| Less cost £90,000 × 28/128 | (19,688) |
|  | 8,312 |
| Less indexation allowance £19,688 × 0.298 | (5,867) |
|  | 2,445 |

(b)                          REPORT

To:      The Board of Directors of STD Ltd
From:   Management Accountant
Date:    4 April 2001
Subject: Chargeable gains

The company has recently been sold by D Ltd to H Ltd.

**If the company received capital assets from D Ltd (or from other companies in the D Ltd group) while D Ltd owned it, those assets would have been treated as transferred at no gain and no loss.** However, since the company is **leaving the D Ltd group within the following six years, it will have chargeable gains on such assets.** The gains will be computed as if the company had, at the time of transfer, sold the assets at their then market values. However, the gains will be included in the company's profits for the year ended 31 March 2001.

Signed: Management Accountant

## 37   CLARISSA LTD

**Pass marks**. The cost of the block of shops had to be apportioned using the values of the shop sold and the shops retained. It would have been wrong to take 1/6 of the cost, because the shops are not of equal value.

(a)  CHARGEABLE GAINS

**The warehouse**

|  | £ |
|---|---|
| Proceeds | 150,000 |
| Less 31 March 1982 value | (38,000) |
|  | 112,000 |
| Less indexation allowance £38,000 × 1.135 | (43,130) |
| Chargeable gain | 68,870 |

**The shop unit**

|  | £ |
|---|---|
| Proceeds | 180,000 |
| Less cost £270,000 × 180/(180 + 720) | (54,000) |
|  | 126,000 |
| Less indexation allowance £54,000 × 1.027 | (55,458) |
| Chargeable gain | 70,542 |

**The property acquired from D Ltd**

|  | £ |
|---|---|
| Proceeds | 115,000 |
| Less 31 March 1982 value | (50,000) |
|  | 65,000 |
| Less indexation allowance £50,000 × 1.166 | (58,300) |
| Chargeable gain | 6,700 |

**Summary**

|  | £ |
|---|---|
| The warehouse | 68,870 |
| The shop unit | 70,542 |
| The property acquired from D Ltd | 6,700 |
|  | 146,112 |

(b) POSSIBLE IMPROVEMENTS TO THE TAX POSITION

**Rollover relief and holdover relief**

If the warehouse and the property acquired from D Ltd **had been used for the purposes of Clarissa Ltd's trade, the gains arising might have been deferred by claims for rollover relief or holdover relief**. These reliefs would be available **if Clarissa Ltd or another company within the capital gains group were to buy qualifying assets within the period from 12 months before each disposal to 36 months after it.** Qualifying assets are assets which are used in the trade of a company within the capital gains group and which fall within one of the following categories.

(i)     Land and buildings (including parts of buildings) occupied as well as used only for the purpose of the trade

(ii)    Fixed (that is, immovable) plant and machinery

(iii)   Ships, aircraft and hovercraft

(iv)    Goodwill

(v)     Satellites, space stations and spacecraft

(vi)    Milk quotas, potato quotas and ewe and suckler cow premium quotas

(vii)   Fish quota

**If the asset acquired is not depreciating** (it has a predictable useful life exceeding 60 years), **rollover relief is obtained: the gain on the old asset is deferred indefinitely by deducting it from the base cost of the new asset. If the new asset is depreciating, the gain on the old asset is only deferred for up to ten years.** Assets under items (ii), (iii) and (v) are always depreciating unless (for item (ii)) they are fixtures in non-depreciating land and buildings.

**The gains on the assets sold are still chargeable immediately, up to the amount of disposal proceeds not reinvested in new assets**.

**The use of capital losses**

Irrespective of whether or not the assets sold had been used in Clarissa Ltd's trade, use might have been made of capital losses accruing to other companies within the capital gains group in the same accounting period or in previous periods. Capital losses cannot be transferred between companies. However  the same effect can be achieved by transferring assets standing at a gain to companies with capital losses before disposing of them outside the group. Alternatively, an election can be made for any company in the group to be deemed to have made any asset disposals which occurred. The gains would then accrue to the companies with the capital losses. Those companies then set the losses against the gains. However, the use of any capital losses that arose before a company joined the group (pre entry capital losses) is restricted.

## 38    S LTD

> **Pass marks**. Heldover gains are deferred they are not deducted from the base cost of the new asset.

(a) (i) **Disposal of rights nil paid.**

As the rights were sold £Nil paid for more than 5% of the value of the shares immediately after the rights issue, a part disposal occurs.

**FA 1985 pool**

|  | No | Cost | Indexed Cost |
|---|---|---|---|
| April 1989 | 20,000 | 120,000 | 120,000 |
| Indexation allowance to November 2000 |  |  |  |
| $0.509 \times £120,000$ |  |  | 61,080 |
|  | 20,000 | 120,000 | 181,080 |
| Part disposal |  |  |  |
| $\dfrac{18,000}{18,000 + (£9 \times 20,000)} \times 120,000/181,080$ |  |  |  |
|  |  | (10,909) | (16,462) |
| Carry forward | 20,000 | 109,091 | 164,618 |

**Sale of rights nil paid**

|  | £ |
|---|---|
| Sale proceeds | 18,000 |
| Cost | (10,909) |
|  | 7,091 |
| Less: indexation allowance |  |
| £(16,462 – 10,909) | (5,553) |
| Capital gain | 1,538 |

(ii) **Business property**

|  | Cost | 31.3.82 |
|---|---|---|
|  | £ | £ |
| Sale proceeds | 175,000 | 175,000 |
| Cost | (80,000) | (90,000) |
|  | 95,000 | 85,000 |
| Less: Indexation allowance |  |  |
| £90,000 × 0.576 | (51,840) | (51,840) |
| Capital gain | 43,160 | 33,160 |

The gain, £33,160, crystallises in April 2000 **under the ten year rule for depreciating assets**.

(iii) S Ltd left the capital gains group when T Ltd disposed of the 40% interest in its shares. **As this was within 6 years of the transfer of the building from T Ltd, the gain that would have arisen on a disposal of the building for its market value on the date of the transfer, crystallises.** The crystallised gain is included in S Ltd's profit chargeable to corporation tax for the year to 31 March 2001.

|  | £ |
|---|---|
| Deemed proceeds | 105,000 |
| Less: Cost | (80,000) |
|  | 25,000 |
| Less: Indexation £80,000 × 0.145 | (11,600) |
| Chargeable gain | 13,400 |

**Summary**

|  | £ |
|---|---|
| Sale of rights nil paid | 1,538 |
| Crystallisation of held over gain | 33,160 |
| Gain arising when S Ltd leaves group | 13,400 |
| Total Capital gains arising in year ended 31 March 2001 | 48,098 |

(b) **Year ended 31 March 2001 without gains**

PCTCT = £140,000
Corporation Tax at 20% (W1)                                              £28,000

**With gains**

|  | £ |
|---|---|
| Other income | 140,000 |
| Gains | 48,098 |
| PCTCT | 188,098 |
| | |
| Corporation tax at 30% (W1) | 56,429 |
| Less: small companies' marginal relief | |
| 1/40 [750,000 – 188,098] | (14,048) |
| | 42,381 |

The corporation tax due on the gain is £14,381 (£42,381 – £28,000)

*Workings*

1    Upper limit for small companies' rate purposes £1,500,000 ÷ 2 = £750,000
     Lower limit for small companies' rate purposes £300,000 ÷ 2 = £150,000
     Without the gains small companies' rate applies.
     With the gains small companies' marginal relief applies.

## 39   AC LTD AND DC LTD

> **Pass marks**. You should have covered not only the ways in which the amounts brought forward could be used but also possible restrictions on their use.

(a)                                          REPORT

|  |  |
|---|---|
| To: | The Board of Directors of AC Ltd |
| From: | Management Accountant |
| Date: | 28 November 2000 |
| Subject: | The use of amounts brought forward by DC Ltd |

### Introduction

This report considers how the trading losses, surplus advance corporation tax (ACT) and capital losses brought forward by the new subsidiary, DC Ltd, may be used.

### Trading losses

**These must be set against the first future profits of the same trade of DC Ltd. They cannot be transferred to AC Ltd.**

No relief is available for losses before the acquisition against profits after the acquisition if, within the period from three years before the acquisition to three years after the acquisition, there is a major change in the nature or conduct of DC Ltd's trade.

Examples of a major change in the nature or conduct of a trade include changes in:

(a)    The type of property dealt in
(b)    The services or facilities provided
(c)    Customers
(d)    Outlets or markets

However, changes to keep up to date with technology or to rationalise existing ranges of products are unlikely to be regarded as major.

**Surplus ACT**

ACT was payable on dividends paid prior to 6 April 1999. Any surplus ACT still existing on that date is carried forward under the shadow ACT system. For any one accounting period, the maximum set off of ACT is equal to 20% of the profits chargeable to corporation tax less any shadow ACT arising in the period. Shadow ACT is the ACT that would have been paid after 6.4.99 if the ACT system had continued.

**DC Ltd may therefore carry the surplus ACT forward to set against the corporation tax liability of the year to 31 March 2001, again subject to the maximum set-off and the set-off of shadow ACT.**

DC Ltd's surplus ACT cannot be used by AC Ltd.

The surplus ACT brought forward may be prevented from being carried forward for set-off against corporation tax of a period after the acquisition of DC Ltd. This will happen if within three years before or three years after the acquisition there is a major change in the nature or conduct of DC Ltd's business.

A further anti-avoidance provision is designed to counter arrangements under which a group purchases a company with unrelieved ACT and transfers assets to the company shortly before their sale in order that the unrelieved ACT can be offset against tax on any gain arising. Where the acquired company brings forward pre-acquisition surplus ACT, and also has chargeable gains on assets which are:

(a)     Acquired in a no gain/no loss transfer from another group member after the acquisition of the company, and

(b)     Disposed of within three years of the acquisition of the company,

a special restriction applies. The limit on ACT set-off for the period of the chargeable gain is reduced by the lower of:

(a)     The pre-acquisition ACT, and

(b)     The ACT in a franked payment equal to the gain and made at the end of that period.

This provision applies whether or not there is a major change in the business of the company which has been acquired.

**Capital losses**

DC Ltd must set its capital losses brought forward against the first gains on assets which:

(a)     It disposed of before its acquisition by AC Ltd,

(b)     It owned before its acquisition by AC Ltd, or

(c)     It bought after its acquisition by AC Ltd from outside the AC Ltd group, provided that since being bought the assets have not been used except for the purposes of a trade which DC Ltd was carrying on immediately before its acquisition and which it continued to carry on until the disposal of the assets.

Because the capital losses are pre-entry losses, they cannot be used in any other way. In particular, if AC Ltd wishes to sell an asset at a gain, there is no point in making an election to treat the asset disposals as having been made by DC Ltd in the hope of using DC Ltd's losses brought forward. It may, however, be worthwhile to make such transfers prior to disposal more than three years after the acquisition of DC Ltd in order to use up DC Ltd's surplus ACT brought forward (see above).

Signed: Management Accountant

(b)                                            REPORT

To:       Directors of AC Ltd Group
From :   A.N. Accountant
Date:    21 June 2000
Subject: Proposed Asset Disposals

The asset disposals proposed for the next accounting period will give rise to the following.

AC Ltd    capital gain
DC Ltd    capital loss

Ideally the group would be in the best position if the capital gain and loss could be matched together in the same company.

It is possible to transfer assets between AC Ltd and DC Ltd on a no gain no loss basis. If this was done prior to the proposed sales both gain and loss would arise in the same company. Alternatively, an election could be made for an asset disposed of by one of the companies to be treated as though it were disposed of by the other company.

Anti-avoidance legislation prevents the full offset of DC Ltd's loss in this way if the asset on which the loss arises was acquired by DC Ltd prior to joining the group (ie prior to 1 April 2000). If this is the case then the capital loss arising must be time apportioned into its pre-1 April 2000 and post-1 April 2000 portions. The post-1 April 2000 portion can be offset against the gain on AC Ltd's asset; the pre-1 April 2000 portion cannot but can only be offset against gain arising on assets owned by DC Ltd prior to joining the group or assets acquired by DC Ltd from third parties since that date.

An alternative method of calculating the pre-1 April 2000 loss is to elect to use the lower of:

(i)    The actual loss arising on the asset sale

(ii)   The loss which would have arisen if the asset was sold at market value on the date the company joined the group (1 April 2000)

Since no figures have been supplied I cannot at this time conclude on whether such an election would be best made. The company has until 2 years after the end of the accounting period of disposal to make the election.

## 40   DIVERSIFY

> **Pass marks.** There is no group relief for capital losses. However, assets can be transferred between group members prior to disposal at nil gain/nil loss or an election can be made for an asset disposed of by one group company to be treated as though it had been disposed of by another group company.

To:     Directors of Holding Company
From:  Management Accountant
Date:   1 March 2000
Subject: Potential Taxation Implications of proposed reorganisation and a VAT group registration.

The following report gives a broad outline of the potential of our proposed disposals and of a VAT group registration.

## Capital gains aspects of reorganisation

Capital gains and losses may arise as a result of the proposed disposal of assets (including goodwill) by group companies and also the sale of shares in subsidiary companies.

The following points need to be taken into account:

1    The general computation of gains is to take the net proceeds of sale and deduct the costs of acquiring the asset (or the value of the asset at 31 March 1982 if the asset was acquired before that date). There is also an allowance for inflation between March 1982 and the date of the disposal, known as indexation allowance. However, this allowance cannot create or increase a loss.

2    **Chargeable gains are taxable as part of the disposing company's profits** at the usual corporation tax rates. This means at 30% where the company pays tax at the full corporation tax rate, at 20% if the company pays tax at the small companies rate, at 10% if it pays at the starting rate or at 32.5% or 22.5% if the company's profits fall into one of the marginal relief bands.

3    **If a capital loss is made by a company, in general, it is first used against chargeable gains of that company** in the same chargeable accounting period. **Any excess gain is then carried forward to subsequent chargeable accounting periods. It is not possible to carry back losses** to previous chargeable accounting periods, **nor to set the loss against income profits, nor to surrender losses to other companies in the same group.**

4    **Where assets are transferred between members of a group of companies,** the **consideration for the disposal is treated as being such as neither a gain nor a loss arises ('no gain/no loss').** Thus the acquiring company takes over the base cost of the asset plus indexation allowance to the date of the transfer. Thus it is possible to move assets around a group in order to match losses and gains.

Alternatively an election can be made so that an asset disposed of by one company is treated as though it were disposed of by another group company. Such an election allows gains and losses to be matched within a group without the need for the asset to be transferred.

However, there are three further provisions which need to be taken into account:

(i)    **If a company leaves a group while it owns assets transferred to it within the previous six years by a no gain/no loss transfer, then the departing company is treated as though it had, at the time of the acquisition of such assets, sold and re-acquired them at their market values on acquisition.** This gain or loss is then brought into the departing company's tax computation for the accounting period in which it leaves the group. The Revenue can collect the tax from the holding company if the tax is unpaid six months after its due date.

(ii)    **If a subsidiary company is acquired, there are rules restricting the use of pre-entry capital losses.** These are losses already made before the subsidiary joined the group and also the pre-entry proportion of losses made on pre-entry assets which are disposed of after the subsidiary joined the group. Such losses can only be used against assets owned by the subsidiary before it joined the group or certain assets acquired by the subsidiary from outside the group. Thus, the pre-entry losses cannot be used against the disposal of assets acquired on a no gain/no loss basis. They also cannot be used against gains accruing as a result of an election made for the asset to be treated as disposed of by the subsidiary.

(iii)    **If a subsidiary company is acquired, there are also rules restricting the offset of losses against pre-entry gains.** These rules only apply to the chargeable

117

accounting period in which the company is purchased, as capital losses cannot be carried back.

5    **There is also relief for replacement of business assets where one member of a group disposes of a business asset ('the old asset') outside the group and either that company or another group company acquires another business asset ('the new asset'), within a period of one year before and three years after the disposal.** If the asset has a useful life of more than 60 years (eg freehold premises, goodwill), the gain on the disposal of the old asset is not chargeable, but is deducted from the base cost of the new asset, thus deferring the gain until the new asset is disposed of. There is a similar relief where the asset has a useful life of 60 years or less (eg leasehold premises where the lease has 60 years or less to run, fixed plant and machinery). In this case the gain on the old asset is deferred for a maximum of ten years. Both reliefs are restricted if less than the amount the proceeds of the old asset are invested in the new asset.

6    Stamp duty is payable by the purchasers of shares in the subsidiaries at the rate of 0.5%. If certain assets are sold, such as freehold or leasehold land and goodwill, stamp duty will be payable by the purchaser at rates between 1% and 4% depending on the value of the assets.

7    VAT may be chargeable on assets sold. However, **if the assets are sold as part of a going concern, such a transfer is generally outside the scope of VAT.**

**VAT group registration**

**Companies under common control may apply for group registration.** The effects and advantages of group registration are as follows.

(i)    Each VAT group must appoint a representative member which must **account for the group's output VAT and input VAT, thus simplifying VAT accounting** and allowing payments and repayments of VAT to be netted off. However, all members of the group are jointly and severally liable for any VAT due from the representative member.

(ii)   **Any supply of goods or services by a member of the group to another member of the group is, in general, disregarded for VAT purposes,** reducing the VAT accounting work. This may also be advantageous from a cash flow point of view. However, VAT does have to be accounted for on certain services supplied to a UK group company via an overseas group member.

(iii)  Any other supply of goods or services by or to a group member is in general treated as a supply by or to the representative member but any special status of the representative member (eg charitable status) is ignored unless the member by or to whom the supply was made also has that special status.

(iv)   Any VAT payable on the import of goods by a group member is payable by the representative member.

**Two or more companies are eligible to be treated as members of a group provided each of them is either established in the UK or has a fixed establishment in the UK, and:**

•    **One of them controls each of the others,** or

•    **One person** (which could be an individual or a holding company) **controls all of them,** or

•    **Two or more persons carrying on a business in partnership control all of them.**

Individual companies which are within a group for company law purposes may still register separately and stay outside the VAT group. This may be done to ensure that a company making exempt supplies does not restrict the input VAT recovery of the group as a whole.

Signed: Management Accountant

## 41  CONTROL

> **Pass marks.** It is important to plan an answer to this type of question otherwise it will be tempting to repeat yourself and wander of the point!

To:       The directors of A Ltd
From:   Management Accountant
Date:    1 March 2001

The purpose of this report is to identify and discuss the tax implications that will arise if A Ltd acquires a majority holding in B Ltd or alternatively if A Ltd acquires the assets, trade and contracts of B Ltd.

1   **Acquisition of majority holding of the voting shares in B Ltd**

In this case, shares in the B Ltd are acquired. **Stamp duty at the rate of 0.5% of the price paid is payable by A Ltd**. The consideration paid for the shares is then the base cost of those shares for a subsequent disposal.

Within A Ltd itself, the tax history of the company is generally preserved. This means that warranties and indemnities should be sought to cover outstanding tax matters and to cover potential tax problems that have arisen in the past eg PAYE or VAT irregularities.

As B Ltd will become an associated company, the effect on the limits for the small companies and the starting rates of tax should be taken into account.

There are some restrictions on the use of losses.

First, **no relief is available for trading losses in accounting periods on one side of a change in ownership of a company in certain circumstances**. These are if the profit making and loss making accounting periods are on the either side of the change in ownership and either there is a major change in the nature or conduct of the trade within 3 years before or after the change in ownership; or after the change in ownership there is a considerable revival of the company's trading activities which at the time of the change had become small or negligible.

Second, **there are restrictions on the use of pre-entry capital losses**. In general, pre-entry losses will only be available to set against gains on assets which B Ltd owned before the take-over or acquired from outside the group of companies. There are also restrictions on the use of losses against pre-entry gains.

Third, **group relief for losses can only be claimed for the period after B Ltd joins the group**. In order to work out what losses are attributable to that period, a time apportionment basis is usually used, although either the company or the Revenue can use another basis if this produces a more 'just and reasonable' result.

2   **Purchase of assets, trade and contracts (including employees)**

Here, the individual assets of the company are acquired, such as stock, premises and goodwill. An allocation of the purchase price to the individual assets is required.

**The disposal of the assets may give rise to trading or capital profits, depending on the nature of the asset.** Thus, there may be possibilities for tax planning to minimise

119

the tax payable. **Balancing charges may be sheltered by trading losses** and chargeable gains may be sheltered by brought forward capital losses, but B Ltd may have capital gains which cannot be relieved.

Stamp duty is payable on the assets such as premises and goodwill. The rate of duty is between 1% - 4% depending on the consideration paid.

There is no scope for using losses in B Ltd such as trading losses and capital losses.

Signed: Management Accountant

## 42    HGJL LTD

> **Pass marks**. Group relief should be surrendered to the group company which suffers tax at the highest marginal rate.

(a)    **Group structure**

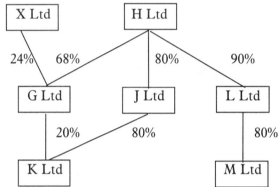

(b)    The **associated companies** in the above structure are:

H Ltd, G Ltd, J Ltd, L Ltd, K Ltd and M Ltd

There is  **capital gains group** consisting of:

H Ltd, J Ltd, K Ltd, L Ltd and M Ltd

There are two **group relief groups** consisting of:

(i)    H Ltd, J Ltd, K Ltd and L Ltd

(ii)    L Ltd and M Ltd.

**Tutorial note**: M Ltd is not in the same group relief group as H Ltd because H Ltd does not hold a 75% effective interest in M Ltd.

There is a **consortium** consisting of

G Ltd, H Ltd and X Ltd

(c)    **Corporation tax computations - year ended 31 March 2001**

|  | H £ | G £ | J £ | L £ | K £ | M £ | X £ |
|---|---|---|---|---|---|---|---|
| Schedule D Case I | 48,000 | 60,000 |  | 30,000 | 90,000 |  |  |
| Schedule D Case III | 4,000 | 5,000 | 6,000 |  | 10,000 | 6,000 |  |
|  | 52,000 | 65,000 | 6,000 | 30,000 | 100,000 | 6,000 | - |
| *Less*: Trade charges | (2,000) | (4,000) | (6,000) |  |  | (6,000) |  |
|  | 50,000 | 61,000 | - | 30,000 | 100,000 | - | - |
| *Less*: Group relief |  |  |  | (30,000) | (64,000) |  |  |
| *Less*: Consortium relief |  | (14,640) |  |  |  |  |  |
| Chargeable profits | 50,000 | 46,360 | - | - | 36,000 | - | - |
| MCT payable at 20% | 10,000 | 9,272 | - | - | 7,200 | - | - |

**Loss memorandum**

|  | J | | M | X |
|---|---|---|---|---|
|  | £ | | £ | £ |
| Schedule D Case I losses | (64,000) | | (42,000) | (24,000) |
| Excess trade charges | | | (2,000) | |
|  | (64,000) | | (44,000) | (24,000) |
| Surrenders to: | | | | |
| L | | | 30,000 | |
| K | 64,000 | | | |
| G(consortium relief) | | | | 14,640 |
| Losses available remaining | - | | (14,000) | (9,360) |

*Notes*

1    As X Ltd is a consortium member, the only option for its loss is to surrender it to G Ltd to utilise 24% of G Ltd's available profits.

2    The only group relief claim that could be made for M Ltd's loss is to surrender £30,000 to L Ltd. This should be done. There is no point in making a s393A ICTA 1988 claim in the current period. (A claim would result in trade charges of £8,000 and losses of £6,000 (£42,000 – £6,000 – £30,000), to carry forward which is the same position as above.)

3    It is not possible for any losses to be surrendered to G Ltd as it is not a member of a group relief group.

4    As there are six associated companies, the lower threshold for small companies' rate purposes is £50,000 (£300,000/6). The surrender to K Ltd hence saves tax at the rate of 32.5% against the profits above £50,000, which fall in the small companies' marginal relief band. The surrender against profits below £50,000 could be made to either H Ltd or K Ltd where tax is saved at the rate of 20%.

## 43    PREPARATION QUESTION: FOREIGN TAX

> **Pass marks**. The four associated companies reduce Mumbo Ltd's upper limit for small companies' marginal relief purposes to £300,000 and this makes marginal relief unavailable. This greatly simplifies the calculation.

**Mumbo Ltd**
**Corporation tax computation**

|  | £ | £ |
|---|---|---|
| Schedule D Case I | | 550,000 |
| Schedule D Case V | | |
| Z Inc: £36,000 × 100/72 | 50,000 | |
| X SA: £38,000 × 100/95 | 40,000 | |
|  | | 90,000 |
|  | | 640,000 |
| Less charge paid | | (60,000) |
| Profits chargeable to corporation tax | | 580,000 |

|  |  | £ |
|---|---|---|
| Corporation tax £580,000 × 30% |  | 174,000 |
| Less double taxation relief (W) |  | (16,000) |
|  |  | 158,000 |
| Less ACT (W) |  | 0 |
| Mainstream corporation tax |  | 158,000 |

*Working: double taxation relief and ACT*

Neither foreign tax rate exceeds the UK corporation tax rate, and the charges can all be set against UK profits. Full relief is therefore available for foreign tax.

|  | Profits | Charges | Net profits | Corporation tax at 30% | DTR |
|---|---|---|---|---|---|
|  | £ | £ | £ | £ | £ |
| UK | 550,000 | 60,000 | 490,000 | 147,000 | 0 |
| Z Inc | 50,000 | 0 | 50,000 | 15,000 | 14,000 |
| X SA | 40,000 | 0 | 40,000 | 12,000 | 2,000 |
| Total | 640,000 | 60,000 | 580,000 | 174,000 | 16,000 |

The franked payment for shadow purposes is £434,000 × 100/80 = £542,500

The shadow ACT is £108,500.

ACT set-off is limited as follows.

|  | 20% of profits | Corporation tax after DTR | Limit (the lower figure) |
|---|---|---|---|
|  | £ | £ | £ |
| UK | 98,000 | 147,000 | 98,000 |
| Z Inc | 10,000 | 1,000 | 1,000 |
| X SA | 8,000 | 10,000 | 8,000 |
|  |  |  | 107,000 |

As the shadow ACT exceeds the maximum set-off it is not possible to set-off any of the real surplus ACT brought forward.

## 44    B AND W LTD

> **Pass marks**. The set off of DTR and ACT must be made on a source by source basis. ACT is set off after DTR. The ACT set off is limited to the lower of 20% of the profits of each source and the tax charge remaining on that source after DTR.

**Mainstream corporation tax**

|  | B Ltd | W Ltd |
|---|---|---|
|  | £ | £ |
| Schedule D Case I | 280,000 | 6,000 |
| Capital gains | 30,000 | 0 |
| Schedule D Case V (× 100/60) | 2,000 | 0 |
| Schedule D Case III | 8,000 | 0 |
| Taxed income | 16,000 | 0 |
| Less charge on income | (18,000) | 0 |
| PCTCT | 318,000 | 6,000 |
| FII | 32,000 | 0 |
| 'Profits' | 350,000 | 6,000 |

*B Ltd*

|  | FY00(2/12) | FY01(10/12) |
|---|---|---|
|  | £ | £ |
| Profits | 58,333 | 291,667 |
| PCTCT | 53,000 | 265,000 |
| Lower limit for small companies rate | 25,000 | 125,000 |
| Upper limit for small companies rate | 125,000 | 625,000 |

As there was no change in tax rates or limits between FY00 and FY01 it was not strictly necessary to make the above split.

|  | £ |
|---|---|
| *FY 00* | |
| £53,000 × 30% | 15,900 |
| Less: $1/40 \, (125,000 - 58,333) \times \dfrac{53,000}{58,333}$ | (1,514) |
| *FY 01* | |
| £265,000 × 30% | 79,500 |
| Less: $1/40 \, (625,000 - 291,667) \times \dfrac{265,000}{291,667}$ | (7,571) |
|  | 86,315 |
| Less DTR (W1) | (543) |
|  | 85,772 |
| Less ACT (W2) | (7,800) |
| Less income tax suffered (£8,000 × 20% + £16,000 × 22%) | (5,120) |
| Mainstream corporation tax | 72,852 |

*W Ltd*

| CT | £ |
|---|---|
| £6,000 × 20% | 1,200 |
| Less: starting rate marginal relief (W3) | |
| 1/40 (£25,000 – £6,000) | (475) |
| Mainstream corporation tax | 725 |

*Workings*

1    **Double tax relief**

|  | UK profits | Schedule D Case V | Total |
|---|---|---|---|
|  | £ | £ | £ |
| Profits | 334,000 | 2,000 | 336,000 |
| Less: charges | (18,000) | – | (18,000) |
|  | 316,000 | 2,000 | 318,000 |

$$CT \; \frac{86,315}{318,000} = 27.14308\%$$

|  | UK profits | Schedule D Case V | Total |
|---|---|---|---|
|  | 85,772 | 543 | 86,315 |
| Less: DTR | | | |
| lower of | | | |
| (i) UK tax (£543) | | | |
| (ii) Overseas tax (£800) | | (543) | (543) |
|  | 85,772 | – | 85,772 |

BPP
PUBLISHING

2   **ACT**

|  | £ |
|---|---|
| Notional franked payment (£236,000 × 100/80) | 295,000 |
| Less: FII for shadow purposes ( × 90/80) | (36,000) |
|  | 259,000 |
| Shadow ACT (£259,000 × 20%) | 51,800 |
| Maximum set off (£316,000 × 20%) | (63,200) |
|  | 11,400 |

Therefore all of the brought forward ACT can be set off in the period.

3   **CT**

The upper and lower limits for starting rate purposes are £25,000 and £5,000 respectively so starting rate marginal relief applies.

45   **J LTD**

**Pass marks**. The three UK subsidiaries meant that small companies' marginal relief was unavailable, the upper limit being £1,500,000/4 = £375,000. This simplified the calculations considerably.

(a)

|  | Total £ | UK profits £ | P Inc £ | L Inc £ |
|---|---|---|---|---|
| Schedule D Case I | 600,000 | 600,000 |  |  |
| Schedule D Case V |  |  |  |  |
| £32,500 × 100/65 | 50,000 |  | 50,000 |  |
| £36,000 × 100/90 | 40,000 |  |  | 40,000 |
| Less charges | (12,000) | (12,000) |  |  |
|  | 678,000 | 588,000 | 50,000 | 40,000 |
| Corporation tax at 30% | 203,400 | 176,400 | 15,000 | 12,000 |
| Less DTR: lower of |  |  |  |  |
| UK tax (£15,000/12,000) |  |  |  |  |
| Overseas (£17,500/£4,000) | (19,000) |  | (15,000) | (4,000) |
| Mainstream corporation tax | 184,400 | 176,400 | 0 | 8,000 |

(b)  **If the holdings had been 10%, underlying tax relief** (for the corporation tax suffered by the overseas companies) **would have been available,** in addition to relief for the withholding tax. Total relief would still be limited to the UK tax on the overseas profits. The overseas profits would have to be grossed up by the underlying tax as well as the withholding tax.

Underlying tax is calculated as:

$$\text{Gross dividend income} \times \frac{\text{Foreign tax paid}}{\text{After-tax accounting profits}}$$

(c)                            MEMORANDUM

To:         The Board of Directors
From:       Management Accountant
Date:       1 November 2001
Subject:    VAT on imports from the USA

**Imports are chargeable to VAT when the same goods supplied in the home market by a registered trader would be chargeable to VAT, and at the same rate.**

When we import goods from the USA we must calculate VAT on the value of the goods imported (the price plus packaging, freight as far as the first destination in the European Community, insurance, commission and customs and excise duties), and account for it at the point of entry into the UK. We can then deduct the VAT payable as input VAT on the next VAT return. HM Customs & Excise issue monthly certificates to importers showing the VAT paid on imports. VAT is chargeable on the sale of the goods in the UK in the normal way. If security can be provided, the deferred payment system can be used whereby VAT and customs duty are automatically debited to our bank account each month rather than payment being made for each import when the goods arrive in the UK.

Signed: Management Accountant

## 46   X LTD

> **Pass marks.** DTR is set off before ACT.
>
> It was important to read the question with care. For instance, you should have taken care not to
>
> (i)   gross up figures which were clearly already stated to be gross
> (ii)  readjust the profit figure which was already given as adjusted

(a)   Capital allowances

|  | FYA £ | Pool £ | Expensive car £ | Total allowances £ |
|---|---|---|---|---|
| WDV b/f | | 102,000 | 18,000 | |
| WDA @ 25% | | (25,500) | (3,000) (max) | 28,500 |
| | | 76,500 | 15,000 | |
| Additions | 12,000 | | | |
| | 23,750 | | | |
| | 35,750 | | | |
| Less: FYA @ 40% | (14,300) | | | 14,300 |
| | | 21,450 | | 42,800 |
| WDV c/f | | 97,950 | 15,000 | |

(b)   **Calculation of profits chargeable to CT**

| | £ |
|---|---|
| Adjusted profit | 220,000 |
| Less:   Capital allowances | (42,800) |
| Schedule D Case I | 177,200 |
| Schedule D Case V | 4,000 |
| Schedule A | nil |
| Patent royalty received | 12,000 |
| Chargeable gains | 28,000 |
| | 221,200 |
| | |
| Less:   Charges on income: | |
| Patent royalties paid (not accruals basis) | (6,000) |
| Gift aid | (2,000) |
| | 213,200 |
| Less:   Schedule A loss relief | (16,000) |
| Non-trading deficit (W1) | (1,000) |
| PCTCT | 196,200 |
| FII | 15,000 |
| | 211,200 |

For the purposes of determining the small companies rate limits, both Z Ltd and Y Ltd need to be treated as associated companies, since they are both deemed to have been associated for the whole period. The limits are therefore £1,500,000/3 = £500,000 and £300,000/3 = £100,000.

*MCT payable by X Ltd*

|  | £ |
|---|---:|
| Tax payable at 30% | 58,860 |

Less: small companies' marginal relief

$$£(500,000 - 211,200) \times \frac{196,200}{211,200} \times \frac{1}{40}$$

|  |  |
|---|---:|
|  | (6,707) |
|  | 52,153 |

Less: DTR re foreign dividend lower of:

(i) UK tax: $\dfrac{4,000}{196,200} \times £52,153 = £1,063$

(ii) Foreign tax: £4,000 × 35% = £1,400

|  |  |
|---|---:|
|  | (1,063) |
| Less: ACT set off (W2) | (nil) |
| Less: Net income tax suffered at source: | (3,120) |
| MCT payable | 47,970 |

*Workings*

### 1   Non trading deficit

|  | £ |
|---|---:|
| Debenture interest (accruals basis) | 14,000 |
| Loan interest from customer | 1,000 |
|  | 15,000 |
| Less: Loss on loan written off | (10,000) |
| Loan interest on let property | (6,000) |
| Non-trading deficit | (1,000) |

### 2   ACT

|  | £ |
|---|---:|
| Notional FP £180,000 × 100/80 | 225,000 |
| Less: FII for shadow purposes (£15,000 × 90/80) | (16,875) |
| FP for shadow purposes | 208,125 |
| Shadow ACT @ 20% | 41,625 |

| Maximum set-off (UK income only | £ |
|---|---:|
| as DTR has reduced tax on non-UK |  |
| income to nil) £192,200 × 20% | 38,440 |
| Less: shadow ACT | (41,625) |
| Surplus shadow ACT | (3,185) |

As shadow ACT exceeds the maximum set off it is not possible to set off any of the surplus ACT b/f

### 3   Income tax suffered

|  | £ |
|---|---:|
| Debenture interest £14,000 × 20% | 2,800 |
| Loan interest received £1,000 × 20% | 200 |
| Patent royalties £12,000 x 22% | 2,640 |
| Income tax retained: |  |
| Loan interest paid £6,000 × 20% | (1,200) |
| Patent royalties £6,000 × 22% | (1,320) |
| Income tax to be set off | 3,120 |

*Note*. Gift Aid donations are paid gross.

## 47    CONTROLLED FOREIGN COMPANY

> **Pass marks**. The proposed dividend has no tax effect until the accounting period in which it is paid. It will then give rise to shadow ACT in the next accounting period.

### A Ltd : corporation tax computation

|  | £ |
|---|---|
| Schedule D Case I | 340,000 |
| Schedule D Case III | 50,000 |
| Schedule A | 20,000 |
| Taxed income | 35,000 |
| Chargeable gains £(150,000 − 40,000) | 110,000 |
|  | 555,000 |
| Less charges £(10,000 + 25,000) | (35,000) |
| Profits chargeable to corporation tax | 520,000 |
| FII | 30,000 |
| 'Profits' | 550,000 |

There are two associated companies, B Ltd and C Inc, making the upper limit £1,500,000 / 3 = £500,000.

| *Corporation tax* | £ |
|---|---|
| £520,000 × 30% | 156,000 |
| Tax on CFC's profits |  |
| £46,000 × 100 / 92 = £50,000 × 30% | 15,000 |
|  | 171,000 |
| Less overseas tax £50,000 × 8% | (4,000) |
|  | 167,000 |
|  |  |
| Less ACT (W1) | (37,500) |
| Mainstream corporation tax | 129,500 |

*Working*

1    ACT

|  | £ |
|---|---|
| Notional franked payment (£341,000 × 100/80) | 426,250 |
| FII for shadow purposes (£30,000 × 90/80 + £10,000) | (43,750) |
|  | 382,500 |
|  |  |
| Shadow ACT = £76,500 |  |
| Maximum ACT set off |  |
| UK profits (£520,000 × 20%) | 104,000 |
| CFC profits (£50,000 × 20%) | 10,000 |
|  | 114,000 |
| Less: shadow ACT | (76,500) |
|  | 37,500 |

∴ £37,500 of the brought forward ACT can be set off in the period.

## 48    ZEBEDEE INC

> **Pass marks**. Only notes were required, not a formal report.

(a)    The profits of a controlled foreign company (CFC) (excluding capital gains) may be apportioned to any corporate UK shareholders entitled to at least 25% of those profits. No apportionment can be made to non-corporate persons. The profits to be apportioned are computed using UK tax rules.

Apportioned profits are brought into the UK company's CT600 corporation tax computation as an amount of tax. The tax rate applicable is always the full rate of corporation tax irrespective of the rate the UK company pays tax on its other profits.

Where CFC profits are apportioned they are reduced by 'creditable tax' which is the aggregate of:

(i)     Any double tax relief (see below) available in the UK in respect of foreign tax due against the chargeable profits

(ii)    Any income tax deducted at source on income received by the CFC

(iii)   Corporation tax payable in the UK on any CFC income taxable in this country.

The CFC rules, where relevant, apply automatically and a UK company must include its share of apportioned profits on its self assessment tax return. A clearance procedure exists for companies who wish to check in advance whether their plans will fall within the CFC rules.

(b)  A CFC profits do not need to be apportioned if:

(i)     **Its chargeable profits for the accounting period do not exceed £50,000 (this is reduced proportionately for short accounting periods)**, or

(ii)    **It is situated in a territory which does not have a lower level of taxation.** A lower level of tax means less than three quarters of the amount which would have been payable had the company been resident in the UK. The Revenue publishes a list of those countries ('excluded countries') which it does not regard as low tax countries, or

(iii)   **It follows an acceptable distribution policy.** This applies where it distributes by way of a dividend, during or within 18 months of the period for which it is due, at least 90% of its net chargeable profits, or

(iv)    **It is engaged in exempt activities** and it has a **real presence** in its territory of residence. For this exclusion to apply there are certain restrictions on the type of income the company may receive and the type of activities that may be carried out.

(v)     **It fulfils the public quotation conditions.** This means it must be quoted on a recognised stock exchange, and dealing must have taken place within twelve months of the end of the accounting period. At least 35% of the voting power must be held by the public with no more than 85% of that power being held by all the company's principal members, or

(vi)    It satisfies the **motive test.** Broadly this means any reduction in UK tax must not have been the main reason for the CFC's existence.

There is an **advance clearance procedure** in respect of the '**exempt activities' test**, the 'motive'; test and the '**acceptable distribution policy**'.

(c)  **EU exports**

The VAT treatment of EU exports depends on whether or not the foreign customer is VAT-registered:

(i)     **If the customer is VAT registered, then we can zero-rate the sale.** The customer will pay VAT at time of importation at the rate that country would normally apply in his country. The customer will be able to claim this as input tax. For us **to apply zero-rating we have to retain documentary evidence of the goods leaving the UK and show the customer's VAT registration number on the sales invoice.**

(ii)    **If the customer is not registered we must charge VAT at the applicable UK rate and account for it to Customers and Excise.** However, if the value of the exports made to non-VAT registered customers in an EU member state exceeds a certain threshold, there would be a requirement for us to register and account for VAT in that foreign country. Alternatively, we could appoint a representative to account for VAT on our behalf in the UK Member State concerned.

(iii)   When the level of our annual trade with EU customers reaches a specified threshold (currently £233,000 or more), it will be necessary for us to submit regular monthly statistical returns known as **Intrastat forms**. It is also likely that we will be required to **submit EC sales statements**.

(iv)    A general rule deems that services are supplied in the country where the supplier belongs. However, there are certain categories of services supplied to VAT-registered traders in the EU which are treated as supplied in the recipient's state and are therefore outside the scope of UK VAT.

## 49    CL PLC

> **Pass marks**. It was not enough in part (a) to merely show that CL plc was controlled by five or fewer participators. You should also have considered the quoted company exemption.

(a)    **Participator**

|  | *Shares owned* | *% holding* |
|---|---|---|
| Mr and Mrs G (associate) | 10,000 | 25 |
| Mr F | 10,000 | 25 |
| Mr H | 2,500 | 6.25 |
|  | 22,500 | 56.25 |

On the basis that **the company is controlled by five or fewer participators, CL plc appears to be close**. It is necessary, however, to establish the total holding of the public.

**Shareholder**

|  | *Shares owned* | *% holding* |
|---|---|---|
| R Ltd (a non-close company) | 10,000 | 25 |
| Members of the public | 5,000 | 12.5 |
|  | 15,000 | 37.5 |

**Where 35% or more of the voting power of a quoted company is held by the public, the company is normally exempted from close company status.** For this exemption to apply, however, **the principal members (the members with the five largest shareholdings, counting associates shares, provided that each holds 5% or more) must not hold more than 85% of the voting power**.

|  | *Shares owned* | *% holding* |
|---|---|---|
| R Ltd | 10,000 | 25 |
| Mr and Mrs G | 10,000 | 25 |
| Mr F | 10,000 | 25 |
| Mr H | 2,500 | 6.25 |
| Miss J | 2,500 | 6.25 |
|  | 35,000 | 87.5 |

Thus since the principal members hold 87.5% of the voting power, the quoted company exemption does not apply and CL plc is a close company.

(b)   If R Ltd sold 3,000 shares to the general public, 37.5% of the company's shares would, as before, be held by the general public but the principal members would hold only 80%:

|  | Shares owned | % holding |
|---|---|---|
| Mr and Mrs G | 10,000 | 25 |
| Mr F | 10,000 | 25 |
| R Ltd | 7,000 | 17.5 |
| Mr H | 2,500 | 6.25 |
| Miss J | 2,500 | 6.25 |
|  | 32,000 | 80.00 |

In this case the quoted company exemption would apply and CL plc would not be a close company.

(c)   As Mr H is not an employee or director, there will be a deemed distribution in respect of the company car. The amount of the deemed distribution is what would have been the Schedule E charge, £4,200, (£12,000 × 35%). The actual cost to the company of providing the car will be a disallowable expense for corporation tax purposes.

## 50   OBJECTIVE TEST QUESTION

1   D   25% × loan is the notional tax payable.

Due on normal due date for small company

ie. 1 October 2002 for y/e 31.12.2001.

## 51   PREPARATION QUESTION: REGISTRATION AND ACCOUNTING

> **Pass marks**. The enquiry clearly came from someone who was ignorant of VAT, so a simple reply was appropriate. However, you should still have been precise about, for example, the registration rules: otherwise, the company might sue you if it were penalised for late registration!

### ABC Management Accountants
### 6 Somewhere Road, London, EC4Y 1SX

The Managing Director
XYZ Ltd
1 Anywhere Street
London, WC2 5SJ

Date: 23 October 2000
Our ref: Misc 1
Your ref: 123

Dear Sir,

Thank you for your recent letter.

We set out below the main points which you need to be aware of in respect of VAT.

**Registration**

If the company makes taxable supplies of goods or services, **it must register with HM Customs & Excise if its taxable turnover in the 12 months down to the end of a calendar month has exceeded the registration limit, or if you anticipate that it will exceed the registration limit in the 30 day period starting on any day.** The company may also register voluntarily so long as it is making taxable supplies of any amount. The registration limit is currently £52,000.

## Accounts

You should **record all income and expenditure exclusive of any VAT**. The VAT should be recorded in a separate account showing the balance due to or from HM Customs & Excise. **The only exception** (when expenditure should be recorded inclusive of VAT) **is expenditure, the VAT on which is irrecoverable**. The main categories are cars with some non-business use and business entertaining.

## Accounting for VAT

VAT is normally accounted for on a **quarterly basis**, the months which end the quarters depending on the type of business you run. You may, however, ask for your VAT quarters to coincide with your own accounting quarters. **If VAT repayment claims normally arise** (because input VAT normally exceeds output VAT), **you can apply for monthly accounting in order to improve cash flow. All VAT returns and payments must be made within one month of the end of the relevant period, and you should note that substantial penalties can be imposed if you are persistently late in paying VAT**.

The normal accounting system for VAT ignores the time when cash is received from debtors and paid to suppliers. Small businesses, in particular, can suffer cash flow problems from the need to account for VAT before receiving payment from customers. Consequently, **taxable persons with an annual taxable turnover of up to £350,000 can use the cash accounting scheme. Users of the scheme account for VAT on the basis of cash receipts and payments**.

**An entirely separate scheme, available when annual taxable turnover does not exceed £300,000, is the annual accounting scheme**. This is designed to reduce the compliance burden on small businesses by requiring only one VAT return each year. VAT payments are made by monthly direct debit for nine months of the year, based on an estimate of the VAT eventually due if annual turnover is £100,000 or more. If annual turnover was less then only four quarterly payments of VAT are required each being 20% of the previous year's VAT liability. If the sum due does not exceed £400, the trader does not need to make the quarterly interim payment. The VAT return for the year is used to calculate the final amount payable or repayable.

Traders cannot apply to join the annual accounting scheme until they have been registered for at least 12 months.

## Records

You will have to **keep VAT records for up to six years** including:

(a)  Details of all input and output VAT together with invoices (copies of invoices issued)

(b)  Details of all credits given or received together with credit notes (copies of credit notes issued)

(c)  Details of errors or corrections

(d)  Details of any self-supplies

(e)  A detailed VAT ledger account

(f)  All other documentation relating to purchases and sales, such as day books.

Finally, we enclose copies of the relevant VAT booklets which you will need. We hope that you have found this letter helpful but if you have any queries, please let us know.

Yours faithfully

ABC Management Accountants

52    PREPARATION QUESTION: VAT COMPUTATIONS

> **Pass marks**. The VAT on purchases attributable to zero rated sales is recoverable, because zero rated sales are *taxable* (at 0%). This is the key distinction between zero rating and exemption.

**The VAT payable for the quarter**

| | £ | £ |
|---|---|---|
| Output VAT on standard rated sales: £172,500 × 7/47 | | 25,691 |
| Input VAT on purchases attributable to standard rated sales: £66,500 × 7/47 | 9,904 | |
| Input VAT on purchases attributable to zero rated sales: £20,350 × 7/47 | 3,031 | |
| | | (12,935) |
| Net VAT payable to HM Customs & Excise | | 12,756 |

**Tutorial notes**

1    The input VAT on motor cars with some non-business use is not recoverable. The only exceptions are cars bought for taxi businesses, self-drive car hire businesses and driving schools.

2    Input VAT is deductible only to the extent that it is attributable to taxable supplies made by the business. Input VAT which is attributable to exempt supplies is not deductible. There is however a de minimis limit (£625 a month and 50% of all input VAT) under which VAT attributable to exempt supplies is deductible.

53    PREPARATION QUESTION: CASH ACCOUNTING AND LAND

> **Pass marks**. This question covers two entirely separate areas of VAT law. The cash accounting scheme is relatively straightforward. The option to tax supplies of interests in land is a more complicated area.

(a)    A company may use the **cash accounting scheme** if:

    (i)    Its **taxable turnover (excluding VAT) does not exceed £350,000 a year,** and

    (ii)    **All returns and VAT payments are up to date, or arrangements have been made to pay outstanding VAT by instalments.**

If the value of taxable supplies has exceeded £437,500 in the 12 months to the end of a VAT accounting period, the trader must leave the scheme immediately.

Under the scheme, **VAT is accounted for on both purchases and sales on the return for the period in which cash was paid or received. This avoids the cash flow difficulties** which could arise if substantial sales were made in one period but cash was not received until a later period. Without the cash accounting scheme, VAT might have to be accounted for before cash was received from the customer. On the other hand, under the cash accounting scheme input VAT cannot be claimed on purchases in respect of a period before the one in which the purchases are paid for.

The other advantages of the scheme are that **bad debt relief is automatic and immediate,** as VAT is not accounted for if the customer does not pay; **and accounting for VAT may be simpler because it can be linked to the cash book.**

(b)    The landlord will be making **exempt supplies when letting out the building. Landlords may elect to treat the supply of interests in land and buildings specified**

**in an election as taxable instead of exempt**. The election covers leases, licences and sales and applies to all future supplies of the specified land and buildings (except a sale of land to an individual to erect a dwelling for his use on it, or to a registered housing association to erect a dwelling or dwellings on it). The landlord must become registered for VAT (if he is not already so registered) in order to make the election.

The point of making the election is that it enables the landlord to recover input VAT. Since he makes taxable supplies with the building (rather than exempt supplies).

The election cannot be made in respect of dwellings or in respect of charity buildings other than offices. The election may be revoked with the consent of Customs after 20 years. Supplies after revocation are exempt.

## 54 OBJECTIVE TEST QUESTIONS

1  A  The retailer's price is inclusive of VAT hence £705 × 7/47 = £105.00 VAT less the £43.75 input VAT on the purchase (£250 × 17.5%) = £61.25.

2  D  Repair of washing machine is the supply of a service. The supply of any form of power or heat is specifically a supply of goods.

3  B  Arun's taxable turnover exceeds £52,000 at the end of November. Arun must notify Customs of a need to register within 30 days, ie by 30 December 2000.

4  D  Arun's taxable turnover exceeds £52,000 at the end of November. Arun must notify Customs of a need to register within 30 days, ie by 30 December 2000.

Customs will register Arun with effect from the end of the month following the end of November, ie from end of December which is effectively from 1 January 2001 onwards.

5  B  A form VAT 1 **must** be completed.

6  C  X inc is overseas and as it has no business establishment in the UK cannot be in a VAT group. E Ltd is only held as to 40% thus insufficient holding to be in the group.

All other companies can be included in a VAT group registration (although may wish to exclude D Ltd since making exempt supplies - question asked for max number so include D Ltd to get answer needed).

7  C  The accountancy service is over 6 months before registration.

The Christmas Party is entertaining. Thus both not allowed. £(25,000 + 10,000) × 7/47 = £5,213.

8  C  **The tax invoice was issued within 14 days of the basic tax point. Hence the invoice date is the tax point**.

9  A  **The date the service was completed is the basic tax point. Since an invoice was not issued within 14 days of this date, the basic tax point becomes the tax point**.

Dates of payment after the service is performed are red herrings.

10  B  Because payment was received before the basic tax point date, the date of payment becomes the tax point.

Zero rated goods **do** have a tax point - item D is totally incorrect.

11  A  Books are zero-rated.

£5,000 of stationery is standard-rated - less 10% discount = £4,500 used to calculate VAT due × 17.5% = £787.50.

12   A   The test for MP is the lower of:

(a)   30% £(100,000 + 32,000 + 30,000) = £48,600
(b)   £1 million

ie £48,600

The error of £30,000 is below this threshold - thus no penalty charged.

13   C   As Customs issued an assessment which was too low and the company failed to notify this within 30 days, the test for MP is the lower of:

(a)   30% × £290,000 = £87,000
(b)   £1 million

ie £87,000

The error of £90,000 (since the assessment only showed £200,000 and not £290,000) exceeds this so the misdeclaration penalty is 15% × £90,000 = £13,500.

14   C   Interest runs from the due date for the VAT return in which the under-declaration was made.

15   C

16   B   Only 50% of the VAT can be reclaimed.

17   D

|  | £ | £ |
|---|---|---|
| Taxable |  | 2,500 |
| Non-attributable |  |  |
| $\dfrac{300k}{400k} = 75\%$ |  |  |
| 75% × £2,800 |  | 2,100 |
|  |  | 4,600 |
| Exempt | 750 |  |
| Non-attributable | 700 |  |
| De-minimis |  | 1,450 |
|  |  | 6,050 |

All the input tax can be recovered as the otherwise non-deductible amount is below the de-minimis limit.

18   C   Debt eligible for bad debt relief if unpaid 6 months after due date of payment.

19   D   Under the cash accounting scheme the date the cash is received becomes the date the supply occurs for VAT accounting purposes.

20   B   VAT is accounted for on the margin (ie basic profit) £(1,100 − 500) × 7/47 = £89.36.

21   D   Drugs and medicines on prescription are zero-rated.

## 55  SELL FOR CASH

> **Pass marks**. It was important to set out the required calculations in appendices attached to the report.

(a)  To:        The directors of P Ltd
     From:      Chief accountant
     Date:      13 March 2000
     Subject:   Sale of assets in order to finance loan repayment

### Introduction

The purpose of this report is to estimate the net proceeds that will arise on the sale of various assets in October 2000 and to advise which asset will realise sufficient funds in order for us to repay our loan which is due to mature in December 2000.

### Estimated chargeable gains

You will see that in Appendix one, I have prepared estimates of the chargeable gains that will arise on the sale of each of the assets that we are considering selling. These estimated chargeable gains are as follows:

|                 | £        |
|-----------------|----------|
| Plot of land    | £289,149 |
| Retail store    | £310,620 |
| Shares in X Ltd | £256,261 |

### Advise on sale of asset

As the company's Schedule D Case I profits are estimated to be £600,000 and we have two wholly owned subsidiary companies, corporation tax at 30% will be payable on any chargeable gain made. I have set out in Appendix two the estimated funds that will remain available after the payment of corporation tax on each of the above gains. You will see that based on our estimates only the sale of the shares will result in sufficient funds to completely repay our loan of £520,000. I therefore recommend sale of the shares.

Signed: Chief Accountant

### Appendix one - chargeable gains

(i)  **The plot of land**

The gain in June 1984 was as follows.

|                                      | £         |
|--------------------------------------|-----------|
| Proceeds                             | 300,000   |
| Less cost                            | (20,000)  |
|                                      | 280,000   |
| Less indexation allowance            |           |
| £20,000 × 0.123                      | (2,460)   |
| Chargeable gain                      | 277,540   |

|  | £ | £ |
|---|---|---|
| The October 2000 disposal |  |  |
| Proceeds |  | 600,000 |
| Less cost | 300,000 |  |
| Less half of rolled over gain | (138,770) |  |
|  |  | (161,230) |
|  |  | 438,770 |
| Less indexation allowance |  |  |
| £161,230 × 0.928 |  | (149,621) |
| Chargeable gain |  | 289,149 |

(ii)    **The retail store**

|  | Cost | 31.3.82 value |
|---|---|---|
|  | £ | £ |
| Proceeds | 600,000 | 600,000 |
| Cost | (80,000) |  |
| October 1980 expenditure | (20,000) |  |
| March 1982 value |  | (90,000) |
| November 1983 expenditure | (20,000) | (20,000) |
| December 1990 expenditure | (25,000) | (25,000) |
|  | 455,000 | 465,000 |
| Less indexation allowance |  |  |
| £100,000 × 1.166 | (116,600) | (116,600) |
| £20,000 × 0.984 | (19,680) | (19,680) |
| £25,000 × 0.324 | (8,100) | (8,100) |
|  | 310,620 | 320,620 |

The chargeable gain is £310,620.

(iii)    **The shares in X Ltd**

|  | Shares | Cost | Indexed cost |
|---|---|---|---|
|  |  | £ | £ |
| Purchase May 1985 | 60,000 | 180,000 | 180,000 |
| Indexed rise to June 1986 |  |  |  |
| £180,000 × 0.027 |  |  | 4,860 |
| Rights issue June 1986 | 20,000 | 80,000 | 80,000 |
|  | 80,000 | 260,000 | 264,860 |
| Indexed rise to July 1990 |  |  |  |
| £264,860 × 0.297 |  |  | 78,663 |
|  |  |  | 343,523 |
| Sale July 1990 | (30,000) | (97,500) | (128,821) |
|  | 50,000 | 162,500 | 214,702 |
| Indexed rise to May 1991 |  |  |  |
| £214,702 × 0.053 |  |  | 11,379 |
|  |  |  | 226,081 |
| Purchase May 1991 | 10,000 | 50,000 | 50,000 |
|  | 60,000 | 212,500 | 276,081 |
| Indexed rise to October 2000 |  |  |  |
| £276,081 × 0.288 |  |  | 79,511 |
|  |  |  | 355,592 |
| Sale October 2000 | (58,000) | ((205,417) | (343,739) |
|  | 2,000 | 7,083 | 11,853 |

|  | £ |
|---|---|
| Proceeds | 600,000 |
| Less cost | (205,417) |
|  | 394,583 |
| Less indexation allowance £(343,739 – 205,417) | (138,322) |
| Chargeable gain | 256,261 |

**Appendix 2** - Available Funds

| Asset | Chargeable gain £ | Corporation tax at 30% £ | Net proceeds £ |
|---|---|---|---|
| Land | 289,149 | 86,745 | 513,255 |
| Retail store | 310,620 | 93,186 | 506,814 |
| Shares | 256,261 | 76,878 | 523,122 |

(b)  To:          The directors of P Ltd
From:        Chief accountant
Date:        31 August 2000
Subject:     Sale of Q Ltd and sale of additional asset to fund the loan repayment due in December 2000

The purpose of this report is to calculate the chargeable gain that arose on the sale of our shareholding in Q Ltd and to indicate whether or not sufficient net proceeds will remain to allow us to invest £485,000 in a new retail outlet in Swindon.

This report will also consider which of our assets would be the best one to sell in order to fund the loan repayment of £520,000 that we are due to make in December 2000.

**Chargeable gain arising on the sale of Q Ltd**

I have calculated that chargeable gain that arose on the sale of the Q Ltd shares as £47,640. (See Appendix 1.) Even though the proceeds from the sale of Q Ltd may be invested in a new retail store it is not possible to defer any of the gain of £47,640 using rollover relief because the gain arose on a sale of shares and shares are not a qualifying asset for rollover relief purposes. This means that the corporation tax arising on the gain will be £14,292 (see Appendix 1). The net proceeds of £485,708 (£500,000 - £14,292) are just sufficient to enable us to invest £485,000 in the new retail store.

**Funding the loan repayment**

In my report of 13 March 2000, I calculated the gains estimated to arise on each of the assets we are considering selling in October 2000 as

|  | £ |
|---|---|
| Land | 289,149 |
| Retail store | 310,620 |
| Shares in X Ltd | 256,261 |

I have previously recommended selling the shares in X Ltd. However, if we are to invest £485,000 in a new retail outlet within the period commencing one year before and ending thirty six months after the above sale, we should consider rollover relief. The gain on the sale of shares cannot be reduced by rollover relief as shares are not a qualifying asset. However, the gain on the land or retail store could be reduced by rollover relief to the extent that the gain exceeds the sale proceeds not reinvested of £115,000 (£600,000 - £485,000). In either case a gain of £115,000 will be left chargeable and after corporation tax on the gain there will be sufficient proceeds to repay the loan of £520,000. (See Appendix 2.)

The sale of any of the assets would achieve the objective of repaying the loan. From a cash flow point of view the sale of the land or retail outlet is better as both of these sales generate additional surplus cash. As the gain rolled over on the sale of the land is smaller, this sale is preferable from a tax point of view to the sale of the retail outlet.

Signed: Chief accountant

137

**Appendix 1**

**Sale of Q Ltd shares**

|  | £ |
|---|---|
| Proceeds | 500,000 |
| Less: cost | (430,000) |
|  | 70,000 |
| Less: indexation | |
| £430,000 × 0.052 | (22,360) |
|  | 47,640 |

Corporation tax at 30% = £14,292

Net proceeds arising from sale

£500,000 - £14,292 = £485,708.

**Appendix 2**

|  | *Gain* | *Rollover* | *Chargeable* |
|---|---|---|---|
|  | £ | £ | £ |
| Land | 289,149 | 174,149 | 115,000 |
| Retail outlet | 310,620 | 195,620 | 115,000 |

Corporation tax on chargeable gains £34,500. Net proceeds from sale £565,500 (£600,000 - £34,500).

## 56  JAY AND CO

> **Pass marks.** This question required no computations. This means that it was particularly important to ensure your written report was concise and answered the question asked.

(a)  To:        Directors of Jay Ltd
     From:      Chief Accountant
     Date:      1 March 2000
     Subject:   Benefits in kind and PAYE requirements

**Reporting requirements**

There are certain reporting requirements in relation to benefits provided to employees. It is important that these are complied with, as there are substantial penalties which can be imposed if they are breached.

There is a distinction between the following two groups of employees:

(i)   Employees earning £8,500 or more pa (including benefits and reimbursed expenses) and directors.

(ii)  Employees earning less than £8,500 pa.

**The first group are assessable on the cost of providing benefits received 'by reason of their employment'** eg medical insurance. It should be noted that the benefit does not have to be provided by the employer directly and the rules also apply if the benefit is provided to members of the employee's family or household. There are also some specific charging provisions eg dealing with the provision of a car (and fuel) available for private use; living accommodation (and expenses connected with such accommodation such as heating and cleaning); and beneficial loans. **It is the employer's responsibility to quantify all benefits in accordance with tax law, which can be onerous and time-consuming. All details of such benefits, and expenses**

reimbursed by the employer to the employee, must be reported on a Form P11D for each relevant employee or director.

**The second group of employees are only assessable on benefits which are convertible into cash** (and then only on the value which would be received on a sale - the 'second-hand' value) and on certain specific benefits such as the provision of living accommodation (but not expenses connected with such accommodation). **These benefits, and any reimbursed expenses, must be reported on a Form P9D for each relevant employee.**

In certain circumstances, it may be possible for the employee to claim a tax deduction in respect of reimbursed expenses. In order to reduce administration, it is possible for the employer to apply to the Inland Revenue for a **dispensation so that such expenses do not have to be included on the P11D or P9D forms**.

**There are a number of tax-free benefits which do not have to be reported.** These include meals in a staff canteen (if available to all employees on broadly similar terms); provision of a parking space at or near the place of work; provision of a mobile telephone; provision of computer equipment worth less than £2,500 to use at home; removal expenses up to £8,000; contributions to approved occupational or personal pension schemes; and certain Inland Revenue approved share schemes.

### Forms P11D and P9D

**These forms must be submitted to the Revenue (and a copy given to the employee) by 6 July following the end of the tax year eg for tax year ended 5 April 2001, by 6 July 2001.** There is an initial penalty of £300 per form not submitted by the due date. There is also a penalty of up to £3,000 for each incorrect form.

### Additional costs that will arise for the company

**Employers must pay Class IA NIC at 12.2% on the taxable value of most taxable benefits. However, benefits are exempt if they are:**

- Within class 1, or
- Covered by a PAYE dispensation, or
- Provided for employees earning at a rate of less than £8,500 a year, or
- Included in a PAYE settlement agreement, or
- Otherwise not required to be reported on P11Ds

In addition, all kinds of childcare provision in kind, for example, where the employer contracts for places in commercial nurseries, are exempt from Class 1A NICs. However, if an employer provides cash to meet or reimburse childcare expenses the cash is 'earnings' for employer and employee Class 1 NIC purposes.

Employers who pay their employee's income tax liabilities via a PAYE settlement agreement (PSA) must, in addition, pay **Class 1B NICs at 12.2%** on both the emoluments subject to NIC included within the PSA and on the tax paid by the employer.

### PAYE requirements

**It will be the company's duty to deduct income tax and NICs from the pay of its employees, whether or not it has been directed to do so by the Revenue.** If the company fails to do this, it (or sometimes the employee) must pay over the tax which it should have deducted and it may be subject to penalties. Interest will run from 14 days after the end of the tax year on any underpaid PAYE.

Officers of the Inland Revenue will be entitled to inspect the company's records in order to satisfy themselves that PAYE tax is being deducted correctly.

**If a new employee joins with a P45, the company must use the information on the P45 to operate PAYE. If a new employee does not have a Form P45, the company must require him to complete Form P46.** The company must then operate PAYE on the basis of information provided on the Form P46.

By 31 May following the end of each tax year, an employer must provide each employee with a Form P60. This form shows taxable emoluments, tax deducted, code number, NI number and the employer's name and address.

By 19 May following the end of each tax year, an employer must send the Revenue end of year returns P14 and form P35.

Signed: Chief Accountant

(b) INFORMATION SHEET: USE OF OWN CAR ON COMPANY BUSINESS

When you use your car on company business, the company will pay you a mileage allowance. This will have one of two tax consequences.

(i) **Consequence one**

Strictly the amount of any mileage allowance received is a taxable benefit which you must report to the Inland Revenue. You will, however, be entitled to claim a tax deduction for any motoring expenses necessarily incurred in the performance of your duties.

(ii) **Consequence two**

As an alternative to the above you can choose to take advantage of the Fixed Profit Car Scheme (FPCS). Under this scheme the Inland Revenue have laid down mileage rates which are dependent on the engine capacity of your car and the number of business miles you travel.

Any mileage allowances you receive of up to the amounts laid down under the scheme is tax free, but any excess mileage allowances is a taxable benefit. If you opt for your mileage allowances to be tax free in this way you will not be entitled to also claim a tax deduction for motoring expenses actually incurred in the performance of your duties. There is one exception: you can claim to deduct the business proportion of any interest paid on a loan taken out to buy your car.

If the mileage allowances the company pays you are below the amount of the allowances laid down under the FPCS and you choose to use the scheme you can claim a tax deduction in respect of the shortfall. The allowances you receive will be tax free.

57 **PGD LTD**

> **Pass marks**. The acquisition of two subsidiaries in part (b) will mean that the small companies upper and lower limits will have to be divided by three and that small companies marginal relief will apply.

(a) REPORT

To:        The directors of PGD Ltd
From:      Chief Accountant
Date:      1 January 2000
Subject:   Estimated corporation tax liability for the year to 30 September 2000, due dates for tax payments and the tax treatment of loan interest

## Introduction

The purpose of this report is to estimate the corporation tax liability of PGD Ltd for the year to 30 September 2000 and to set out the dates on which PGD Ltd will have to make tax payments. The report will also explain how loan interest is dealt with for tax purposes.

## Estimated corporation tax liability

As you will see in Appendix 1, I have used the budgeted profit and loss account figures you have provided to compute an estimated corporation tax liability of £37,280. To arrive at this figure I have computed capital allowances as £39,700 based on the details of expected sales and purchases provided to me (see Appendix 1). I have assumed that we will make the maximum claim for capital allowances possible. I have computed Schedule D Case I profits as £169,600 and profits chargeable to corporation tax as £196,600 (see Appendix 1).

## Loan interest

Loan interest is dealt with on an accruals basis for tax purposes. **Interest payable/receivable on a loan taken out for trading purposes is included in the computation of Schedule D Case I profits whilst interest receivable on a loan taken out for non trading purposes is taxed under Schedule D Case III.**

Interest payable on a non trading loan is deducted firstly from Schedule D Case III income. A net deficit may be

(i)    Set against other income or the same accounting period

(ii)    Surrendered as group relief

(iii)    Carried back and set against any Schedule D Case III income arising in the previous twelve months on loan taken out for non-trading purposes

(iv)    Carried forward against future non-trading profits.

I have dealt with the interest we expect to be payable/receivable as follows:

## Treatment of loan interest

(i)    **Debenture interest payable of £12,000**

     This is interest payable on a loan raised for trading purposes and has been treated as an expense (on the accruals basis) for Schedule D Case I

(ii)    **Loan interest receivable of £6,000**

     This is interest receivable on a loan entered into for non-trading purposes and is treated as a receipt (on the accruals basis) for Schedule D Case III.

(iii)    **Loan interest paid of £8,000**

     This is interest paid on a loan raised for non-trading purposes. This is deducted from the interest received on the loan raised for non-trading purposes and the net deficit of £2,000 is set against PGD Ltd's PCTCT for the year ended 30 September 2000.

## Tax payments

I have estimated the mainstream corporation tax that will be due in respect of the year as £37,280 (Appendix 1). This amount will be due for payment on 1 July 2001.

Income tax withheld from interest/charges must be paid throughout the year. You will see from Appendix 2, that I have estimated that £1,200 will be due on 14.1.00 and £1,200 will be due on 14.7.00. Both of these amounts will be repaid in the following quarter.

Signed: Chief Accountant

### Appendix 1

(i) **Capital allowances**

| | FYA £ | Pool £ | Motor cars £ | Short-life asset £ | Expensive car £ | Allowances £ |
|---|---|---|---|---|---|---|
| WDV b/f | | 46,000 | 21,500 | 12,000 | 11,200 | |
| Transfer | | 21,500 | (21,500) | | | |
| Additions | | 10,500 | | | | |
| Disposals | | (8,000) | | (4,000) | | |
| BA | | | | 8,000 | | 8,000 |
| | | 70,000 | | | 11,200 | |
| WDA 25% | | (17,500) | | | (2,800) | 20,300 |
| Addition qualifying for FYA (W) | 16,000 | | | | | |
| FYA at 40% | (6,400) | | | | | 6,400 |
| | | 9,600 | | | | |
| Addition qualifying for FYA (W) | 5,000 | | | | | 5,000 |
| FYA at 100% | (5,000) | | | | | |
| Allowances | | | | | | 39,700 |
| WDV c/f | | 62,100 | | | 8,400 | |

*Working*

Plant will cost £18,800 inclusive of VAT. Capital allowances are given on the VAT exclusive cost of £16,000 (£18,800 × 100/117.5). The computer will cost £5,875 inclusive of VAT. Capital allowances are given on the VAT exclusive cost of £5,000 (£5,875 × $\frac{100}{117.5}$). Similarly, the disposal proceeds deducted in respect of the plant and the computer are the amounts exclusive of VAT.

(ii) **Schedule D Case I profit**

| | £ | £ |
|---|---|---|
| Net profit before taxation | | 231,300 |
| Add: loan interest | 8,000 | |
| patent royalties | 10,000 | |
| depreciation | 11,000 | |
| | | 29,000 |
| Less: loan interest receivable | 6,000 | |
| rents | 7,000 | |
| patent royalties | 30,000 | |
| FII | 8,000 | |
| Capital allowances | 39,700 | |
| | | (90,700) |
| Schedule D Case I | | 169,600 |

(iii) MAINSTREAM CORPORATION TAX LIABILITY FOR PGD LTD

| | £ |
|---|---|
| Schedule D Case I | 169,600 |
| Schedule A | 7,000 |
| Patent royalties received | 30,000 |
| | 206,600 |
| Less: Patent royalties paid (£10,000 – £2,000) | (8,000) |
| | 198,600 |
| Less: Deficit on non-trading interest (£6,000 – £8,000) | (2,000) |
| PCTCT | 196,600 |
| FII | 8,000 |
| Profits | 204,600 |

The year ended 30 September 2000 falls 6 months into FY99 and 6 months into FY00. The small companies lower limit is £300,000 for both financial years, so the small companies rate applies to both years:

*Corporation tax*

|  | £ | £ |
|---|---|---|
| £196,600 × 20% |  | 39,320 |
| Less: income tax suffered |  |  |
| Loan interest (£6,000 × 20%) | 1,200 |  |
| Patent royalties (£30,000 × 22%) | 6,600 |  |
|  | 7,800 |  |
| Income tax retained |  |  |
| Debenture interest (£12,000 × 20%) | (2,400) |  |
| Loan interest (£8,000 × 20%) | (1,600) |  |
| Patent royalties (£8,000 × 22%) | (1,760) |  |
|  |  | (2,040) |
| Mainstream corporation tax payable (MCT) |  | 37,280 |

## Appendix 2

### Tax payments throughout the year

|  | Income tax suffered | Income tax withheld | Net payment (repayment) | Due date |
|---|---|---|---|---|
| 1.10.99 - 31.12.99 |  | 1,200 | 1,200 | 14.1.00 |
| 1.1.00 - 31.3.00 | 1,200 |  | (1,200) |  |
| 1.4.00 - 30.6.00 |  | 1,200 | 1,200 | 14.7.00 |
| 1.7.00 - 30.9.00 | 6,600 | 3,360 | (1,200) |  |

(b) To: The directors of PGD Ltd
From: Chief Accountant
Date: 1 October 2000
Subject: Actual corporation tax liability for the year to 30.9.00

PGD Ltd's profits chargeable to corporation tax for the year to 30.9.00 were £196,600. I have calculated the mainstream corporation tax liability on these profits as £49,844 (see Appendix one). This amount will be due for payment on 1 July 2001. It differs from the estimates made in my report of 1.1.00 because the existence of the two wholly owned subsidiaries alters the tax rate that must be paid by PGD Ltd.

Signed: Chief Accountant

### Appendix one

Small companies rate lower limit $= \dfrac{£300,000}{3} = £100,000$

Upper limit $= \dfrac{£1,500,000}{3} = £500,000$

As 'profits' of £204,600 (see report of 1.1.00) are between the limits, small companies marginal relief applies:

**Corporation tax**

|  |  | £ |
|---|---|---:|
| £196,600 × 30% | | 58,980 |
| Less: marginal relief | | |
| 1/40 (£500,000 – £204,600) × $\frac{196,600}{204,600}$ | | (7,096) |
| | | 51,884 |
| Less: | Income tax suffered (part a) | (2,040) |
| | | 49,844 |

## 58   P LTD

> **Pass marks**. You had to use your imagination to answer part (a). Basically the answer is 'anything which can enter into the computation of a PAYE code'.

(a)   **REPORT TO THE ACCOUNTANCY ASSISTANT OF P LTD FROM THE CHIEF ACCOUNTANT HIGHLIGHTING THOSE AREAS IN WHICH PAYE CODE ERRORS ARE MOST LIKELY TO OCCUR**

**Introduction**

As discussed at out recent meeting I would like you to conduct an initial investigation into the PAYE code numbers of our company employees with a view to identifying any errors present therein. Please report back to me by 15 February.

To assist you in your work I outline below those areas in which PAYE code errors are most likely to occur.

**Summary of potential errors**

There are four main areas where errors in PAYE codes may occur:

(i)     Giving the correct level of allowances

(ii)    Making the correct adjustments for benefits in kind, for example

    (1)  Car benefits may be based on the wrong cost

    (2)  Car benefits may fail to take account of business mileage

    (3)  Car benefits may fail to take account of the age of the car

    (4)  Car benefits may fail to take account of contributions by the employee

    (5)  Fuel benefits may be for the wrong cylinder capacity

    (6)  Fuel benefits may be for the wrong type of fuel (petrol or diesel) in small engined car

    (7)  The benefit of a low-interest loan may be miscomputed

    (8)  The benefit of living accommodation may be miscomputed

(iii)   Making the correct adjustment to collect tax underpaid in previous years

(iv)   Making the correct adjustments for allowable expense payments.

I hope the above is helpful. If you have any problems, please do not hesitate to contact me.

Signed

Chief Accountant

23 January 2001

(b) **REPORT FOR THE BOARD OF DIRECTORS OF P LTD OUTLINING THE TAXATION IMPLICATIONS OF THE PROPOSED IMPROVEMENT TO STAFF REMUNERATION.**

**Introduction**

The Board has proposed making two improvements to staff remuneration:

(i)    Setting up an approved occupational pension scheme

(ii)   Providing certain key employees with motor cars for both business and private use.

The purpose of this report is to look at the tax implications for both the company and the employees of each proposal.

**An approved occupational pension scheme**

(i)    The **company's contributions will be tax-deductible**, and **will not give rise to national insurance contributions or to taxable benefits for the employees**.

(ii)   The **employees' contributions (up to 15% of their emoluments**, with emoluments limited to the earnings cap) **will be tax-deductible, but will not reduce their salaries for national insurance purposes**.

(iii)  If the scheme is **contracted out, the national insurance contributions payable by both the company and the employees will be reduced**.

(iv)   **When pensions are paid, they will be taxed as earned income** of the pensioners.

**Motor cars for senior staff**

(i)    The company could either buy or lease motor cars. The **deductions from taxable profits will be capital allowances at 25% of the reducing balance for purchase, or the lease rentals for leasing**. These deductions are not affected by private motoring, but they are restricted for cars with a purchase price of over £12,000. **Capital allowances are limited to £3,000 a year, and the deductible fraction of any lease rental is:**

       **(£12,000 + purchase price)/(2 × purchase price)**

(ii)   If a director, or an employee earning £8,500 or more a year, uses a company car for private motoring, he or she must pay tax on an amount of deemed income which depends on the car's original list price. The **basic annual charge is 35% of this price, although the percentage is reduced from 35% to 25% or 15% for substantial business mileage. The benefit is multiplied by $\frac{3}{4}$ for cars over four years old**. For cars over 15 years old and worth more than £15,000 and more than their original list price, their value is used instead of that price. However, in all cases the price or value for tax purposes is limited to £80,000.

(iii)  **If fuel is provided for private motoring and the cost is not fully reimbursed, the employee must pay tax on an amount of deemed income, on a set scale** based on the car's cylinder capacity and, for small engined cars, the type of fuel used.

(iv)   **The company (not the employees) must pay class 1A national insurance contributions of 12.2% of any taxable car and fuel benefits.**

### Reporting requirements

The taxable value of any car or fuel benefits must be recorded by the company **on a form P11D for each employee**. The company must supply **both the employee and the Revenue with a copy of this P11D by 6 July following the end of the tax year ended**.

(c) **TO THE FINANCE DIRECTOR OF P LTD**

*Report from the Chief Accountant on the adjusted results of the year ended 31 March 2001.*

### Introduction

The purpose of this report is to advise you of P Ltd's estimated Schedule D Case I results for the year ended 31 March 2001.

Our auditors have prepared draft accounts for the year which show a trading loss of £110,000. I have adjusted this loss for tax purposes and have arrived at a Schedule D Case I loss of £84,000. The adjustment is shown in the appendix attached to this report.

You provided me with a list of potential taxation issues following a review of the accounts and in my report below I outline their impact (if any) on the accounting results.

### Salary and NICs of director seconded to national charity

**Expenditure on employees seconded to charities and educational bodies is specifically deductible as a Schedule D Case I** expense so no adjustment is needed to the Schedule D Case I loss.

### Debenture interest

**Our debenture was issued for a trading purpose** (to acquire a building used in the trade) **and thus the interest payable is allowed as a Schedule D Case I expense** on an accruals basis. This means no adjustment is needed to the Schedule D Case I loss.

### Loan interest

The loan was used to acquire a subsidiary company (an investment). **This was a non-trading purpose and the interest is, therefore, not a Schedule D Case I expense which means that it must be added back to the above loss. Non-trading loan relationships fall under Schedule D Case III. The interest accruing during the year will be deducted from any income under this Case. Any excess amount accruing will be dealt with as a non-trading deficit.**

### Refurbishment expenditure

As the office was **usable at the date of the acquisition, the refurbishment is a revenue expense and therefore deductible** for Schedule D Case I purposes (Odeon Associated Theatres v Jones). This means that no adjustment is required to the Schedule D Case I loss.

### Bad debts

**An increase or decrease in a general provision is not allowed**. Thus the £8,000 (£24,000 – £16,000) of income included in profit when the provision was decreased is deducted when calculating the above loss.

**Specific provision movements are allowed. Trade debts written off or recovered are trading items** that should be included within the Schedule D Case I results. This means that no adjustment is required in respect of these items.

**The loan to the customer written off is not an allowable expense,** and must be added back to the loss. As this is a non trading debt written off it will be dealt with as a non-trading deficit.

### Redundancy repayments

Statutory redundancy costs are allowable expenses as is extra redundancy paid up to three times the statutory amount. Thus £3,000 plus $3 \times £3,000 = £12,000$ per employee is allowed. With ten employees this totals £120,000. The extra £30,000 (£150,000 less £120,000 ) is disallowed and must be added back to the above loss.

### Insurance proceeds

The reimbursement from the insurers of the repair costs incurred on the business premises is taxable income in the Schedule D Case I computation of profits because the expense was a Schedule D Case I deduction last year. The reimbursement of repair costs for the let property is not in respect of the trade and instead falls under Schedule A. Thus it is deducted from Schedule D Case I profit.

### Sale of goods at overvalue

The transfer pricing rules do not apply between UK resident companies and so no adjustment is required.

I hope the above is helpful. If you have any queries please feel free to contact me.

Signed

Chief Accountant

27 June 2001


### APPENDIX

### Loss for the year ended 31 March 2001

|  | £ |
|---|---:|
| Loss per the accounts | (110,000) |
| Add: | |
| Secondment costs | - |
| Debenture interest | - |
| Loan interest | 6,000 |
| Refurbishment of office | - |
| Loan to customer written off | 10,000 |
| Extra redundancy costs | 30,000 |
|  | (64,000) |
| Deduct: | |
| General provision decrease | (8,000) |
| Reimbursed expenses for let property | (12,000) |
| Inflated price to subsidiary | - |
| Schedule D Case I loss | (84,000) |

59   **WJ LTD**

**Pass marks**. A long period of account is split into two accounting periods. The first accounting period is always twelve months long.

(a)                                                    REPORT

To:          The Finance Director of WJ Ltd
From:       The Chief Accountant
Date:        31 March 2001
Subject:    Report on our tax computations for the accounting period 1 November 1999 to 28 February 2001.

**Introduction**

The Board of Directors decided, shortly before October 2000, to change the accounting date for WJ Ltd from 31 October to 28 February and consequently a 16 month set of accounts to 28 February 2001 was prepared. Such a long accounting period will be split for tax purposes into two periods as follows:

•      12 months to 31 October 2000
•      4 months ended 28 February 2001.

**Capital allowances**

I have calculated the capital allowances available for the two periods as £68,100 and £16,742 respectively.

My computations of these figures is shown in Appendix 1 of this report.

**Corporation tax computation**

I have calculated mainstream corporation tax due for the year ended 31 October 2000 as £72,593 and the mainstream corporation tax due for the 4 month period to 28 February 2001 as £154,495.

Appendix 2 to this report outlines the calculation of the above liabilities plus associated workings.

There will be surplus ACT of £27,268 which remains to be carried forward at 28 February 2001.

I hope that this is useful. If you have any queries regarding the calculations please do not hesitate to contact me.

Signed: Chief Accountant

## APPENDIX 1

### Capital allowances calculations

| | £ | General pool £ | CAA90 pool £ | Exp car 1 £ | Short-life asset £ | Exp car 2 £ | Capital allowances £ |
|---|---|---|---|---|---|---|---|
| **Y/e 31 October 2000**: | | | | | | | |
| Balances b/f | | 140,000 | 28,000 | 20,000 | 8,000 | | |
| Car pool transferred | | 28,000 | (28,000) | | | | |
| Additions | | | | | | 14,000 | |
| Disposals | | (6,000) | | (11,000) | | | |
| | | 162,000 | | 9,000 | 8,000 | 14,000 | |
| Balancing allowance | | | | (9,000) | | | 9,000 |
| WDAs @ 25% | | (40,500) | | | (2,000) | (3,000) | 45,500 |
| FYA additions: | | | | | | | |
| Plant – 10.3.00 | 10,000 | | | | | | |
| FYA at 40% | (4,000) | | | | | | 4,000 |
| Lorry – 10.7.00 | 24,000 | | | | | | |
| FYA at 40% | (9,600) | | | | | | 9,600 |
| Balances c/f | | 20,400 | | | | | |
| | | 141,900 | | | 6,000 | 11,000 | 68,100 |
| **4 months ended 28 February 2001** | | | | | | | |
| **Disposal** | | | | | (2,000) | | |
| | | 141,900 | | | 4,000 | 11,000 | |
| Balancing allowance | | | | | (4,000) | | 4,000 |
| WDAs @ 25% × 4/12 | | (11,825) | | | | (917) | 12,742 |
| Balances c/f | | 130,075 | | | | 10,083 | |
| | | | | | | | 16,742 |

## APPENDIX 2

### Corporation tax computations

| | Y/e 31.10.00 £ | Y/e 31.10.00 £ | 4 m/e 28.2.01 £ | 4 m/e 28.2.01 £ |
|---|---|---|---|---|
| Trading profits (time-apportioned) | | 451,500 | | 150,500 |
| Less: Capital allowances | | (68,100) | | (16,742) |
| Schedule D Case I | | 383,400 | | 133,758 |
| Capital gains | 40,000 | | 360,000 | |
| Less: Capital losses b/f | (30,000) | | 0 | |
| | | 10,000 | | 360,000 |
| Schedule A Rents accruing | | | | |
| (12 × £1,500)/(4 × £5,000) | | 18,000 | | 20,000 |
| Patent royalties (gross) | | | | 24,000 |
| | | 411,400 | | 537,758 |
| Less: Gift aid donation | | (8,000) | | |
| Less: Non-trading deficit (W1) | | (5,000) | | |
| PCTCT | | 398,400 | | 537,758 |
| FII | | 20,000 | | |
| 'Profits' | | 418,400 | | 537,758 |

| | FY99 and FY00 £ | FY00 4/12 £ |
|---|---|---|
| PCTCT | 398,400 | 537,758 |
| Profits | 418,400 | 537,758 |
| Upper limit | 1,500,000 | 500,000 |
| Lower limit | 300,000 | 100,000 |
| | *Small companies' marginal relief* | *Full rate* |

**MCT payable - y/e 31 October 2000**

| | £ | £ |
|---|---|---|
| FY99 and FY00 | | |
| £398,400 × 30% | | 119,520 |
| Less 1/40 (1,500,000 – £418,400) × $\frac{398,400}{418,400}$ | | (25,747) |
| | | 93,773 |

| | | |
|---|---|---|
| Less: ACT | | |
| Shadow ACT calculation | | |
| (£252,000 × 100/80) | 315,000 | |
| Deduct FII (£20,000 × 90/80) | (22,500) | |
| | 292,500 | |
| | | |
| Shadow ACT @ 20% | 58,500 | |
| Maximum set-off £398,400 × 20% | (79,680) | |
| Maximum ACT offset | 21,180 | (21,180) |
| | | |
| MCT payable | | 72,593 |

**MCT payable - P/E 28 February 2001**

| | £ | £ |
|---|---|---|
| £537,758 × 30% | | 161,327 |
| Less: ACT: | | |
| Shadow ACT (£424,000 × 20/80 = £106,000) | 106,000 | |
| Surplus ACT b/f (balancing figure) | 1,552 | (1,552) |
| Maximum set-off £537,758 × 20% | 107,552 | |
| Less: Income tax suffered at source: | | |
| Patent royalties (£24,000 × 22%) | | (5,280) |
| MCT payable | | 154,495 |

*Working*

1   **Non trading deficit**

| | £ |
|---|---|
| Schedule D Case III | 10,000 |
| Loan interest paid | (15,000) |
| | (5,000) |

2   **ACT**

| | £ |
|---|---|
| Surplus ACT b/fwd at 1.11.99 | 50,000 |
| Less: | |
| Utilised in y.e. 31.10.00 | (21,180) |
| | 28,820 |
| Utilised in p.e. 28.2.01 | (1,552) |
| Surplus ACT c/fwd forward at 28.2.01 | 27,268 |

(b)                          REPORT

| | |
|---|---|
| To: | The Board |
| From: | Chief Accountant |
| Date: | 31 March 2001 |
| Subject: | Implications of making supplies which are exempt from VAT |

**Introduction**

WJ Ltd presently produces only goods which are standard-rated for VAT when sold within the UK.

In the near future the company will, for the first time, make supplies which are exempt from VAT. These exempt supplies will account for approximately 25% of the turnover of WJ Ltd on an annual basis.

This report sets out the VAT implications of the change in the status of our sales mix.

(i)   VAT is currently charged at $17\frac{1}{2}$% on all of our goods. However, VAT will not be charged on supplies which are exempt from VAT.

(ii)  Input tax is, in general, recoverable on purchases which relate to taxable supplies. Currently, since only taxable supplies are made nearly all input tax we currently incur is fully recoverable.

**Input tax which is attributable to exempt supplies is only recoverable if it does not exceed a de minimis limit of:**

(1)  **£625 per month on average,** and
(2)  **50% of the total input tax incurred.**

This means that when we starting making exempt supplies some of our input tax is likely to be non-deductible.

(iii) When exempt and taxable supplies are both being made we will have to analyse all input tax incurred into the following three categories:

(1)  Wholly attributable to taxable supplies

(2)  Wholly attributable to exempt supplies

(3)  Not directly attributable to a single type of supply (this is called non-attributable input tax).

(iv)  It is inevitable that some input VAT will not be directly attributable to taxable or exempt supplies (eg general overheads). This unallocated amount is then normally allocated using the following method.

(1)  **Attributable to taxable supplies.**

$$\text{Non-attributable input tax} \times \left( \frac{\text{Value of taxable supplies made}}{\text{Total supplies made (taxable and exempt)}} \right) \star$$

*Round up to nearest percentage

As exempt supplies will account for 25% of total turnover, the amount attributable to taxable supplies will be:

Non-attributable input tax $\times$ 75%

(2)  The rest of the unallocated amount is attributable to exempt supplies and is added to the directly attributable amount calculated above. This total amount is not recoverable (unless it is within the *de minimis* limits mentioned above).

If you would like further clarification of the above, please do not hesitate to contact me.

Signed: Chief Accountant

**60    ZAD LTD**

> **Pass marks**. Loan relationships are an extremely popular topic with this examiner.

(a)   (i)                                REPORT

To:          Accounting assistant of ZAD Ltd
From:        Management Accountant
Date:        1 May 2001
Subject:     The tax treatment of the loan made to a supplier now in liquidation

**Introduction**

Thank you for preparing the draft corporation tax computations of ZAD Ltd for the year ended 31 March 2001.

I understand that during the year a supplier went into liquidation owing ZAD Ltd £65,000 on a loan made to it earlier this year and that interest of £2,600 on this loan had been received by ZAD Ltd prior to the supplier going into liquidation. I also understand that you have provisionally included both of these amounts in our Schedule Case I profits.

**Schedule D Case I or III**

The £2,600 gross interest received on the loan to the supplier must not be included in the Schedule D Case I profits. **It is, instead, taxable under Schedule D Case III since it is interest on a non-trading loan relationship**.

The deduction of the £65,000 capital value of the loan written off can be deducted from the Schedule D Case III income to give a net deficit of £62,400 on non trading loan relationships. The £65,000 must be added back in the computation of Schedule D Case I profits.

The net non-trading deficit of £62,400 can be relieved in a number of ways. I outline the best option below.

**Non-trading deficit**

My advice is to set the £62,400 non-trading deficit against the £286,000 chargeable profits of JWD Ltd in the year ended 31 March 2001. This is preferable to set-off ZAD Ltd's profits in this year because of the respective marginal tax rates. As there are two associated companies for small companies' rate purposes, the upper and lower limits are £750,000 and £150,000. Hence, JWD Ltd pays corporation tax at a marginal rate of 32.5% compared to 20% for ZAD Ltd. It is therefore beneficial to set the deficit against JWD Ltd's chargeable profits.

From a cashflow point of view there would be no point in carrying the deficit forward. Assuming that ZAD Ltd paid tax at 20% in the previous year there would also be no point in carrying the deficit back.

Please do not hesitate to contact me if you require any further help with this matter.

Signed: Management Accountant

(ii)

REPORT

To:        The Finance Director
From:    Management Accountant
Date:     1 April 2001
Subject:  Industrial buildings allowances

**Introduction**

ZAD Ltd occupies a factory acquired in June 1997. The company is considering acquiring two further factories. All three factories will qualify for Industrial Buildings Allowances (IBAs) and the purpose of this report is to quantify the industrial buildings allowances that will be available for the year to 31.3.02.

**IBAs due for year ended 31 March 2002**

Assuming that the newly constructed factory is not in an enterprise zone, the maximum IBAs which may be claimed by ZAD Ltd for its 12 month accounting period to 31 March 2002 is £17,920.

The calculation of this allowance is set out in Appendix One to this report.

**Enterprise zone**

I understand that it may be possible to acquire the newly constructed factory in an Enterprise Zone. If we do this the IBAs due will increase to £209,920.

The increase is due to the special 100% initial allowance available on the full costs incurred (£200,000) of purchasing an enterprise zone building. However, industrial buildings allowances on this building will not then be available in later years.

I have set out my calculations in Appendix 2.

If you have any queries on this, please do not hesitate to contact me.

Signed: Management Accountant

**APPENDIX** 1

| | £ |
|---|---|
| The old factory: £148,000 × 4% (notes) | 5,920 |
| The secondhand factory | |
|   Remaining tax life = 20 years | |
|   £80,000/20 | 4,000 |
| The new factory: £200,000 × 4% | 8,000 |
| Maximum IBAs | 17,920 |

*Notes*

1    The cost of land is excluded when calculating IBAs.

2    The £52,000 spent on offices in the old factory exceeds the 25% limit on non-industrial expenditure within the purchase of an industrial building. Hence of the £200,000 spent only £148,000 qualifies for IBAs.

**APPENDIX** 2

If the new factory had been in an enterprise zone, the result would have been as follows.

|  | £ |
|---|---|
| The old factory | 5,920 |
| The secondhand factory | 4,000 |
| The new factory £200,000 (all commercial buildings qualify) × 100% | 200,000 |
| Maximum IBAs | 209,920 |

(b)                                                REPORT

| To: | Payroll Clerk |
|---|---|
| From: | Management Accountant |
| Date: | 30 April 2001 |
| Subject: | P11D Queries |

**Introduction**

Thank you for your memo of 6 April 2001. As you are obviously aware, the benefits in kind we provide to directors must be quantified, using special rules under Schedule E, and recorded on a form P11D for each director.

**Benefits in kind**

The value of the benefits you outlined in your memo are:

|  | £ |
|---|---|
| Use of house | 1,000 |
| Purchase of asset at undervalue | 200 |
| Low interest loan | 1,200 |
| Gift of dishwasher | 280 |
| Provision of medical insurance | 1,200 |

For your information, the calculation of these benefits is outlined in Appendix A to this report.

**National insurance contributions**

Class 1A NICs at 12.2% must be paid by ZAD Ltd on the taxable value of all benefits in kind. The total amount of Class 1A NICs due in respect of the above benefits is therefore £473.36 (12.2% × £3,880).

I hope the above is helpful. The quantification of benefits in kind forms an important part of our work, so you will need to study this topic very carefully when you reach it in your study pack.

Signed: Management Accountant

**APPENDIX A**

(a) **The use of a private house which cost £80,000**

Two calculations are required.

(i)   The living accommodation benefit

|  | £ |
|---|---|
| Annual value | 2,000 |
| Less contribution by director | (1,500) |
|  | 500 |

(ii)    The additional charge for expensive accommodation

£(80,000 – 75,000) × 10%                           £500

The total benefit is £(500 + 500) = £1,000.

(b)   **The purchase of a company asset at an undervalue**

The benefit is the greater of:

(i)    The asset's current market value, and

(ii)    The asset's market value when first provided, less the total benefits taxed during the period of use.

The acquisition price paid by the director is deducted from whichever of (i) and (ii) is used.

|  | £ | £ |
|---|---|---|
| Market value when first provided |  | 1,500 |
| Less: taxed in 1997/98 (20% of market value) | 300 |  |
|         taxed in 1998/99 (20%) | 300 |  |
|         taxed in 1999/00 (20%) | 300 |  |
|  |  | (900) |
|  |  | 600 |

The figure of £600 is taken (as greater than the current market value of £500).

Benefit taxed in 2000/01

|  | £ |
|---|---|
| Initial market value minus benefits already taxed | 600 |
| Less amount paid by director | (400) |
| Benefit | 200 |

(c)   **A low-interest loan to a director to purchase his sole residence**

There will be a benefit of £20,000 × (10 – 4)% =£1,200.

(d)   **The gift of a dishwasher to a director**

The general measure of a benefit for an employee earning £8,500 or more a year or a director is the cost to the employer of providing it. The benefit is thus £280.

(e)   **The provision of medical insurance**

For the same reason as in (d) above, the benefit is £1,200.

**61   Z LTD**

> **Pass marks**. The payment of corporation tax by quarterly instalments is an extremely popular topic with this examiner.

(a)                                      REPORT

To:       The Board of Directors of Z Ltd
From:    Chief Management Accountant
Date:     10 September 2001
Subject: Corporation tax paid and payable by the company for the year ended 31 December 2000.

The purpose of this report is to calculate the amount of corporation tax that Z Ltd must pay for the year to 31 December 2000 and to set out the due dates for payment of this tax. The report will also explain why the company has already paid certain amounts of corporation tax and it will calculate the balance remaining to be paid now.

## Corporation tax due

The total mainstream corporation tax liability of Z Ltd for the year to 31.12.00 is £169,000. I have set out the calculation of this amount in Appendix one which is attached to this report.

## Payment dates

As Z Ltd pays corporation tax at the full rate of 30%, it is a 'large' company for payment purposes and must make quarterly interim payments of its CT liability. For the year to 31 December 2000, 72% of the mainstream corporation tax due £121,680 (72% × £169,000), should have been paid in quarterly instalments starting on 14 July 2000. The balance of the tax, £47,320 (28% × £169,000) is due for payment on 1 October 2001. I have set out the schedule of due dates in Appendix two. Note that for the year to 31 December 2001, 88% of our corporation tax liability will be due in instalments and in the following year 100% will be due by instalments.

## Schedule of payments

In June 2000 the previous Chief Management Accountant estimated that the corporation tax liability of Z Ltd for the year to 31 December 2000 would be £100,000.

In January 2001, based on information available at that date, I revised this estimate to £120,000.

Thus corporation tax based on these estimates has been paid as follows prior to the date of this report.

| Due date | Amount due calculated as | £ | £ |
|---|---|---|---|
| 14 July 2000 | ¼ (72% × (£100,000) | | 18,000 |
| 14 October 2000 | ¼ (72% × £100,000) | | 18,000 |
| 14 January 2001 | ¼ (72% × £120,000) | 21,600 | |
| | plus underpaid 2 × £(21,600 - 18,000) | 7,200 | |
| | | | 28,800 |
| 14 April 2001 | ¼ (72% × £120,000) | | 21,600 |
| Tax paid to date | | | 86,400 |

Corporation tax of £86,400 has been paid to date. The under paid instalments of £35,280 (see below) should be paid immediately. The balance of tax £47,320 is due on 1 October 2001. This is calculated as:

| | | £ |
|---|---|---|
| 1 October 2001 | Balance of instalments (72% × £169,000) less £86,400 | 35,280 |
| | Balance of tax due 28% × £169,000 | 47,320 |
| Total due to be paid | | 82,600 |
| Paid by instalments | | 86,400 |
| Total tax paid for year ended 31 December 2000 | | 169,000 |

Signed

Chief Management Accountant

**APPENDIX ONE**

**Mainstream corporation tax of Z Ltd for the year ended 31.12.2000**

|  | UK<br>£ | P Inc<br>£ | QSA<br>£ | Total<br>£ |
|---|---|---|---|---|
| Schedule D Case I | 500,000 |  |  | 500,000 |
| Schedule D Case V |  | 100,000 | 80,000 | 180,000 |
| Less: charges on income | (10,000) |  |  | (10,000) |
| PCTCT | 490,000 | 100,000 | 80,000 | 670,000 |
|  |  |  |  |  |
| Corporation Tax @ 30% (W1) | 147,000 | 30,000 | 24,000 | 201,000 |
| Less: DTR (W2) |  | (28,000) | (4,000) | (32,000) |
| MCT | 147,000 | 2,000 | 20,000 | 169,000 |

*Workings*

1  Upper limit (£1,500,000 ÷ 3)  = £500,000
   Profits                       = £670,000

   The full rate of corporation tax applies.

2  Double tax relief (DTR)

   Lower of

   (i)   UK tax on overseas income
   (ii)  Overseas tax suffered

   *P Inc*              *Q SA*
   (i)   £30,000        (i)   £24,000
   (ii)  £28,000        (ii)  £4,000

         Take £28,000         Take £4,000

**APPENDIX TWO**

| **Due date** | £ |
|---|---|
| 14 July 2000 | 30,420 |
| 14 October 2000 | 30,420 |
| 14 January 2001 | 30,420 |
| 14 April 2002 | 30,420 |
|  | 121,680 |

1 October 2001 (balance) = £47,320

(b)                        **MEMO**

To:       Jonas Tomelty
From:     Chief Management Accountant
Date:     23 September 2001
Subject:  VAT - instalment payments

Thank you for your memo dated 22 September 2001 to which I reply below.

There are provisions under which certain businesses have to make monthly payments on account of their VAT liability during a prescribed accounting period. Any under- or over-payment is settled when the return for the period is submitted.

Broadly speaking, this requirement affects businesses whose net VAT payments exceed £2m per annum based on a reference period (ie year to 31 March, 30 April or 31 May, depending upon the trader's return periods).

A first payment on account is required by the end of the month following the first month of a period, a second one a month later, the balance being cleared by submission of the return at the end of the month following the period end.

There is provision for escaping this requirement where, in a subsequent 12-month period, the net VAT liability falls below £1.6m.

The payments on account required at the end of the first and second months of a VAT quarter are each one twenty-fourth of the annual liability, estimated by reference to the previous year's liability, using a reference period ending on 31 March, 30 April or 31 May. The balance is payable on the normal due date.

Z Ltd wholesales food which is a zero-rated or standard rated supply for VAT hence the company is VAT registered. However, in the year ended 31 December 2000 the profits of Z Ltd totalled £500,000 based on a UK turnover of £1.5 million.

However, on a £1.5 million turnover (even if all of that was of standard rated food) Z Ltd is a long way off having a VAT liability of £2 million, (£1.5 million × 17.5% is only £262,500).

Thus Z Ltd is not 'large' enough from a VAT point of view to pay VAT by instalments.

I hope this answers your queries.

Signed

Chief Management Accountant


62   **ABCD LTD**

> **Pass marks**. It is not always advantageous to include a company in a VAT group registration. There are several factors to consider.

(a)                                         REPORT

To:         The Board of Directors
From:       Management Accountant
Date:       31 August 2000
Subject:    The tax effects of various group asset transfers planned for September 2000

At our recent meeting you outlined a series of asset transactions planned for September 2000. This report outlines the tax effects of those proposed transactions.

### Transfer of building to B Ltd

The building transferred from A Ltd to B Ltd will be transferred at such a value as gives rise to no gain/no loss for chargeable gains purposes. This means the transfer value would be £100,800 (£60,000 + 0.680 × £60,000). **If B Ltd and A Ltd cease being members of the same group within six years of the transfer, B Ltd will be deemed to have disposed of the asset at its market value, £110,000, on the date of the transfer. The gain arising will be taxed in the accounting period in which the group relationship is broken.**

### Disposals by B Ltd

The chargeable gain arising on B Ltd on the disposal of the warehouse totals £42,000. There will also be a gain of £10,400 arising on the sale of the factory unit.

Appendix 1 to this report details the calculation of these gains.

## Purchase of new bakery plant

As B Ltd and D Ltd are in the same capital gains group and D Ltd will purchase a qualifying asset for rollover relief purposes, a claim can be made to rollover some of B Ltd's gains. A rollover relief claim is not available to defer any of the gain on the warehouse, because the proceeds not reinvested in the bakery (£45,000) are larger than the gain arising. A rollover relief claim is, however, available to defer some of the gain on the factory unit. The proceeds on the sale of the factory unit which are not reinvested by the group in the bakery are £5,000 (£140,000 – £135,000). This amount is immediately chargeable but the remainder of the gain £5,400 (£10,400 – £5,000), can be deferred.

## Pre-entry loss

There would be no point in transferring the warehouse or the factory unit to C Ltd prior to disposal because C Ltd's losses of £40,000 are pre-entry capital losses and will not be available to set against gains arising on assets transferred from another group member. Similarly, there will be no point in making an election for the asset disposals to be treated as having been made by C Ltd.

Signed: Management Accountant

## APPENDIX 1

B Ltd will have the following gains.

*Warehouse*

| | £ |
|---|---|
| Proceeds | 180,000 |
| Less cost | (92,000) |
| | 88,000 |
| Less indexation 0.5 × £92,000 | (46,000) |
| Chargeable gain | 42,000 |

*Factory unit*

| | Cost £ | 31.3.82 mv £ |
|---|---|---|
| Proceeds | 140,000 | 140,000 |
| Less cost/M82 value | (50,000) | (60,000) |
| | 90,000 | 80,000 |
| Less £60,000 × 1.160 | (69,600) | (69,600) |
| | 20,400 | 10,400 |

The chargeable gain is £10,400.

(b)

REPORT

| To: | The Board of Directors |
|---|---|
| From: | Management Accountant |
| Date: | 1 May 2001 |
| Subject: | VAT group registration and corporation tax self assessment |

Following your recent meeting I have looked into the proposal raised of a VAT group registration. The first part of this report looks at the impact this would have on the group.

The second part of this report advises the board of its responsibilities under Corporation Tax Self Assessment (CTSA) in respect of C Ltd's recent change of accounting date.

## VAT Group Registration

**Two or more companies which are UK resident or have an established place of business in the UK may apply to be treated as members of a group for VAT purposes as long as they are under common control.**

### Advantages of VAT group registration

The advantages of VAT group registration for the group are

(i)     **One of the companies would be treated as the representative member and would submit one VAT return on behalf of those companies from the group included in the VAT group registration.** This should **reduce the overall amount of VAT accounting** work to be done but it does mean that one of the companies is likely to have to do more work.

(ii)    **Supplies of goods and services between group registered companies would be disregarded for VAT** purposes, again **reducing the amount of VAT accounting.**

It may be better to exclude some of the group companies from a group registration for the following reasons

(i)     **Including B Ltd, which makes exempt supplies, in the group will lead to partial exemption rules applying to the VAT registered group as a whole. This can lead to a loss of input VAT recovery.** However, the situation needs to be reviewed carefully as the inclusion of B Ltd in a VAT group may improve the group's overall VAT position.

(ii)    **C Ltd is an exporter and thus makes zero rated taxable supplies. C Ltd reclaims VAT and can obtain a cash flow advantage by making monthly returns. The advantage would be lost if its VAT figures were merged into a group's position.**

(iii)   **Any companies which would find it difficult to get their VAT figures to the representative member in good time to avoid penalties for late returns should be excluded from the group.** Thus the position of D Ltd must be considered carefully. It would be best to keep D Ltd out of the group until it's compliance systems are fully operational and working to ensure speedy delivery of returns.

(iv)    **Any financially unstable company should be excluded from the group as group members are jointly and severally liable for the VAT due.** Thus again the position of D Ltd must be carefully considered. D Ltd should therefore not be included into the group until the Directors have found that the company is financially fit.

(v)     **If significant amounts of group supplies are made to or from one company it may be better to register that company separately and take advantage of a cash flow benefit that can arise when different VAT periods mean that input VAT on the intra-group supplies is reclaimed up to two months before the group has to pay the output tax.**

### CTSA and C Ltd

Accounts for C Ltd were made up for the 15 month period from 1.4.99 to 30.6.00. However, for corporation tax purposes, there are in fact two chargeable accounting periods, one running from 1.4.99 to 31.3.00 ('Period 1') and one from 1.4.00 to 30.6.00 ('Period 2')

The tax for Period 1 is due on 1 January 2001 and that for Period 2 is due on 1 April 2001. However, the self assessment return itself for both periods does not have to be filed until 12 months after the end of the long period of account, ie by 30 June 2001.

Please let me know if you require any further information.

Signed: Management accountant

**63   HAPPY MAIDS LTD**

> **Pass marks**. In part (a) you were asked to write a letter. It is important to present your answer in the format required.

(a)

Huntley Accountants
2 The High Street
Jesmond
Newcastle NE1

Mrs Beth Jones
Happy Maids Ltd
24 Haldane Road
Jesmond
Newcastle. NE2

Dear Beth,

TAXATION QUERIES

I outline below the impact of taxation on the various aspects of Happy Maid Ltd's business which we discussed at our recent meeting.

**Impact of VAT on the Business**

> VAT is charged on
> - supplies
> - of taxable goods and services
> - made in the UK
> - by a taxable person
> - in the course or furtherance of business.

The provision of cleaning services by Happy Maids Ltd is a taxable supply of services for VAT and will be subject to VAT at the standard rate of 17.5% once the company becomes a 'taxable person'.

A 'Taxable person' is someone who is or should be registered for VAT. Essentially the company needs to be registered for VAT once its turnover exceeds a certain threshold (currently £52,000), although it can register voluntarily before the compulsory date if it wishes. If the level of turnover remains fairly similar to that incurred in the first 4 months the company will have to register early in the new year when the turnover of £52,000 is due to be exceeded. The company could register voluntarily at any time before this date. The compulsory registration date must not be missed as penalties can be imposed by Customs and Excise.

Let us say that by the 28 February 2001 the company's cumulative turnover to date totalled £52,100 and thus exceeded the compulsory registration threshold. The company would have to notify Customs of this fact and apply to register for VAT by 30 March 2001. Customs would register the company for VAT from 31 March 2001. Once registered for VAT the company must charge 17.5% VAT on all invoices to customers. This will result in a 17.5% price increase for all domestic customers. However, commercial customers will not be affected by the price increase if they are registered for VAT and can recover the VAT that has been charged to them.

Once registered, Happy Maids Ltd can recover VAT paid by it on acquisitions for the business. It will also have to complete quarterly VAT returns showing the VAT charged to customers (output tax) in the quarter, the VAT suffered on purchases (input tax) and the net amount payable or repayable. VAT returns must be completed accurately and submitted with any payment due within one month of the quarter end to avoid interest or penalties being imposed on the business.

161

## Tax implications of employees engaged by the company.

There are two taxes to consider for any company taking on an employee – Income Tax and National Insurance Contributions (NIC).

The cost of employing staff are fully deductible expenses when calculating the Schedule D Case I profit of the business. Such costs will include wages, mileage allowances and NIC costs. Every pay day the company must also deduct the income tax and NIC payable by its employees under the PAYE system.

Special code numbers for each of the employees will be used together with tax calculation tables (both of which are issued by the Inland Revenue) to work out how much tax to deduct from each pay packet and these amounts are then paid over to the Inland Revenue 14 days after the end of each tax month.

When an employee leaves a form P45 must be prepared. This shows the employee's code and the tax paid to date. The P45 is given to the new employer who sends a section of it to his tax office. If a new employee is taken on without a P45 then form P46 must be completed and sent to the tax office.

At the end of the tax year the employer must by 31 May give each employee a P60 showing the pay and tax deducted in the tax year. These amounts are summarised on form P35 and sent to the Revenue by 19 May. In addition forms P11D or P9D (dependant on amount paid to employee) must be completed giving details of benefits in kind made available to employees in the year and copies must be given to the employee.

Penalties and interest may be incurred if taxes are not paid on time or forms submitted on time.

### Employee business mileage allowances

If an employee uses his own car on employer's business and is paid a mileage allowance for doing so strictly this mileage allowance is taxable income for the employee (and tax deductible as a business expense for the employer). The employee may make a claim to deduct any motoring expenses incurred wholly, exclusively and necessarily in the performance of his duties from his taxable income.

However, as an alternative to the above, employees can take advantage of the Fixed Profit Car Scheme (FPCS) under which the Revenue have laid out mileage rates dependant on the engine size of the car and the business miles travelled. The employee can receive tax free mileage allowances up to the amounts laid down under the scheme. Any excess allowance received is a taxable benefit. Allowances received in excess of the FPCS rates are also subject to Class I national insurance contributions.

I hope my letter have explained clearly the problem areas you raised in our meeting. However if you wish me to clarify any of the points made or if you have any other queries please do not hesitate to contact me.

Yours sincerely,

N. Advisor

(b) **Draft VAT return for the quarter to 31 August 2000**

| | £ | £ |
|---|---:|---:|
| Output tax | | |
| £20,000 × 17.5% | | 3,500 |
| Input tax | | |
| Leaflet mailing | 1,000 | |
| Cleaning packages 10 × £495 | 4,950 | |
| Cleaning products £200 × 3 | 600 | |
| Van | 5,000 | |
| Computer | 1,000 | |
| | 12,550 | |
| × 17.5% | | (2,196) |
| VAT payable | | 1,304 |

(c) **Schedule D Case I profit for the four months to 30 September 2000**

| | £ | £ |
|---|---:|---:|
| Turnover | | 25,250 |
| Expenses: | | |
| Wages | 18,000 | |
| Brochure delivery service | 1,000 | |
| Cleaning products £200 × 4 | 800 | |
| Capital allowances (W1) | 3,000 | |
| | | (22,800) |
| Schedule D Case I | | 2,450 |

*Note.* Turnover is the net of VAT figure

*Working*

1    **Capital allowances 4 months to 30.9.2000**

| | £ | *General pool* £ | *Total allowances* £ |
|---|---:|---:|---:|
| B/fwd | | Nil | |
| Additions | | | |
| Van | 5,000 | | |
| FYA 40% | (2,000) | | 2,000 |
| | | 3,000 | |
| Computer | 1,000 | | |
| FYA 100% | (1,000) | | 1,000 |
| | | Nil | |
| C/fwd | | 3,000 | |
| Total allowances | | | 3,000 |

*Notes*

* FYAs are not restricted for a 4 month period

* No WDAs are available on assets on which an FYA was available in the period.

* The computer qualifies for a 100% FYA since the business meets the definition of small.

* The 'cost' of additions is net of VAT since all VAT has been recovered in (b). If there was any irrevocable VAT then the 'cost' for capital allowance purposes would include this amount.

(d) Only bad debts incurred in the course of a business are deductible for Schedule D Case I purposes. General bad debt provisions are not deductible but specific provisions and write-offs against individual debts are deductible.

(e) Where a discount is offered for prompt payment VAT is chargeable on the net amount, regardless of whether or not the discount is taken up.

Thus for a supply by Happy Maids Ltd for £500 plus VAT where a 5% prompt payment discount is available VAT will be calculated as follows.

£500 × 95% × 17.5%

Thus if the invoice is paid promptly the following will be due from the customer.

|  | £ |
| --- | --- |
| £500 less 5% discount | 475 |
| VAT | 83 |
|  | 558 |

If the invoice is not paid promptly

|  | £ |
| --- | --- |
| Amount in full | 500 |
| VAT | 83 |
|  | 583 |

*Paper 5*

*Business Taxation*

## *BTX*

INSTRUCTIONS TO CANDIDATES

| |
|---|
| *You are allowed three hours to answer this question paper.* |
| *Answer the ONE question in section A (consisting of seven sub-questions).* <br> *Answer the ONE question in section B.* <br> *Answer TWO questions ONLY from section C.* |

**DO NOT OPEN THIS PAPER UNTIL YOU ARE READY
TO START UNDER EXAMINATION CONDITIONS**

## SECTION A - 14 MARKS

## ANSWER *ALL* SEVEN SUB-QUESTIONS

*Each of the sub-questions numbered from 64.1 to 64.7 inclusive, given below, has only* ONE *right answer.*

REQUIREMENT:

*On the* SPECIAL ANSWER SHEET *provided at the end of this question, place a circle 'O' around the letter (either **A**, **B**, **C**, or **D**) that gives the right answer to each sub-question.*

*If you wish to change your mind about an answer, block out your first attempt and then encircle another letter. If you do not indicate clearly your final choice, or if you encircle more than one letter, no marks will be awarded for the sub-question concerned.*

---

**64.1**   A Ltd has one wholly owned subsidiary, B Ltd, one 51% subsidiary, C Ltd and one 75% subsidiary, D Ltd. All of the companies pay tax at the small companies rate.

Which of the companies can enter into the group payment arrangements whereby one group company pays the corporation tax liability on behalf of all group members?

**A**   A Ltd, B Ltd and C Ltd
**B**   A Ltd, B Ltd, C Ltd and D Ltd
**C**   A Ltd and B Ltd
**D**   None of the companies

---

**64.2**   Aura Ltd was 12 months late notifying Customs of it's liability to register for VAT.

A VAT return was duly completed covering the missing period showing

| | |
|---|---|
| Output tax | £12,900 |
| Input tax | £10,700 |

How much penalty will be charged by Customs?

**A**   £50
**B**   £110
**C**   £220
**D**   £1,290

---

**64.3**   D Ltd's bad debt account for the year to 31.3.01 showed the following.

| | £ | | £ |
|---|---|---|---|
| Trade debts written off | 15,000 | Balances b./f | |
| Loan to former employee | 18,000 | General provision | 10,000 |
| General provision | 8,000 | Special provision | 12,000 |
| Special provision | 12,000 | Profit and loss account | 31,000 |
| | 53,000 | | 53,000 |

What amount must be added back when calculating Schedule D Case I profits?

**A**   £18,000
**B**   £16,000
**C**   £20,000
**D**   £2,000

BPP PUBLISHING

**64.4**   Zeta Ltd sells £10,000 worth of furniture to Gamba Gmbh, a company based in Germany.

Which of the following statements best describes the VAT position of this transaction.

**A**   The goods are subject to VAT at 17.5% since furniture is a standard rated supply

**B**   The goods are a zero-rated export thus no VAT is charged

**C**   Since Germany is in the EU no VAT is charged on the sale. The invoice issued by Zeta Ltd must state 'EU sale'

**D**   If Gamba Gmbh is VAT registered in Germany the supply to the company can be zero-rated if Gamba Gmbh's VAT number is supplied to Zeta Ltd

**64.5**   Paul is seconded to the New York office of his employer company Mega Bank Ltd for a 2 year assignment. His wife Catherine and 6 year old daughter Flora remain in London.

Mega Bank Ltd allows Paul's family to visit him 3 times a year and pay all associated expenses.

During 2000/01 Catherine and Flora visit Paul as follows:

|                              | *Cost of visit* |
| ---------------------------- | --------------- |
| 2 weeks in April 2000        | £3,000          |
| 4 weeks in August 2000       | £5,000          |
| 2 weeks in December 2000     | £3,000          |

How much benefit in kind will Paul be taxed on in 2000/01 in respect of these visits paid for by the employer?

**A**   Nil
**B**   £3,000
**C**   £3,333
**D**   £10,000

**64.6**   P Ltd prepares accounts for the twelve months to 31.12.01. Its corporation tax liability for the period is £100,000. It has always paid corporation tax at the full rate. On what date will P Ltd make its first payment of corporation tax in respect of this period and how much will this be?

**A**   £18,000   14 July 2001
**B**   £18,000   14 October 2001
**C**   £22,000   14 July 2001
**D**   £22,000   14 October 2001

**64.7**   A Ltd lends an employee £4,000 to purchase a season ticket. The employee has no other loans from A Ltd. A Ltd also pays £300 a year to provide the employee with a parking space at work. What is the total amount of taxable benefits arising in respect of these items?

Assume the official rate of interest is 10%.

**A**   £400
**B**   £300
**C**   £700
**D**   £nil

# PILOT PAPER EXAMINATION

SPECIAL ANSWER SHEET FOR SECTION A

64.1            A            B            C            D

64.2            A            B            C            D

64.3            A            B            C            D

64.4            A            B            C            D

64.5            A            B            C            D

64.6            A            B            C            D

64.7            A            B            C            D

BPP PUBLISHING

---

SECTION B - 46 MARKS

THIS QUESTION IS COMPULSORY

---

**65    L LTD**

**SCENARIO - PART 1**

**BACKGROUND INFORMATION**

**(a)**    You are the management accountant of L Ltd, a UK company with no associated companies. L Ltd commenced trading on 1 February 1999. It made up accounts to 31 January 2000 but decided that 30 September would be a more appropriate accounting date. It therefore made up its second set of accounts to 30 September 2000.

The following information refers to the first three periods of trading:

| | *12 months to 31 January 2000* | *8 months to 30 September 2000* | *12 months to 30 September 2001 (budgeted)* |
|---|---|---|---|
| *Income* | £ | £ | £ |
| Schedule D Case I profit | 17,000 | 24,000 | |
| Schedule D Case I loss | | | (62,000) |
| Schedule A | 3,000 | 2,000 | 4,000 |
| Patent royalties received (gross figures) [received 1 May each year] | 6,000 | 4,000 | 2,000 |
| Chargeable capital gains | 7,000 | | 4,000 |
| Allowable capital losses | | (8,000) | |
| | | | |
| *Charges paid* (Gross figures) | | | |
| Patent royalties (paid 1 June each year) | 4,000 | 3,000 | 5,000 |
| Gift Aid (paid 1 September) | - | 2,000 | - |

L Ltd manufactures equipment used in e-commerce. The trading loss expected in the year ended 30.9.2001 will be exceptional and profits are expected in the future.

To date activities have been confined to the UK but L Ltd is looking to expand and to set up operations in overseas countries, both within and outside of the European Community. The company hopes to be selling to overseas customers and buying from overseas suppliers before the end of 2001.

REQUIREMENT:

Prepare a report dated 1 October 2000 for the Finance Director:

**(i)**    Computing the mainstream corporation tax (MCT) payable for each of the first two accounting periods, without taking account of the trading loss for the year ended 30 September 2001.    **6 Marks**

**(ii)**    On the assumption that relief for the trading loss for the year ended 30 September 2001 is claimed at the earliest opportunity, showing the effect of such a claim on all of the accounting periods, identifying the amount of tax which will be saved as result of the claim.    **10 Marks**

**(iii)**    Showing the amounts which will be available for carry forward at 30 September 2001.    **2 Marks**

**(iv)**    Explaining the important features of the taxation implications of L Ltd's decision to expand its sales and purchases overseas. Your answer should deal with both direct tax and VAT.    **8 Marks**

Corporation tax rates were:

| | FY99 | FY98 |
|---|---|---|
| Full rate | 30% | 31% |
| SCR | 20% | 21% |

Presentation and style                                                    **5 Marks**

Note that your computations should be shown in appendices attached to your report.

**Total Marks = 31**

**SCENARIO - PART 2**

**(b)**    You receive the following memo:

---

**MEMORANDUM**

To:        Chief Accountant of L Ltd
From:      Managing Director of L Ltd
Date:      1 May 2001
Subject:   Expansion Plans

At the last board meeting the directors of the company decided to set up an operation in a country where the rate of corporation tax is 10%.

They are considering two alternative approaches:

(a)    to run the overseas operation as a branch of the UK company; or
(b)    to run it as a foreign-registered subsidiary of the UK company.

Can you please draft a report to the board on the taxation implications of each of the alternative proposals.

Signed


Managing Director

1 May 2001

---

REQUIREMENT:

You are required to answer the Managing Director's memo                   **11 Marks**

Presentation and style                                                    **4 Marks**

**Total Marks = 15**

**Total Marks = 46**

SECTION C – 40 MARKS

ANSWER *TWO* QUESTIONS ONLY

**66    STD LTD**

STD Ltd, a UK resident company which manufactures concrete slabs, owns 8,000 shares in CCD Ltd, a retail company which sells building materials to the public. This holding represents 80% of the share capital of CCD Ltd.

STD Ltd needs to raise approximately £512,000 in order to repay a loan which is due for repayment in June 2001.

The directors of the company advised you in October 2000 that they were considering the sale of two assets, each of which could be sold for £700,000. They sought your advice on which of the two assets would generate sufficient funds, after taking into account any corporation tax payable on the resultant gain, to repay the outstanding loan. It was the directors' intention to sell the appropriate asset in December 2000, during STD Ltd's accounting period of twelve months to 31 March 2001.

Details of the two assets, only ONE of which was to be sold, are as follows;

(a)    A plot of land which had cost £110,000 in June 1986 and which is used for the storage of finished products.

This purchase had been funded by the sale in May 1985, for £120,000, of another plot of land, used for parking the company's vehicles. This land had cost £70,000 in May 1978 and had a market value at 31 March 1982 of £80,000.

On the occasion of this first sale, the maximum possible rollover relief was claimed.

(b)    The 80% holding of shares in CCD Ltd

These shares had cost £40,000 in May 1980 and had a market value at 31 March 1982 of £2.50 per share.

Prior to the current proposed disposal, STD Ltd had not made any other disposals since May 1985.

You establish that STD Ltd's other chargeable income for the year ended 31 March 2001 will be £150,000 and that this will be used to pay a dividend in June 2001.

REQUIREMENTS:

**(a)**    Compute the chargeable gain which will arise as a result of EACH of the two proposed disposals.
**10 Marks**

**(b)**    Advise the directors of STD Ltd which asset will generate sufficient funds, after taking into account the corporation tax payable on the gain, to allow them to repay the outstanding loan.
**5 Marks**

**(c)**    Advise the directors of any other tax implications arising as a result of the sale of the shares in CCD Ltd.    **5 Marks**

Please note that this question does NOT require you to calculate the TOTAL corporation tax payable by STD Ltd.

*Indexation factors which may be used in answering this question are:*

| | | |
|---|---|---|
| March 1982 | – December 2000 | 1.179 |
| March 1982 | – May 1985 | 0.199 |
| June 1986 | – December 2000 | 0.769 |

**Total Marks = 20**

**67    JAY LTD**

Jay Ltd is an unquoted UK company which runs a number of fast food outlets based in city centres.

Jay Ltd prepares and packages much of the food sold through the outlets. Until December 1999, this work had been carried out in a rented factory owned by Bee Ltd, a company in the same trade. During 1999, Bee Ltd had run into financial difficulties and ceased trading in November 1999. Jay Ltd was able

172

to acquire the factory on 1 January 2000 for £100,000. It was established that it had been bought new by Bee Ltd for £80,000 on 1 January 1994 and had been used for manufacturing purposes ever since. Jay Ltd was able to acquire, also on 1 January 2000, at a cost of £24,000, wrapping and processing machinery which was already installed in the factory.

Jay Ltd had been making up accounts each year to 31 December, but, during 1999, the directors decided that a March year ending would be more appropriate. They therefore made up accounts for the FIFTEEN months to 31 March 2001.

The following capital transactions, in addition to those mentioned above, took place during that period:

| Purchases | | Cost |
| --- | --- | --- |
| | | £ |
| Meat slicers | 28 June 2000 | 2,500 |
| | 15 January 2001 | 6,000 |
| Wrapping machine | 2 February 2001 | 12,000 |
| Delivery vehicles | 5 July 2000 | 28,000 |
| | 20 March 2001 | 32,000 |
| New shop front for recently acquired retail unit | 12 August 2000 | 14,000 |
| Motor cars for newly-appointed managers: | | |
| VW Polo | 12 September 2000 | 11,600 |
| Lexus | 1 January 2001 | 24,000 |
| New computer (including software £4,000) | 10 January 2000 | 14,000 |

| Disposals | | Proceeds |
| --- | --- | --- |
| | | £ |
| 30 March 2000 | Plant (original cost (£12,000) | 8,000 |
| 3 July 2000 | Motor car (original cost £11,000) | 6,000 |
| 3 January 2001 | Expensive car (1) | 14,000 |
| The computer bought in January 2000 proved useless and was sold in February 2001 for | | 3,000 |

(This item should be treated in the most advantageous manner.)

The balances brought forward for capital allowances purposes at 1 January 2000 were:

| *General pool* | *Car pool* | *Expensive car (1)* |
| --- | --- | --- |
| £36,000 | £12,000 | £9,000 |

Jay Ltd has 200 employees and in the fifteen months to 31 March 2001 it has a turnover of £5 million.

REQUIREMENT:

Compute the maximum capital allowances, including industrial buildings allowance (IBA), which may be claimed by Jay Ltd for EACH of the above accounting periods. **20 Marks**

---

**68** **C LTD**

You are the chief accountant of C Ltd, a company which owns a number of hotels, bars and restaurants.

You have been asked to attend a board meeting to advise the directors on the taxation implications of a number of transactions which have taken place during the recently-completed financial year.

Each of the costs and income items notes below have been reflected as revenue items in the company's profit and loss account for the year.

(a) The company had been negotiating to buy a hotel in the north of England and had incurred valuation fees of £8,000 and solicitors ' fees of £5,000. The proposed purchase was abandoned.

(b) A major refurbishment of a number of hotels was undertaken and this was funded by means of a bank loan. To secure this loan, a full valuation of the company's assets was required, and this cost £60,000.

(c) Legal fees to draw up the loan agreement were £15,000, and a finder's fee of £5,000 was paid to AB & Co.

(d) A firm of accountants was engaged to prepare a report on a group of companies which C Ltd wished to acquire. The firm's fees amounted to £45,000.

(e)    The purchase of the appropriate share capital of the companies in this group went ahead, and legal and accountancy fees of £38,000 were incurred.

(f)    The group taken over included two restaurants which were unsuitable. One was sold, incurring legal costs of £5,000, and the other was leased. The cost of setting up the lease was £3,000.

(g)    In order to build up cash to finance further future acquisitions, the company raised £5,000,000 by means of a rights issue, incurring professional fees of £380,000.

(h)    In the previous accounting period, a fire had seriously damaged a major hotel, and the repairs cost £160,000. This had been charged in last year's accounts and had been allowed as a deduction in arriving at the trading profit. There was a protracted dispute with the insurers who finally paid during the current accounting period a sum of £140,000. This amount was credited to the profit and loss account.

REQUIREMENT:

Write brief notes on EACH of the above transactions, in preparation for the meeting. Your notes should explain, with reasons, how each item would be dealt with in arriving at the adjusted trading profit, bearing in mind that they are all already reflected in the net profit figure shown in the accounts. Where any of the transactions have additional taxation implications, these should be explained.    **20 Marks**

---

69    **PGD LTD**

PGD Ltd, a UK company with no associated companies, provides the following information in respect of its twelve-month accounting period ended 31 March 2001.

The company has an outstanding debenture for £200,000 with an annual rate of interest of 12%. The interest is payable half-yearly on 30 September and 31 March, and both amounts due during the year to 31 March 2001 were paid on the due dates. The debenture was taken out for non trading purposes.

You are advised that the company received the following patent royalties during the year – net amounts after deduction of basic rate income tax:

| | |
|---|---|
| 20 May 2000 | £6,240 |
| 23 November 2000 | £37,440 |

You also establish that the company had other chargeable profits, before taking the above into account, for the year ended 31 March 2001 of £2,150,000. In previous years, the company had a similar level of profits.

REQUIREMENTS:

**(a)**    Prepare tables showing the amounts of income tax payable or repayable for each of the quarterly settlement periods involved, indicating the appropriate dates.    **6 Marks**

**(b)**    Compute the mainstream corporation tax due in respect of the year to 31 March 2001, state the due dates of payment of this liability and state from when interest will run on the late payment of tax.    **12 Marks**

**(c)**    State the date by which PGD Ltd must file its corporation tax return for the year to 31 March 2001.    **2 Marks**

**Total Marks = 20**

---

174

# ANSWERS

**DO NOT TURN THIS PAGE UNTIL YOU HAVE COMPLETED THE MOCK EXAM**

# A PLAN OF ATTACK

What's the worst thing you could be doing right now if this was the actual exam paper? Sharpening your pencil? Wondering how to celebrate the end of the exam in 2 hours 59 minutes time? Panicking, flapping and generally getting in a right old state?

Well, they're all pretty bad, so turn back to the paper and let's sort out a **plan of attack**!

## First things first

It's usually best to **start with the objective test questions**. You'll always be able to do at least a couple of them, even if you really haven't done as much preparation as you should have done. And answering even a couple of them will give you the confidence to attack the rest of the paper. **Don't even look at the other questions before doing Section A**. If you see something you don't recognise or which you don't think you can do, you'll only panic! Allow yourself **25 minutes** to do the objective test questions. No more. You can always come back to them at the end of the exam if you have some spare time.

## The next step

Now spend a good 5 minutes looking through Sections B and C in detail working out which optional questions to do and the order in which to attack the questions. You've then got **two options**.

## Option 1 (if you're thinking 'Help!')

If you're a bit worried about the paper, do the questions in the order of how well you think you can answer them. You will probably find the optional questions in Section C less daunting than the case study in Section B so start with Section C.

• If you are totally happy with chargeable gains calculations then start with **question 66**. If you feel you are doing these computations correctly, it will boost your confidence. Allow yourself 36 minutes to answer the question but make sure that you don't spend too long on part (a) (18 minutes at the most) – you need to leave 18 minutes for part (b) and (c).

• **Question 67** is another computational question. If you are happy with capital allowances and you like the computations this question could give you another confidence boost.

• If you prefer written questions you might wish to do **question 68**. However if you do this question ensure you give your reasons for the treatment of the various items and that you write your answer concisely.

• The requirements of **question 69** are broken down and are pretty clear cut which might mean that you would prefer it to **questions 67 and 68**. Again this question is mainly computational.

When you've spent the allocated time on the two questions in Section C turn to the compulsory question in Section B. You should have 1 hour and 20 minutes left at this point in the exam. Read the compulsory question through thoroughly before you launch into it. Once you start make sure you allocate your time to any parts within the question according to the marks available and that, where possible, you attempt the easy marks first. Also, remember that there are presentation and style marks available for this question: don't throw these away.

Lastly, what you mustn't forget is that you have to **answer the ONE question in Section B, and TWO questions from Section C**. Once you've decided on your two questions from Section C, it might be worth putting a line through the other questions so that you are not tempted to answer them!

177

## Option 2 (if you're thinking 'It's a doddle')

It never pays to be over confident but if you're not quaking in your shoes about the exam then **turn straight to the compulsory question** in Section B. You've got to do it so you might as well get it over and done with.

Once you've done the compulsory question, choose two of the questions in Section C.

- If you prefer working with numbers rather than providing written answers it might be best to avoid **question 68** in Section C.

- Unless you really have problems with corporation tax computations, **question 69** might be a better option than **question 67** because the requirements are clear cut and the question is shorter.

## No matter how many times we remind you....

Always, always **allocate your time** according to the marks for the question in total and then according to the parts of the question. And **always, always follow the requirements** exactly. Question 68, for example, asks you to give reasons for your treatment of each item. So give reasons. You are asked for brief notes in question 68. So don't provide a report.

## You've got spare time at the end of the exam.....?

If you have allocated your time properly then you **shouldn't have time on your hands** at the end of the exam. But if you find yourself with five or ten minutes to spare, **go back to the objective test questions** that you couldn't do or to **any parts of questions that you didn't finish** because you ran out of time.

## Forget about it!

And don't worry if you found the paper difficult. More than likely other candidates will too. If this were the real thing you would need to **forget** the exam the minute you leave the exam hall and **think about the next one**. Or, if it's the last one, **celebrate**!

## SECTION A

64.1 D    For a group to participate in the group payment arrangements at least one company in the group must be liable to quarterly instalments (ie must pay tax at the full rate).

64.2 C    The notification is over 9 months but under 18 months late.

   10% penalty applies.

   10% of net VAT due on the return.

   £(12,900 − 10,700)    = £2,200 × 10%
                         = £220

64.3 B

|  | £ |
|---|---|
| Loan to former employee | 18,000 |
| Less: decrease in general bad debt provision | (2,000) |
|  | 16,000 |

64.4 D

64.5 B    Where an employee works abroad for 60 continuous days or more he can claim a deduction equal to the BIK of up to two family visits per tax year if his employer pays for or reimburses the cost of those visits.

   Thus £11,000 BIK for Paul but can deduct first 2 visits leaving £3,000 taxable.

64.6 C    88% of the CT liability is due in four quarterly instalments commencing 14 July 2001.

64.7 D    Both benefits are exempt.

## SECTION B

### 65    L LTD

> **Pass marks**. The tricky point in this question was working out how much of the loss could be carried back to set off in the twelve months to 31.1.00. However, even if you got this wrong you should still have been able to score enough marks to pass the question.

(a)                                            **REPORT**

To:        The finance director of L Ltd
From:      Management Accountant
Date:      1 October 2000
Subject:   A report outlining the tax impact of the loss making period and on the effects of the proposed expansion

#### Introduction

This report is divided into two sections, the first of which deals with the first three accounting periods of L Ltd and the impact of the expected loss to be made in the third period of account.

The second part of this report looks at the effects of the proposed expansion of the business into overseas markets.

#### First three periods of account

The mainstream corporation tax payable for the first two accounting periods, if no account is taken of the third period's anticipated trading loss is:

|  | £ |
|---|---|
| Year ended 31 January 2000 | 5,388 |
| Period ended 30 September 2000 | 4,624 |

**BPP** PUBLISHING

Appendix 1 to this report outlines the calculation of these figures.

If relief for the loss of the year ended 30 September 2001 is claimed at the earliest opportunity then a claim under S393A will be made to offset the loss against other income in the year ended 30 September 2001 and then to carry the loss back to offset against income arising in the 12 months prior to the loss making accounting period.

The carry back claim will result in a total saving of corporation tax of £6,842 as outlined in Appendix 2 to this report.

At 30 September 2001 there will be a capital loss available to carry forward of £4,000 and a trading loss available to carry forward under S393(1) of £23,000. Appendix 3 contains the details of these amounts.

**Expanding overseas**

This section of the report is divided into two areas: Direct tax and VAT.

(a)  **Direct tax**

    (i)    Profits from sales overseas are taxable in the ordinary way. The cost of purchases overseas is deductible in the ordinary way.

    (ii)    The points made in (i) above apply whether operations are conducted in the UK or in an overseas branch. However, if an overseas branch is set up, its profits may well be taxed abroad. Credit for that tax can be claimed against UK corporation tax, up to the UK tax on those profits.

    (iii)    The company may prefer to set up overseas subsidiaries instead of branches. Their results (profits or losses) will then be isolated from the UK company's results. Their profits will only be taxable in the UK if:

        (1)    They are remitted to the UK, for example as dividends, interest or royalties

        or

        (2)    The controlled foreign companies rules apply. These rules tax in the UK profits which are being rolled up in low-tax countries.

        Where profits are taxed in the UK, relief will be given both for foreign withholding tax on remittances and for foreign corporation tax (underlying tax). Relief will not be available in the UK for overseas subsidiaries' losses.

(b)  **Value added tax**

    (i)    Imports from outside the European Community (the EC) are chargeable to VAT at the same rate as would apply if the goods had been purchased in the UK. This VAT is payable at the time of import or (in certain circumstances) in the following month, and it counts as input VAT.

    (ii)    Taxable acquisitions (purchases from registered traders in other EC states) are treated in the same way as imports from outside the EC, except that the VAT due on the acquisition is accounted for on the next VAT return.

    (iii)    Exports to outside the EC are zero rated.

    (iv)    Sales to VAT registered traders in other EC states are zero rated.

    (v)    Sales to unregistered persons in other EC states are treated like sales in the UK.

    (vi)    If annual trade within the EC exceeds £233,000, monthly Intrastat forms must be submitted. Sales to EC customers also require the completion of EC sales listings.

Signed: Chief Accountant

## APPENDIX 1

MCT payable for first two accounting periods

| | *y/e 31.1.00* | *p/e 30.9.00* |
|---|---|---|
| | £ | £ |
| Schedule D Case I | 17,000 | 24,000 |
| Schedule A | 3,000 | 2,000 |
| Taxed income (patent royalty) | 6,000 | 4,000 |
| Chargeable gain | 7,000 | nil |
| Total profits | 33,000 | 30,000 |
| Less: charges on income | | |
| patent royalties paid (gross) | (4,000) | (3,000) |
| gift aid payment | | (2,000) |
| PCTCT | 29,000 | 25,000 |

*MCT payable*

| | | £ | £ |
|---|---|---|---|
| FY 98 | | | |
| £29,000 × 21% × 2/12 | | 1,015 | |
| FY 99 | | | |
| £29,000 × 20% × 10/12 | | 4,833 | |
| FY 99 2/8 × £25,000 × 20% | | | 1,250 |
| FY 00 6/8 × £25,000 × 20% | | | 3,750 |
| Less: Starting rate marginal relief (£33,333 – £25,000) × 1/40 × 6/8 | | | (156) |
| Less: Net income tax suffered (£1,000 × 22%) | | | (220) |
| | £ | | |
| £6,000 × 23% | 1,380 | | |
| £4,000 × 23% | (920) | (460) | |
| MCT payable | | 5,388 | 4,624 |

**Tutorial note.** The upper limit for starting rate purposes is £50,000 × 8/12 = £33,333.

## APPENDIX 2

Effect of loss on all accounting periods

| | *y/e 31.1.00* | *p/e 30.9.00* | *y/e 30.9.01* |
|---|---|---|---|
| | £ | £ | £ |
| Schedule DI | 17,000 | 24,000 | nil |
| Schedule A | 3,000 | 2,000 | 4,000 |
| Taxed income (patent royalty) | 6,000 | 4,000 | 2,000 |
| Chargeable gain | 7,000 | Nil | Nil (W) |
| Total profits | 33,000 | 30,000 | 6,000 |
| Less: S 393A(1) c/y loss claim | | | (6,000) |
| Less: trade charges on income (gross) | (4,000) | (3,000) | |
| | 29,000 | 27,000 | |
| Less: S 393A(1) c/b loss claim to | | | |
| p/e 30.9.00 | | (27,000) | |
| S 393A(1) c/b loss claim to | | | |
| y/e 31.1.00 maximum relief | | | |
| 4/12 × £33,000 | (11,000) | | |
| PCTCT | 18,000 | Nil | Nil |

181

BPP
PUBLISHING

The gift aid payment becomes unrelieved as a result of the carry back claim.

|  | y/e 31.1.00 £ | p/e 30.9.00 £ | y/e 30.9.01 £ |
|---|---|---|---|
| *MCT payable* |  |  |  |
| FY 98 |  |  |  |
| £18,000 × 21% × 2/12 | 630 |  |  |
| FY 99 |  |  |  |
| £18,000 × 20% × 10/12 | 3,000 |  |  |
| Less:   Net income tax suffered | (460) |  |  |
| MCT payable after loss relief | 3,170 | nil | nil |
| Less:   original MCT payable | (5,388) | (4,624) | nil |
| Repayment | (2,218) | (4,624) | nil |

*Working*

| 1. Chargeable gain y/e 30.9.01 | 4,000 |
|---|---|
| Less: loss b/f | (4,000) |
| Chargeable gain | Nil |

Total tax saving is £6,842 (£2,218 + £4,624).

## APPENDIX 3

Amounts available to carry forward at 30 September 2001

|  | £ |
|---|---|
| Loss incurred y/e 30.9.01 | 62,000 |
| Less:   S 393A(1) c/y claim | (6,000) |
|        S 393A(1) c/b claim to p/e 30.9.00 | (27,000) |
|        S 393A(1) c/b claim to y/e 31.1.00 | (11,000) |
| Loss unrelieved | 18,000 |
| Add:   unrelieved trade charges y/e 30.9.01 | 5,000 |
| Loss available to c/f under s 393(1) | 23,000 |
| Capital loss available to c/f £(8,000 – 4,000) | 4,000 |

(b)                              **REPORT**

To:         Managing Directors of L Ltd
From:     Chief Accountant
Date:      2 May 2001
Subject:   Taxation implications of the overseas operation

The purpose of this report is to set out the tax implications which will arise if we set up either a branch or a foreign registered subsidiary to run our overseas operations.

(a) **UK taxation arises on the profits of an overseas branch, and any losses of such a branch will, provided that the branch is controlled in the UK, be aggregated with the profits or losses of the UK division. UK taxation will,** subject to paragraph (c) below, **only arise on the profits of an overseas subsidiary controlled abroad to the extent that those profits are remitted to the UK (for example as dividends, or as interest on loans). Losses of an overseas subsidiary cannot be relieved against the UK company's profits,** as group relief is only normally available between UK resident companies.

(b) **Foreign tax will arise on the profits of both branches and subsidiaries,** as these will constitute permanent establishments. There may also be foreign withholding taxes on profits of a subsidiary remitted to the UK. **To the extent that the same profits suffer both foreign and UK taxation, double taxation relief will be available,** either under a treaty or under the UK's unilateral relief provisions. The usual effect is that the overall tax rate is the higher of the average UK rate on the UK company's profits and the foreign rate.

(c) If a subsidiary is **set up in a country where the tax on profits is less than three quarters of the amount it would be in the UK,** the 'controlled foreign companies' **rules may apply.** This means it will be necessary to impute profits (excluding chargeable gains) and creditable overseas tax to the UK company, so that the profits become subject to UK corporation tax.

In computing the profits and creditable tax to be apportioned and the corresponding UK tax, a number of assumptions are made.

(i)     The company is deemed to be UK resident.

(ii)    The company is deemed not to be a close company.

(iii)   The company is given the maximum amount of tax reliefs (except group relief), though the holding company may require that certain claims be deemed not to have been made.

(iv)    The full range of capital allowances is available, subject to anti-avoidance rules.

The legislation does not currently apply if any one of the following conditions is met.

(i)     The **annual profits of the overseas company are £50,000 or less.**

(ii)    The **overseas company follows an acceptable distribution policy.** An acceptable distribution policy is one where at least 90% of non-capital profits are remitted as a dividend within 18 months of the end of the accounting period to which the dividend relates.

(iii)   The **overseas company is engaged in exempt activities.** In broad terms, exempt activities are those which require a permanently occupied business establishment in the country concerned, do not involve frequent cross-frontier transactions and are not in the course of certain, mostly finance-oriented, businesses.

(d) A subsidiary will only be treated as not UK resident if it is not incorporated in the UK and its central management and control are abroad.

Signed: Chief Accountant

## SECTION C

## 66    STD LTD

> **Passmarks**. The question emphasised that you were not required to calculate the total corporation tax payable by STD Ltd. You would not have gained any marks for doing so.

(a)   **Gain on disposal of land in May 1985**

|  | £ |
|---|---|
| Sale proceeds in May 1985 | 120,000 |
| Less cost | (70,000) |
|  | 50,000 |
| Indexation allowance (£80,000 × 0.199) | (15,920) |
|  | 34,080 |
| Gain rolled over | (24,080) |
| Proceeds retained (£120,000 – £110,000) | 10,000 |

### Sale of land

|  | £ | £ |
|---|---|---|
| Sale proceeds | | 700,000 |
| Less : Cost | 110,000 | |
| Less: 50% gain rolled | (12,040) | |
| | | (97,960) |
| | | 602,040 |
| Indexation allowance (£97,960 × 0.769) | | (75,331) |
| Chargeable gain | | 526,709 |

### CCD Ltd shares

|  | £ | £ |
|---|---|---|
| Cost: 31 March 1982 | | |
| Proceeds | 700,000 | 700,000 |
| Less cost/31.3.82 | (40,000) | (20,000) |
| | 660,000 | 680,000 |
| Indexation allowance £40,000 × 1.179 | (47,160) | (47,160) |
| | 612,840 | 632,840 |
| Take lower gain | £612,840 | |

(b) **Funds for loan repayment**

As STD Ltd and CCD Ltd are associated companies, the small companies rate thresholds are divided by two, giving upper and lower limits for small companies rate purposes of £750,000 and £150,000 respectively. Because of the other chargeable income of £150,000 for the year ended 31 March 2001, the chargeable gains will bear corporation tax at the marginal rates of 32.5% on £600,000 and 30% on any excess.

|  | Plot of land | CCD Ltd Shares |
|---|---|---|
| | £ | £ |
| Proceeds | 700,000 | 700,000 |
| Corporation tax at marginal rate of 32.5% | (171,180) | (195,000) |
| Corporation tax at marginal rate of 30% | | (3,852) |
| Net sale proceeds | 528,820 | 501,148 |

The directors need approximately £512,000 in order to repay the loan, so only the sale of the land generates sufficient net sale proceeds to repay the loan.

They should be advised to sell the plot of land rather then the shares, since this generates more net cash after taking into account the corporation tax that must be paid on the chargeable gain.

In addition, if either STD Ltd or CCD Ltd buys further capital assets qualifying for rollover relief within the next three years, the gain arising on the sale of the land can once more be deferred through rollover relief.

(c) To:       The Directors
From:    Management Accountant
Date:    30 October 2000
Subject:  Tax implications of the sale of shares in CCD Ltd

A capital gain would arise on the sale of shares in CCD Ltd. In addition the following tax implications will arise following the sale.

A group relief group will no longer exist so the companies will no longer be able to transfer losses to each other, and any assets transferred between the two companies in future will give rise to a chargeable gain as a capital gains group will no longer exist.

Gains on any assets transferred from STD Ltd within the six years prior to CCD Ltd leaving the group, will crystallise.

STD Ltd will no longer have any associates. As a result, the upper and lower limits for determining the rate of corporation tax will no longer be divided by two. At the current level of trading profits, this will enable STD Ltd to take advantage of the small companies rate.

Stamp duty will be payable by the purchaser on the purchase of the shares.

The purchaser of shares may require tax warranties and indemnities to be given regarding the tax status of CCD Ltd.

## 67    JAY LTD

> **Passmarks**. It was vital to adopt a good layout when answering this question.
>
> Note that the company is a small or medium sized enterprise for first year allowance purposes. This means that FYAs of 40% are available in respect of all purchases except cars. FYAs are not pro-rated in short periods, although writing down allowances are pro-rated.

### Industrial buildings allowance

Jay Ltd is entitled to IBAs on the lower of the building's original cost and its subsequent purchase price, ie £80,000. The remaining tax life is 19 years. The industrial building allowances available are therefore as follows:

12 months to 31 December 2000, WDA is £80,000/19 = £4,211
3 months to 31 March 2001, WDA is £4,211 × 3/12 = £1,053

*BPP* PUBLISHING

*Plant and machinery - 12 months to 31 December 2000*

| | | General pool £ | Car pool £ | Exp car 1 £ | Exp car 2 £ | Short life asset £ | Allowances £ |
|---|---|---|---|---|---|---|---|
| Tax WDV b/f | | 36,000 | 12,000 | 9,000 | | | |
| Transfer | | 12,000 | (12,000) | | | | |
| Addition | | 11,600 | | | | | |
| Disposals | | (14,000) | | | | | |
| | | 45,600 | | 9,000 | | | |
| WDA 25% | | (11,400) | | (2,250) | | | 13,650 |
| *Acquisitions qualifying for FYA* | | | | | | | |
| 28.6.00 | 2,500 | | | | | | |
| 5.7.00 | 28,000 | | | | | | |
| 1.1.00 | 24,000 | | | | | | |
| 10.1.00 | | | | | | 14,000 | |
| | 54,500 | | | | | | |
| FYA 40% | (21,800) | | | | | (5,600) | 27,400 |
| | | 32,700 | | | | | |
| | | 66,900 | | 6,750 | | 8,400 | |
| *3 months to 31 March 2001* | | | | | | | 41,050 |
| Addition | | | | | 24,000 | | |
| Disposals | | | | (14,000) | | (3,000) | |
| | | | | (7,250) | | 5,400 | |
| Balancing charge/(allowance) | | | | 7,250 | | (5,400) | (1,850) |
| WDA 25% × 3/12 | | (4,181) | | | (750) | max | 4,931 |
| *Acquisitions qualifying for FYA* | | | | | | | |
| 15.1.01 | 6,000 | | | | | | |
| 2.2.01 | 12,000 | | | | | | |
| 20.3.01 | 32,000 | | | | | | |
| | 50,000 | | | | | | |
| FYA @ 40% | (20,000) | | | | | | 20,000 |
| | | 30,000 | | | | | |
| Tax WDV c/f | | 92,719 | | | 23,250 | | |
| Capital allowances | | | | | | | 23,081 |

## 68    C LTD

> **Pass marks**. For each item you should have given a clear statement stating whether the amount should be deducted, added or left unadjusted.

**Deductibility of costs in calculating adjusted Schedule D Case I trading profits for corporation tax purposes**

(a)  **Valuation fees and solicitors fees**

Both the valuation fees of £8,000 and solicitors fees of £5,000 are disallowed as they were incurred on abortive capital expenditure in respect of a hotel which was never acquired for use in C Ltd's trade. Both amounts must be added back in computing Schedule D profits.

(b)  **Asset valuation**

These asset valuation fees are allowed in calculating adjusted trading profits because they are admissible expenses of bringing into existence a loan relationship entered into for trading purposes. This means that no adjustment to trading profits is needed.

(c)  **Legal and finders fees**

These fees are also allowed in calculating adjusted trading profits because they are admissible expenses of bringing into existence a loan relationship entered into for trading purposes. Again, no adjustment to trading profits is needed.

(d)  **Accountants report and legal and accountancy fees**

The fees for preparing the report are disallowed as they were incurred in respect of a proposal to acquire share capital in a corporate group, a capital transaction. Similarly, the legal and accountancy fees associated with the purchase of the share capital are disallowed. All of these costs will form part of C Ltd's capital gains base cost in the shares acquired with regard to any future disposal of C Ltd's equity investment. They must however be added back in computing Schedule D Case I profits.

(e)  **Legal costs re restaurants**

The legal fees on the sale of the unsuitable restaurant are also disallowed as they were incurred in respect of the disposal of a capital asset, but they will be a deductible cost in calculating the chargeable gain or capital loss on the sale of the restaurant. The fees must be added back on computing Schedule D profits.

The legal costs of setting up a new lease (as distinct from renewing a short lease where costs are deductible) are a capital expense and therefore disallowed. Again, the costs must be added back in computing Schedule D profits.

(g)  **Professional fees**

These professional fees are disallowed as they were incurred in respect of an issue of shares, which is a capital transaction. This in contrast to incidental costs of raising debt funding which are allowable under the loan relationship rules. The professional fees must be added back in computing Schedule D profits.

(h)  **Insurance proceeds**

The insurance proceeds are taxable, being regarded as trading income in the year of recovery, offsetting substantially the tax deduction allowed for repairs in the previous year. This means that no adjustment to trading profit is needed.

69   **PGD LTD**

> **Passmarks**. The quarterly payments regime for corporation tax is an extremely topical subject.

(a)

| Return period | Income tax Withheld £ | Income tax Suffered £ | Tax paid (repaid) £ | Due date |
|---|---|---|---|---|
| 1.4.00 - 30.6.00 | | (1,760) | | 14.7.00 * |
| 1.7.00 - 30.9.00 | 2,400 | | 640 | 14.10.00 |
| 1.10.00 - 31.12.00 | | (10,560) | (640) | 14.1.01 * |
| 1.1.01 - 31.3.01 | 2,400 | | | 14.4.01 * |
| | 4,800 | (12,320) | | |

The excess income tax suffered can be deducted from the mainstream corporation tax liability.

* These are the due dates for the return. There is no due date for the repayment of tax.

(b)  Mainstream corporation tax

|  | £ |
|---|---|
| Other chargeable profits | 2,150,000 |
| Patent royalties ($\times$ 100/78) | 56,000 |
| Less: Debenture interest | (24,000) |
| Profits chargeable to corporation tax | 2,182,000 |

|  | £ |
|---|---|
| Mainstream corporation tax |  |
| £2,182,000 $\times$ 30% | 654,600 |
| Less: income tax suffered (para (a)) | (7,520) |
|  | 647,080 |

As PGD Ltd pays corporation tax at the full rate it is a 'large' company and it must pay 72% of its corporation tax liability for the year to 31 March 2001 in quarterly instalments. The quarterly instalments are due as follows.

|  | *Amount due* |
|---|---|
|  | £ |
| 14.10.00 | 116,474 |
| 14.01.01 | 116,474 |
| 14.4.01 | 116,475 |
| 14.7.01 | 116,475 |
|  | 465,898 |

The balance of £181,182 is due for payment on 1 January 2002.

Interest on any late paid instalment will run from the due date for that instalment. The position is looked at cumulatively after the payment of each instalment.

Interest on the balancing payment runs from the due date, 1 January 2002.

(c)  The corporation tax must be filed on the later of:

(i)   31 March 2002
(ii)  Three months after a notice requiring the return to be filed was made.

*Business Taxation*

# *BTX*

INSTRUCTIONS TO CANDIDATES

| |
|---|
| *You are allowed three hours to answer this question paper.* |
| *Answer the ONE question in section A (consisting of seven sub-questions).*<br><br>*Answer the ONE question in section B.*<br><br>*Answer TWO questions ONLY from section C.* |

**DO NOT OPEN THIS PAPER UNTIL YOU ARE READY
TO START UNDER EXAMINATION CONDITIONS**

## SECTION A - 14 MARKS

## ANSWER *ALL* SEVEN SUB-QUESTIONS

*Each of the sub-questions numbered from 70.1 to 70.7 inclusive, given below, has only ONE right answer.*

REQUIREMENT:

*On the* SPECIAL ANSWER SHEET *provided at the end of this question, place a circle 'O' around the letter (either* **A**, **B**, **C**, *or* **D***) that gives the right answer to each sub-question.*

*If you wish to change your mind about an answer, block out your first attempt and then encircle another letter. If you do not indicate clearly your final choice, or if you encircle more than one letter, no marks will be awarded for the sub-question concerned.*

---

**70.1**   J Limited, a manufacturing company which is registered for VAT, seconds a trainee accountant to an accounting firm, sending the firm an invoice for the exact cost of the trainee's salary.

The supply of the trainee's services to the accounting firm for VAT purposes is:

**A**   Exempt
**B**   Zero rated
**C**   Standard rated at 17.5%
**D**   Outside the scope of VAT

---

**70.2**   SD LTD, a retail clothes shop, prepares accounts to 31 December each year. The accounts to 31 December 2000 show that a Jaguar car was sold for £13,000 and the following assets were bought:

| | | £ |
|---|---|---|
| 14 January 2000 | New general lighting | 1,200 |
| 18 January 2000 | New shop front | 900 |
| 3 June 2000 | New computer | 5,500 |

The tax written down values at 1 January 2000 were:

| | £ |
|---|---|
| General pool | 8,300 |
| Jaguar car | 27,000 |

The company qualifies for FYA where relevant. The company's maximum capital allowances for the year ended 31 December 2000 are:

**A**   £23,135
**B**   £21,575
**C**   £18,275
**D**   £19,115

---

**70.3**   The entertainment account of S Ltd showed:

| | £ |
|---|---|
| Staff tennis outing for 30 employees | 1,800 |
| 2,000 tee shirts with firm's logo given to race runners | 4,500 |
| Advertising and sponsorship of an athletic event | 2,000 |
| Entertaining customers | 7,300 |
| Staff Christmas party (30 employees) | 2,400 |

The amount to be added back in arriving at the taxable profits is:

**A**   £7,300
**B**   £11,800
**C**   £16,300
**D**   £21,100

**70.4** The form used to report the benefits of employees earning over £8,500 per annum under the PAYE system is:

A   P9D
B   P11D
C   P45
D   P60

**70.5** BD Ltd is a building company which insists on being paid before starting a contract for a particular customer. It issued an invoice for the full amount on 1 September 2000, received half the amount on 9 September 2000 and the balance on 14 September 2000. It started the work on 20 September 2000 and finished it on 1 October 2000.

The correct VAT tax point is:

A   1 September 2000
B   9 September 2000
C   14 September 2000
D   1 October 2000

**70.6** M Ltd, a large company, has a corporation tax liability of £240,000 in respect of its accounting year 31 March 2001.

On which date will the company be required to pay the final quarterly instalment of the liability?

A   14 April 2001
B   14 July 2001
C   31 July 2001
D   1 October 2001

**70.7** A company with an accounting year to 30 September 1999 does not submit its CT600 corporation tax self assessment return until 30 November 2000.

What is the latest date by which the Inland Revenue can normally open an enquiry into the return?

A   30 September 2001
B   30 November 2001
C   31 December 2001
D   31 January 2002

BPP PUBLISHING

PILOT PAPER EXAMINATION

SPECIAL ANSWER SHEET FOR SECTION A

70.1          A        B        C        D

70.2          A        B        C        D

70.3          A        B        C        D

70.4          A        B        C        D

70.5          A        B        C        D

70.6          A        B        C        D

70.7          A        B        C        D

BPP
PUBLISHING

---

SECTION B - 46 MARKS

THIS QUESTION IS COMPULSORY

---

71 **X LTD**

(a) X Ltd is a UK resident company which manufactures household appliances. Until 1994 its shares were wholly owned by the members of the Smith family. During 1994 80% of the shares were acquired by Z Ltd, a UK company which owns a chain of retail outlets selling household appliances. The remaining 20% of the shares continue to be held by Mr J Smith, aged 43, who is employed as general manager of X Ltd.

The directors of X Ltd are also directors of Z Ltd.

For the purpose of this scenario you are the chief accountant of X Ltd.

At a meeting arranged by you with the directors of X Ltd held in April 2000, you are provided with their estimates of the results for the year to 31 March 2001, together with additional information which may have a bearing on the taxation liability of the company. They express surprise that you have requested this information at such an early stage.

The estimates are as follows.

| | | £ |
|---|---|---|
| Income | Trading profits | 820,000 |
| | Loan interest receivable (see below) | 5,000 (gross) |
| | Patent royalties received | 10,000 (gross) |
| | Rental income | 15,000 |
| Payments | Loan interest payable (see below) | 12,000 (gross) |
| | Gift Aid | 4,000 |

Notes

1 The loan interest receivable was in respect of a loan of £50,000 made by X Ltd to a major supplier S Ltd, two years ago.

2 The loan interest payable was on a loan from a finance company (which was not a bank) to finance the purchase of equipment.

3 Interest is received and paid net of 20% tax.

In addition to the above, you establish that the company had a corporation tax (CT) liability of £270,000 for the year ended 31 March 2000 based on chargeable income of £900,000.

It had surplus advance corporation tax (ACT), generated in the year to 31 March 1999, brought forward at 31 March 2000 of £30,000. The directors had decided to pay a dividend of £624,000 during May 2000 in respect of the year ended 31 March 2000. There was no FII received in any year.

REQUIREMENTS:

Prepare a report to the directors of X Ltd.

(i) Producing your calculation of the estimated corporation tax liability of the company for the year ended 31 March 2001 **8 Marks**

(ii) Illustrating, by means of a schedule, how and when this liability will be settled **6 Marks**

(iii) Advising them of the effect of paying the dividend in May 2000 **3 Marks**

(iv) Explaining why it is necessary to have reliable estimates of the chargeable income **2 Marks**

(v) Advising them of their statutory obligations under the Corporation Tax Self Assessment (CTSA) system. **3 Marks**

Presentation and style **5 Marks**

**Total Marks = 27**

Note that your calculations, in arriving at the corporation tax liability and the schedule of payments should be shown in appendices attached to your report.

The schedule of payments should cover the period for April 2000 to January 2002.

(b) During the year to 31 March 2001 X Ltd's parent company, Z Ltd, experienced cash flow problems. On 31 December 2000 Z Ltd sold its holding in X Ltd to B Ltd, a UK company which already owned two UK subsidiaries. You are aware that X Ltd owned an asset which had been transferred to by Z Ltd under group arrangements in August 1996. The gain on this transaction at the time of the transfer was £30,000.

In May 2001 you have a meeting with the directors of B Ltd who have been provided with a copy of your report made to X Ltd in April 2000 and they provide you with the following information:

- Apart from the trading profit, which was £810,000, all of the other estimates shown in Part (a) were accurate.

- The supplier, S Ltd, to whom the loan of £50,000 was made, became insolvent on 31 January 2001 and nothing was recoverable.

- During January 2001, the directors of B Ltd considered that Mr Smith, the general manager of X Ltd, was unsatisfactory and dismissed him, making him a gratuitous payment of £24,000. This has not been treated as a deduction in the reported profits of X Ltd. Mr Smith later sold his 20% holding in X Ltd to B Ltd.

REQUIREMENTS:

Prepare a report for the directors of B Ltd;

(i) Producing your calculation of the corrected corporation tax liability for the year ended 31 March 2001 and indicating whether there has been an over or under payment of corporation tax to date **6 Marks**

(ii) Explaining the reasons for the difference between the projected and actual liability for the year ended 31 March 2001 **4 Marks**

(iii) Explaining how the over/under payment will affect the quarterly payment position by producing a revised schedule of payments. **5 Marks**

Presentation and style **4 Marks**

**Total Marks = 19**

**Total Marks = 46**

Any detailed calculations should be shown in appendices attached to your report.

SECTION C – 40 MARKS

ANSWER *TWO* QUESTIONS ONLY

72    **PAYE**

The advertising company of which you are chief accountant is about to reorganise the method of remunerating certain members of staff. Until recently a number of individuals had been acting as freelance agents. They were not on the company's payroll, and had been paid gross.

As a result of a major investigation by the Inland Revenue the company has been advised that these individuals should now become employees subject to the rules of Schedule E.

It is the intention that each of these individuals will be given the use of a company-owned motor car and provided with fuel to cover both business and private mileage. A number of them will need to move house and the company has undertaken to give each person affected an amount of £5,000 towards their relocation costs. In addition, some of them will be given interest-free loans in order to enable them to refurnish their new homes.

This will be the first time your company has provided this range of benefits (apart from motor cars which are provided to the directors). The Board is anxious to ensure that it will be complying with the rules for both quantifying and reporting the benefits in kind. It also wishes to be in a position to explain to these new staff members the effect of the benefits on their monthly PAYE deduction.

REQUIREMENTS:

(a)    Prepare a report to the head of payroll, briefly setting out the rules for quantifying each of the above benefits. Your report must also deal with:

•    the compliance rules for returning details of the benefits to the Inland Revenue, and

•    the company's responsibilities under income tax self assessment rules, making references to the documentation, deadlines and penalties.                                    **15 Marks**

(b)    Prepare a brief information sheet for staff members, explaining the method by which they will be taxed on their benefits in kind and the effect of this on their PAYE Code Numbers.        **5 Marks**

**Total Marks = 20**

73    **W LTD**

W Ltd, a company engaged in the manufacture of machine tools, prepares its accounts annually at 31 March.

The following information relates to transactions during the year ended March 2001.

During the years 1998 and 1999 the company invested heavily in plant and machinery, mainly to take advantage of the first year allowances (FYA) available to it under the capital allowances system. This has resulted in a low pool value brought forward and the company has decided to sell plant which is now surplus to its requirements.

The various values brought forward at 1 April 2000 are:

| General pool | Expensive car (1) | Expensive car (2) | Computer SLA |
|---|---|---|---|
| £36,000 | £22,000 | £30,000 | £18,000 |

The following transactions took place during the year ended 31 March 2001:

Disposals

•    Two items in the general pool were sold for £60,000
     In each case the selling price was less than the original cost

•    Expensive car (2) was sold for £22,000

•    The computer, which had been de-pooled under the Short Life Asset (SLA) rules, was sold for £20,000

196

Purchases:
- A new lorry was bought for £18,000

- A piece of machinery was bought for £20,000
  This could, if wished, be treated as a SLA

The factory in which the trade is carried on was bought new on 1 April 1992 for £120,000 and an extension costing £40,000 was added on 1 April 1994. Neither of these payments had qualified for initial allowance. On 1 April 2000 the factory was sold for £100,000 and, on the same day, the company took occupation of a second-hand factory for which they paid £210,000. This factory had been bought by the original owners for £180,000 on 1 April 1990 and first used by them on that date.

The company is one which qualifies for FYA where appropriate and if claimed.

REQUIREMENTS:

**(a)** Calculate the maximum possible capital allowances (including industrial buildings allowances) which could be claimed by W Ltd in respect of the year ended 31 March 2001.       **14 Marks**

**(b)** State clearly how you have treated the purchases of the lorry and the new piece of machinery.
       **2 Marks**

**(c)** State clearly why you have chosen this approach given that there are two possible approaches, one of which produces significantly higher capital allowances than the other.       **4 Marks**

**Total Marks = 20**

---

**74    D LTD**

The following information relates to events and transactions involving D Ltd, a UK resident company, 90% of whose share capital is owned by T Ltd, another UK resident company. D Ltd made up accounts for the year ended 31 December 2000.

(a)   In May 1994 D Ltd had sold a building for £280,000 which had cost £120,000 in May 1980 and which had a market value (MV) of £130,000 at 31 March 1982. On the occasion of this disposal D Ltd had made a global election to use MV at 31 March 1982 for all sales of assets held at that date.

Of the proceeds, £270,000 was used to purchase new plant and machinery and the maximum possible holdover relief was claimed. This plant and machinery was scrapped in May 2000 and £10,000 was recovered for its scrap value.

(b)   In June 1997 the ownership of a factory was transferred to D Ltd from its parent company, T Ltd, at the agreed market value of £260,000. The factory had cost T Ltd £180,000 in June 1989. In May 2000, T Ltd sold 20% of its holding in D Ltd, reducing the holding to 70%.

(c)   In June 2000, D Ltd sold, for £300,000, an office block which had been held as an investment property and let. It had cost £180,000 in June 1978 and its MV at 31 March 1982 was £150,000.

(d)   In September 2000, D Ltd sold for £180,000 two plots of land which had been used for the purpose of the trade. These are part of a block of nine plots which had been bought by D Ltd in June 1992 for a total amount of £500,000. The market value of the seven unsold plots at 30 September 2000 was £1,200,000.

REQUIREMENTS:

**(a)** Compute any chargeable gain or allowable loss arising from each of the above events.  **16 Marks**

**(b)** Explain briefly whether any of the above gains could be deferred.       **4 Marks**

**Total Marks = 20**

Indexation factors which may be used.

| | |
|---|---|
| March 1982 – May 1994 | 0.821 |
| June 1989 – June 1997 | 0.365 |
| June 1997 – May 2000 | 0.067 |
| March 1982 – June 2000 | 1.116 |
| June 1992 – September 2000 | 0.209 |

### 75    M LTD

M Ltd is a UK resident company which owns controlling interests in two other UK resident companies and in two non-resident companies.

It also has the following interests in three non-resident companies:

| Company | Shareholding | Rate of Withholding tax | Profits post tax y/e 31.03.01 | Foreign tax paid |
|---------|--------------|-------------------------|-------------------------------|------------------|
|         | %            | %                       | £                             | £                |
| A Inc   | 6            | 15                      | 400,000                       | 80,000           |
| B P G   | 8            | 25                      | 900,000                       | 300,000          |
| C S A   | 12           | 20                      | 800,000                       | 200,000          |

M Ltd had experienced a prolonged period of poor trading and, as a result of losses brought forward from earlier years, its chargeable Schedule DI income for the year ended 31 March 2001 is only £20,000.

During the year, patent royalties of £75,000 (gross) had been paid and these had been added back in arriving at the adjusted Schedule DI income.

The only other income received by M Ltd during the year consisted of dividends from the above three companies, each of which had substantial undistributed profits. The figures (net of withholding tax) were:

|       | £       | Date received |
|-------|---------|---------------|
| A Inc | 170,000 | 1.6.00        |
| B P G | 150,000 | 10.9.00       |
| C S A | 120,000 | 31.12.00      |

REQUIREMENTS:

**(a)** Compute the MCT payable by M Ltd in respect of the year ended 31 March 2001. Your answer should show clearly your treatment of the patent royalties payment and of the foreign taxes suffered. You should explain why you are dealing with items in a particular way and you should use a columnar layout.

**16 Marks**

**(b)** Explain briefly what the taxation implications would be if C S A were deemed to be a controlled foreign company

**4 Marks**

**Total Marks = 20**

# ANSWERS

DO NOT TURN THIS PAGE UNTIL YOU
HAVE COMPLETED THE MOCK EXAM

## A PLAN OF ATTACK

As you turned the page to start this exam any one of a number of things could have been going through your mind ranging from the sublime to the ridiculous.

The main thing to do is take a deep breath and do not panic. It's best to sort a plan of attack before the actual exam so that when the invigilator tells you that you can begin and the adrenaline kicks in you are using every minute of the three hours wisely.

## Your approach

This paper has three sections, The first section contains seven objective test questions which are compulsory. The second contains one compulsory 46 mark scenario based question. The third has four twenty mark questions and you must answer two of them.

## First things first

It's usually best to **start with the objective test questions**. You'll always be able to do at least a couple of them, even if you really haven't done as much preparation as you should have done. And answering even a couple of them will give you the confidence to attack the rest of the paper. **Don't even look at the other questions before doing Section A**. If you see something you don't recognise or which you don't think you can do, you'll only panic! Allow yourself **25 minutes** to do the objective test questions. No more. You can always come back to them at the end of the exam if you have some spare time.

You then have a choice.

- Read through and answer Section B before moving on to Section C.

- Go through Section C and select the two questions you will attempt. Then go back and answer the questions in Section B first.

- Select the two questions in Section C, answer them and then go back to Section B.

You must give yourself a couple of minutes to go through the question(s) you are going to do. Time spent at the start of each question confirming the requirements and producing a plan for the answers is time well spent.

## Question selection

When selecting the two question's from Section C make sure that you read through all of the requirements. It is painful to answer part (a) of a question and then realise that parts (b) and (c) are beyond you, by then it is too late to change your mind and do another question.

When reviewing the requirements look at how many marks have been allocated to each part. This will give you an idea of how detailed your answer must be.

## Doing the exam

Actually doing the exam is a personal experience. There is not a single *right way*. As long as you submit complete answers to the questions in Sections A and B and any two from the questions in Section C after the three hours are up then your approach obviously works.

## One approach

Personally, I would look at the optional question's before I tackled the compulsory scenario style question. I need to know what I will be doing (you may be less curious and launch straight into the compulsory question).

A quick look at the optional questions would tell me that:

- Question 72 required a report covering PAYE and benefits in kind

- Question 73 covers capital allowances

- Question 74 requires the computation of chargeable gains and allowable losses

- Question 75 is a corporation tax computation which clearly includes double tax relief. Controlled foreign companies are covered in part (b).

I may already be deciding that I am not strong on PAYE requirements, whereas I can calculate capital allowances.

I will look at **all** of the requirements though. I don't want to fall into the trap of doing a question because I can do the calculation then find that I cannot answer the written part of the question in part (b). So I go through the requirements.

**Q72.** Am I confident that I can prepare a report quantifying each of the benefits and also dealing with the compliance rules and the company's responsibilities under income tax self assessment. Can I explain the effect of benefits on code numbers for part (b)?

**Q73.** Can I calculate the figures required for part (a)?

**Q74.** Can I calculate the figures required for part (a)? Can I answer part (b) on the deferral of gains?

**Q75.** Can I calculate the figures in part (a)? Can I identify the tax implications of CFC's for part (b)?

Always look at the requirements. You may find that a subject you find difficult is examined in a more straight forward way than one of your stronger subjects.

Having taken a few minutes to select two questions, I would then tackle the compulsory senario based question. You have 80 minutes to answer the scenario question and it is important to allocate your time so that you make an attempt on each part of the question. Don't forget that there will be marks for presentation and style in this question so ensure your answer is in the form required.

You should have approximately one hours and ten minutes left at this point as you go on to answer the two questions you selected earlier.

## Time allocation

Be disciplined. Allocate you time according to the marks available but never go over the time allocation. The last few marks in a question are the hardest to earn.

Be sure to follow the requirements. If four advantages are required, give four. No extra credit will be given for five. Two advantages will only get you half marks.

Answer all of the question. Having a go at every part of all four questions you are required to do will put you in a better position to pass than, say, only doing three questions. However difficult that fourth question seems at first there are easy marks to be earned.

If you have time left at the end of the exam ensure that you have attempted every part of every question. If you have, then scan through and ensure you completed any part of an answer you left earlier. Use the full three hours working towards a pass.

## Marking the exam

When you mark your exam, be honest. Don't be too harsh though. Give yourself credit for the things you did well, but don't kid yourself with 'I would have done that in the real exam'. It may be worth your while making two lists; strengths and weaknesses.

Strengths will be areas of the syllabus you are confident with and also good exam technique (maybe you remembered to lay the capital allowances computation out correctly).

Weaknesses will be holes in your knowledge and poor exam technique (maybe you ran out of time and couldn't answer all the requirements of the last question).

Making this list will help you focus your last days of revision on the areas which require attention whilst reminding you of the areas you excel in.

## SECTION A

70.1   C     The supply is a standard rated management charge at 17.5%

70.2   B

|  |  | General pool | Jaguar car | Allowances |
|---|---|---|---|---|
|  | £ | £ | £ | £ |
| TWDV b/f |  | 8,300 | 27,000 |  |
| Disposals |  | _____ | (13,000) |  |
|  |  | 8,300 | 14,000 |  |
| WDA @ 25% |  | (2,075) |  | 2,075 |
| Balancing allowance |  | _____ | (14,000) | 14,000 |
|  |  | 6,225 |  |  |
| Additions for qualifying for FYA | 5,500 |  |  |  |
| FYA @ 100% | (5,500) |  |  | 5,500 |
|  |  | 6,225 |  | 21,575 |

**Tutorial note.** Capital allowances are not available in respect of expenditure on the general lighting or on the shop front.

70.3   A

|  | £ |
|---|---|
| Entertaining | 7,300 |
|  | 7,300 |

70.4   B     Form P11D is used for these employees.

70.5   A     The basic tax point is 1 October 2000. However, as an invoice was issued before the basic tax point, the date on which the invoice was issued becomes the actual tax point.

70.6   B     The instalments are due on the 14th of the month. For a twelve month accounting period the first instalment is due in the seventh month and thereafter at three monthly intervals.

70.7   D     Quarter date after anniversary of return ∴ 31.1.02.


## SECTION B

### 71    X LTD

> **Pass marks**. Remember that in scenario questions there are nine marks available for presentation and style.

(a)   To:          The Directors of X Ltd
      From:        Chief Accountant
      Date:        30 April 2000
      Subject:     Estimated corporation tax liability of X Ltd and due dates of payment of corporation tax

**Introduction**

The purpose of this report is to estimate the corporation tax liability of X Ltd for the year to 31 March 2001 and to set out the dates by which X Ltd will have to pay corporation tax.

It is necessary to make the most precise estimates of the corporation tax (CT) liability for the year to 31 March 2001 to allow us to make accurate quarterly payments during the current period.

Failure to make adequate payments on their due dates could result in interest and penalties for the company imposed by the Inland Revenue.

Thus at our recent meeting you used you management accounting expertise to provide accurate estimates of our profits for the year ahead from which I have estimated out likely CT liability.

**Estimated corporation tax liability**

As you will see from Appendix 1, I have used the estimates of the company's results for the year to 31 March 2001. I have used these estimates to calculate that corporation tax of £238,600 will be due in respect of the year.

On 1 April 2000 the company had brought forward ACT of £30,000. Subject to the maximum set off limit, this ACT can be set against the CT liability arising in the period to 31 March 2001. The maximum ACT set off will be equal to 20% of the company's profits chargeable to corporation tax. I have estimated this as £166,800 in Appendix 1.

However, the maximum set off of ACT must reduced by any 'shadow' ACT that arises on a dividend paid during the accounting period. If X Ltd pays a dividend of £624,000 during May 2000, shadow ACT of £156,000 will arise and the set off of brought forward ACT in the year to 31 March 2001 will be restricted to £10,800. Although the remaining unrelieved ACT will be carried forward for relief in future periods, this clearly has cash flow disadvantages and we should consider carefully whether it might be worth reducing the amount of dividend to be paid next month.

**Due dates of payment of corporation tax**

As X Ltd pays corporation tax at the full rate it is required to pay its corporation tax liability in quarterly instalments commencing during the accounting period concerned. The system of paying corporation tax by quarterly instalments was being phased in. 60% of the corporation tax liability due for the year to 31 March 2000 is due in instalments. This percentage increases to 72% for the year to 31 March 2001, and then to 88% and 100% for the subsequent periods.

I have set out the amounts of tax payable on various dates in Appendix 2. The amounts for the year to 31 March 2001 are based on the estimates that you gave me earlier this month. It is important to note that interest runs from the due date on under or overpaid instalments. The Revenue may impose penalties if it believes that the company has deliberately or flagrantly failed to pay instalments of sufficient size. This means that it is very important that we make reliable estimates of chargeable income.

It will be important that we carefully monitor the CT which we need to pay by instalments because, as you can see, these will have a significant cash flow effect throughout the year.

**Statutory obligations under the corporation tax self assessment (CTSA) system**

Under the new CTSA system we are normally obliged to file a CT return for each period by the later of:

(i)    3 months after a notice requiring the return was issued
(ii)   12 months after the end of the accounting period

Thus the return for the year ended 31 March 2001 will be due on 31 March 2002 assuming the Revenue issue a timely notice. The Revenue has a further 12 months to decide whether or not to enquire into the return

We are required to keep the records on which a return is based, normally until six years after the end of an accounting period. The standard of records maintained is high and goes beyond the Company Act requirements. If the Revenue enquire into a return we may also be required to produce documents.

If you wish any further clarification on any of the items discussed above please do not hesitate to contact me

Signed: Chief Accountant

**Appendix 1**

May I draw your attention to the significant outflow of nearly £151,000 during January 2001 when the balance of tax for the year ended 31 March 2000 falls due in addition to a quarterly instalment for the year ended 31 March 20001.

*Estimated CT liability for the year ended 31 March 2001*

|  | £ |
|---|---:|
| Schedule D Case I (£820,000 – £12,000) | 808,000 |
| Schedule D Case III | 5,000 |
| Taxed income | 10,000 |
| Schedule A | 15,000 |
| Less: Gift Aid | (4,000) |
| Profits chargeable to corporation tax | 834,000 |

*FY 2000*

|  | £ |
|---|---:|
| £834,000 × 30% (W1) | 250,200 |
| Less: ACT (W2) | (10,800) |
| Less: Income tax suffered (W3) | (800) |
| Estimated CT payable | 238,600 |

*Workings*

1    *Upper limit*

As there are two associated companies, the upper limit is £750,000 and the full rate of corporation tax applies.

2    *ACT*

|  | £ |
|---|---:|
| Notional franked payment (× 100/80) | 780,000 |
| Shadow ACT @ 20% = £156,000 | |

|  | £ |
|---|---:|
| Maximum set off (£834,000 × 20%) | 166,800 |
| Less: Shadow ACT | (156,000) |
| Maximum offset surplus ACT b/f | 10,800 |

3    *Income tax suffered*

|  | £ |
|---|---:|
| Loan interest (£5,000 × 20%) | 1,000 |
| Patent royalties (£10,000 × 22%) | 22,200 |
| Less: Loan interest payable (£12,000 × 20%) | (2,400) |
| Income tax suffered | 800 |

Note that payments under the gift aid scheme are made gross.

Appendix 2: Schedule of payments of CT

**Year to 31 March 2000**

CT liability          £270,000

60% × £270,000 = £162,000 is due in four quarterly instalments of £40,500 commencing on 14 October 1999.

40% × £270,000 = £108,000 is due nine months after the end of the accounting period, 1 January 2001.

*Year to 31 March 2001*

CT liability          £238,600

72% × £238,600 = £171,792 is due in four quarterly instalments of £42,948 each commencing on 14 October 2000. The balance of 28% × £238,600 = £66,808 is due **nine** months after the end of the accounting period, 1 January 2002.

The schedule of payments of CT from April 2000 is therefore:

|  | *Date* | *Amount due* |
|---|---|---|
|  |  | *£* |
| 3rd instalment for y/e 31.3.00 | 14.4.00 | 40,500 |
| 4th instalment for y/e 31.3.00 | 14.7.00 | 40,500 |
| 1st instalment for y/e 31.3.01 | 14.10.00 | 42,948 |
| Balancing payment for y/e 31.3.00 | 1.1.01 | 108,000 |
| 2nd instalment for y/e 31.3.01 | 14.1.01 | 42,948 |
| 3rd instalment for y/e 31.3.01 | 14.4.01 | 42,948 |
| 4th instalment for y/e 31.3.01 | 14.7.01 | 42,948 |
| 1st instalment for y/e 31.3.02 | 14.10.01 | (amount not calculated) |
| Balancing payment for y/e 31.3.01 | 1.1.02 | 66,808 |

(b)  To:          The Directors of B Ltd
      From:      Chief Accountant
      Date:      1 May 2001
      Subject:   Actual corporation tax liability of X Ltd for the year to 31 March 2001 and due dates of payment of corporation tax

**Introduction**

The purpose of this report is to advise the directors of B Ltd of X Ltd's actual liability to corporation tax for the year ended 31 March 2001 and to set out the dates by which payment of corporation tax is due. In my report dated 30 April 2000 the CT liability was estimated at £238,600. A number of events have taken place since that estimate was made which have resulted in the liability being less than the forecast figure.

**Actual corporation tax liability for the year ended 31 March 2001**

As outlined in Appendix 1 the calculation of X Ltd's actual corporation tax liability for the above year is £233,200 as opposed to the estimated corporation tax liability for the year of £238,600. The reasons for the difference between the actual and estimated liability are as follows:

(i)    As Z Ltd sold its shares in X Ltd during the period, the gain that would have arisen at the time of the transfer of the chargeable asset from Z Ltd to X Ltd crystallises. This means that chargeable profits increase by £30,000.

(ii)   Actual trading profits are £10,000 below the estimate and an additional deduction of £24,000 can be made in respect of the compensation payment made to Mr Smith

(iii)   A loan of £50,000 became irrecoverable. This amount is deducted firstly from Schedule D Case III income and then from total profits.

However the reduction of the actual chargeable profits to £780,000 means that it is not possible to set off any of the surplus ACT brought forward.

**Payment of corporation tax**

72% of the actual corporation tax liability for the year is due in quarterly instalments as shown in Appendix 2. To date quarterly instalments have been overpaid by a total of £2,916. The company will receive interest on this overpaid amount and will only need to pay tax of £39,060 on 14 July 2001. The balancing payment which is due on 1 January 2002 will be £65,296 rather than the £66,808 originally estimated.

**Appendix one**

*Actual corporation tax liability for the year ended 31 March 2001*

|  | £ |
|---|---|
| Schedule D Case I | |
| (£810,000 – £12,000 – £24,000) | 774,000 |
| Taxed income | 10,000 |
| Schedule A | 15,000 |
| Chargeable gain | 30,000 |
| Less: Gift Aid | (4,000) |
| | 825,000 |
| Less: Non-trade deficit (£5,000 – £50,000) | (45,000) |
| Profits chargeable to corporation tax | 780,000 |

*FY 2000*

|  | £ |
|---|---|
| £780,000 × 30% (WI) | 234,000 |
| Less: ACT (W2) | - |
| Less: income tax suffered | (800) |
| CT liability | 233,200 |

*Workings*

1   There are 5 associated companies. Thus the upper limit becomes £300,000. Full rate of CT is thus still due.

2   ACT

|  | £ |
|---|---|
| Maximum set-off (£780,000 × 20%) | 156,000 |
| Less: Shadow ACT (part one) | (156,000) |
| Set-off of ACT b/f | Nil |

**Appendix two: due dates for the payment of tax**

*Year ended 31 March 2001*

72% × £233,200 = £167,904 is due in four quarterly instalments of £41,976. The due dates are as follows.

| Dates | Amount due £ | Amount paid £ | Overpaid £ |
|---|---|---|---|
| 14.10.00 | 41,976 | 42,948 | (972) |
| 14. 1.01 | 41,976 | 42,948 | (972) |
|  |  |  | (1,944) |
| 14.4.01 | 41,976 | 42,948 | (972) |
|  |  |  | 2,916 |
| 14.7.01 | 41,976 |  |  |
|  | (2,916) |  |  |
|  | 39,060 |  |  |
| 1.01.02 | 65,296 |  |  |

# SECTION C

## 72    PAYE

> **Pass marks**. In part (a) a report was asked for so it was important to present your answer in report format.

### REPORT

To:      The head of payroll
From:   Chief Accountant
Date:    1 April 2000
Subject: Benefits in kind

### Introduction

The purpose of this report is to set out the rules for quantifying for tax purposes the various benefits that we will be providing to certain members of staff. It also deals with the compliance rules for returning details of benefits to the Revenue and the company's responsibilities under the income tax self-assessment rules to employees. The requirement to pay NIC on certain benefits is also discussed.

### Quantifying various benefits

*Cars and car fuel*

For employees earning £8,500 or more a year and directors, a car provided by reason of the employment gives rise to a taxable benefit. The taxable benefit each year is found as follows:

£ (Price of car – capital contributions) × % × age factor

The price of the car is the sum of:

(i)    The list price of the car (up to a maximum of £80,000) at the time of first registration, including charges for delivery and standard accessories, and

(ii)   The price (including fitting) of all optional accessories provided when the car was first provided to the employee or, if fitted later, costing at least £100 each.

The cost of mobile telephones and equipment needed by a disabled employee are not included.

Capital contributions are payments by the employee in respect of the price of the car or accessories. The maximum deductible capital contributions is £5,000: contributions beyond that total are ignored.

The 'percentage' for 2000/01 depends on the **business** mileage in the tax year:

| Business mileage | First car |
|---|---|
| Less than 2,500 | 35% |
| At least 2,500, less than 18,000 | 25% |
| At least 18,000 | 15% |

If the car is at least four years old at the end of the tax year, then the age factor is ¾. Otherwise it is 1.

The benefit is pro rated on a time basis if the car is not available for a continuous period of at least 30 days in the tax year. The mileage factor limits of 2,500 and 18,000 are also pro rated in such cases.

The benefit is reduced by any payment the user must make for the private use of the car (as distinct from a capital contribution to the cost of the car).

If we provide fuel for the company cars there will be a further benefit on a set scale in addition to the car benefit. No taxable fuel benefit will, however, arise if the employee or director reimburses the company with the cost of ALL fuel used for private purposes. Unlike most benefits, a reimbursement of only part of the cost of such fuel does not reduce the scale charge.

The fuel benefit is reduced in the same way as the car benefit if the car is not available for 30 days or more, but it is not adjusted for business mileage.

*Relocation costs*

There will be no taxable benefit for any employee or director in respect of the first £8,000 of relocation costs. Thus the proposed £5,000 payment will be tax-free for the recipients.

*Interest free loans*

No taxable benefit will arise in respect of interest free loans which do not exceed £5,000 at any time in a tax year. For employees earning in excess of £8,500 per annum and directors, the taxable benefit of loans in excess of £5,000 is the amount of the loan multiplied by the Inland Revenue's official rate of interest. If any part of the loan is written off a taxable benefit will also arise equal to the amount written off in a tax year.

### Compliance rules for reporting benefits to the Revenue

A form P11D quantifying benefits in kind must be completed for each director and employee earning £8,500 or more a year. These forms must be submitted to the Inland Revenue by 6 July following the end of the tax year.

### Company responsibilities under the income tax self assessment rules

Employees must be given details of the information included in their P11D by 6 July following the end of the tax year. This will enable employees to complete their self-assessment returns and as such are cross referenced into those returns. Penalties may be imposed on the company if the P11D returns are incorrect or late.

### National Insurance Contributions (NICs)

Class 1A NICs are due to be paid by the company no later than 19 July following the end of the tax year in which any benefits-in-kind were provided to employees. These NICs are calculated at a rate of 12.2 % on the value of the benefit as outlined above. Class 1A NICs must be returned on Form P11D(b).

**Information sheet for staff members**

The purpose of this information sheet is to set out how you will be taxed on any benefits in kind you receive from the company and to explain how these benefits will effect your PAYE code.

There will be no taxable benefit in respect of the first £8,000 of relocation costs you receive and there will be no taxable benefit in respect of any interest free loans if the total loans made to you do not exceed £5,000. However, if you earn at least £8,500, your company car will give rise to a taxable benefit and there will be a further benefit in respect of fuel provided for private use. There will also be a taxable benefit in respect of loans in excess of £5,000 and in respect of any loan written off.

The tax on taxable benefits will be collected throughout the year under the PAYE system. The way the Revenue collect the tax is to deduct the taxable value of your benefits from the allowances given to you in your PAYE code. This means that at each pay date you will be taxed on a proportion of the value of your benefits and that at the end of the year you should have paid the correct amount of income tax.

You could, however, find that you still owe some tax at the year end. This will occur if the Revenue underestimate the taxable value of the benefits included in your PAYE code. It may also occur if the taxable value of your benefits exceed allowances as the company is then restricted in the amount of tax that it can deduct from your cash pay on each pay day.

**Example**

If you are provided with a 1995 cc car with a list price of £15,000 and you drive 20,000 miles on business the benefit in kind will be calculated as:

|  | £ |
|---|---|
| £15,000 × 15% = | 2,250 |
| If any private petrol is paid for by the company | 2,170 |
| Taxable benefit-in-kind | 4,420 |

Tax at 22% on this equals £972 which would be collected over the tax year at £81 per month.

---

**73    W LTD**

> **Pass marks**. The planning element in this question is to recognise that by NOT claiming a FYA on the lorry and by NOT depooling the new piece of machinery as a short-life asset, the capital allowances are significantly greater.

(i)  **Plant and machinery**

|  | General pool £ | Expensive car (1) £ | Expensive car (2) £ | SLA £ | Allowances £ |
|---|---|---|---|---|---|
| TWDV b/f | 36,000 | 22,000 | 30,000 | 18,000 | |
| Additions | 38,000 | | | | |
| Disposals | (60,000) | | (22,000) | (20,000) | |
| | 14,000 | 22,000 | 8,000 | (2,000) | |
| Less: WDA @ 25%/ (restricted) | (3,500) | (3,000) | | | 6,500 |
| Balancing allowance | | | (8,000) | | 8,000 |
| Balancing charge | | | | 2,000 | (2,000) |
| TWDV c/f | 10,500 | 19,000 | - | - | 12,500 |

(ii)  **Industrial buildings allowances**

**Factory one**

|  | £ |
|---|---|
| Cost | 120,000 |
| Y/e 31.3.93/31.3.94 | (9,600) |
|  | 110,400 |
| Y/e 31.3.95 |  |
| Addition | 40,000 |
|  | 150,400 |
| WDA @ 4% cost | (6,400) |
|  | 144,000 |
| Y/e 31.3.96 – 31.3.00 |  |
| 5 × £6,400 | (32,000) |
| Residue before sale | 112,000 |

The factory was sold for £100,000, so a balancing allowance of £12,000 is available.

**Factory two**

Industrial buildings allowances are available on the lower of the original cost (£180,000) and the purchase price (£210,000), ie on £180,000.

Allowances are available over the remaining tax life of the building = 15 (25 – 10) years.

∴ the industrial buildings allowance available in the year ended 31.3.01 is:

$$\frac{£180,000}{15} = \underline{£12,000}$$

Capital allowances

The maximum capital allowances for the year ended 31 March 2001 are therefore £36,500 (£12,500 + £12,000 + £12,000).

First year allowances have not been claimed in respect of the lorry or the new piece of equipment. In addition, an election has not been made to de-pool the new piece of equipment. This avoids the balancing charge that would otherwise arise on the general pool. The position if FYAs were claimed and a SLA election made would be:

|  | Gen Pool £ | FYA £ | SLA £ | Total £ |
|---|---|---|---|---|
| 1 April 2000 b/f | 36,000 | - | - |  |
| Purchases |  | 18,000 | 20,000 |  |
| FYA 40% |  | (7,200) | (8,000) | 15,200 |
| Disposals | (60,000) |  |  |  |
| Bal Charge | (24,000) |  |  | (24,000) |
| Allowances as before: |  |  |  |  |
| Expensive car (1) |  |  |  | 3,000 |
| (2) |  |  |  | 8,000 |
| SLA charge |  |  |  | (2,000) |
| Total capital allowances |  |  |  | 200 |
| First method capital allowances |  |  |  | 12,500 |
| Difference |  |  |  | 12,300 |

The IBAs would be unchanged.

Clearly this is less beneficial than the position shown where no FYA's are claimed and a SLA election is not made.

**74    D LTD**

> **Pass marks**. The examiner considers this type of question to be 'core' knowledge. Ensure that you can answer it well.

(a)  (i)    Sale of building in May 1994

| | £ |
|---|---:|
| Disposal proceeds | 280,000 |
| Less: M82 value | (130,000) |
| | 150,000 |
| Less: indexation (£130,000 × 0.821) | (106,730) |
| Gain | 43,270 |

An amount equal to the proceeds not reinvested, £10,000, was immediately chargeable. The remainder, (£33,270) was held over and is chargeable on the disposal (ie the scrapping) of the plant and machinery in May 2000.

(ii)    Transfer of building

The transfer of the building from T Ltd in June 1997 would have been made on a no gain/no loss basis for chargeable gains purposes.

On the sale of 20% of T Ltd's holding in D Ltd in May 2000 T Ltd and D Ltd cease to be members of the same capital gains group. The gain that would have arisen in June 1997 on the transfer of the factory for its market value then crystallises.

| | £ |
|---|---:|
| Market value in June 1997 | 260,000 |
| Less: cost | (180,000) |
| | 80,000 |
| Less: Indexation (£180,000 × 0.365) | (65,700) |
| Chargeable gain | 14,300 |

The gain of £14,300 is chargeable in the year that D Ltd and T Ltd ceased to be members of the same group, the year ended 31 December 2000.

(iii)

| | £ |
|---|---:|
| Sale proceeds | 300,000 |
| Less: M82 value | (150,000) |
| Unindexed gain | 150,000 |
| Less: indexation | |
| (£150,000 × 1.116) (restricted) | (150,000) |
| | Nil |

**Tutorial note 1.** As a rebasing election had previously been made, the March 1982 value must be used in this computation.

**Tutorial note 2.** Indexation cannot turn a gain into a loss, it can only reduce the gain to £nil.

(iv)    Disposal of two plots of land

| | £ |
|---|---:|
| Sale proceeds | 180,000 |
| Less: Cost (£500,000 × $\dfrac{180,000}{180,000 + 1,200,000}$ ) | (65,217) |
| Unindexed gain | 114,783 |
| Less: indexation (£65,217 × 0.209) | (13,630) |
| Chargeable gain | 101,153 |

(b)   It is not possible to rollover the gain of £33,270 which was previously held over on the acquisition of the plant and machinery.

It is not possible to rollover the gain that crystallises when D Ltd and T Ltd cease to be members of the same group.

No deferral is possible on the investment property because it is not a gain arising on a business asset.

Rollover relief will be available to defer the gain arising on the disposal of the two plots of land providing a qualifying asset is purchased in the period commencing one year before and ending three years after the disposal and also dependant on how much of the £180,000 proceeds are reinvested in the new asset.

## 75   M LTD

> **Pass marks**. The main point in this question is to ensure that any deductible charges are first deducted from UK income with the balance of charges being deducted from that part of foreign income bearing the LOWEST rate of foreign tax. This allows a maximisation of the foreign tax credits.

(a)   Year ended 31 March 2001

|  | Total £ | UK £ | A Inc £ | B PG £ | C SA £ |
|---|---|---|---|---|---|
| Schedule D Case I | 20,000 | 20,000 | | | |
| Schedule D Case V (W1) | 587,500 | - | 200,000 | 200,000 | 187,500 |
|  | 607,500 | 20,000 | 200,000 | 200,000 | 187,500 |
| Less: Charge on income | (75,000) | (20,000) | (55,000) | - | - |
| Profits chargeable to corporation tax | 532,500 | - | 145,000 | 200,000 | 187,500 |
| CT @ 30% | 159,750 | - | 43,500 | 60,000 | 56,250 |
| Less: DTR (W2) | (136,250) | - | (30,000) | (50,000) | (56,250) |
| Mainstream corporation tax | 23,500 | - | 13,500 | 10,000 | - |

In order to maximise the set off of double tax relief, charges are allocated firstly to UK profits and then to overseas sources of income that have suffered the lowest rate of overseas tax. There are five associated companies so the full rate of corporation tax applies.

(b)   If C SA were deemed to be a controlled foreign company (CFC), then an amount equal to M Ltd's interest in C SA's profits would be included in M Ltd's profits chargeable to corporation tax. This would be equal to £96,000 worth of extra profit (ie £800,000 × 12%) taxable for M Ltd.

The tax on C SA's profits would be calculated using the supplementary page for CFCs contained in Form CT600. This tax would be due for payment on the same date(s) as the rest of M Ltd's CT.

If C SA were to distribute at least 90% of its profits to M Ltd, M Ltd would be taxable on the dividends received in any accounting period. The CFC rules would not then apply.

*Workings*

1    Dividend from C SA

     Since M Ltd's shareholding in C SA is at least 10%, relief for underlying tax is available:

|  | £ |
|---|---|
| Dividend from C SA | 120,000 |
| Withholding tax ($\times$ 20/80) | 30,000 |
|  | 150,000 |
| Underlying tax |  |
| $£150,000 \times \dfrac{200,000}{800,000}$ | 37,500 |
| Gross dividend | 187,500 |

2     *Overseas dividends*

|  |  |  | Net £ | Tax credit £ | Gross £ |
|---|---|---|---|---|---|
| A | Inc | (15%) | 170,000 | 30,000 | 200,000 |
| B | PG | (25%) | 150,000 | 50,000 | 200,000 |
| C | SA | (20%) | 120,000 | 67,500 | 187,500 |

3     *Double tax relief*

|  | A Inc £ | B pg £ | C Sa £ |
|---|---|---|---|
| Lower of |  |  |  |
| (i) UK tax | 43,500 | 60,000 | 56,250 |
| (ii) Overseas tax | 30,000 | 50,000 | *67,500 |
|  | £30,000 | £50,000 | £56,250 |

\* Underlying tax + withholding tax.

# TAX RATES AND ALLOWANCES

A   INCOME TAX

1   *Allowances*

|  | 1999/00 | 2000/01 |
|---|---|---|
|  | £ | £ |
| Personal allowance | 4,335 | 4,385 |

2   *Car fuel scale charges*

|  | 2000/01 | |
|---|---|---|
|  | *Petrol* | *Diesel* |
|  | £ | £ |
| Cars having a cylinder capacity | | |
| 1,400 cc or less | 1,700 | 2,170 |
| 1,401 cc to 2,000 cc | 2,170 | 2,170 |
| More than 2,000 cc | 3,200 | 3,200 |
| Cars not having a cylinder capacity | 3,200 | 3,200 |

3   *Fixed profit car scheme - 2000/01 rates*

|  | *On first 4,000 miles* | *On each mile over 4,000* |
|---|---|---|
| Size of car engine | | |
| Up to 1,000 cc | 28p | 17p |
| 1,000 cc - 1,500 cc | 35p | 20p |
| 1,501 cc - 2,000 cc | 45p | 25p |
| Over 2,000 cc | 63p | 36p |

4   *Personal pension contribution limits*

| *Age* | *Maximum percentage* |
|---|---|
|  | % |
| Up to 35 | 17.5 |
| 36 – 45 | 20.0 |
| 46 – 50 | 25.0 |
| 51 – 55 | 30.0 |
| 56 – 60 | 35.0 |
| 61 or more | 40.0 |

Subject to earnings cap of £90,600 for 1999/00 and £91,800 for 2000/01

B    CORPORATION TAX

1    *Rates*

| Financial year | Full rate % | Small companies rate % | Starting rate | Marginal relief Fraction | Lower limit for starting rate £ | Upper limit for starting rate £ | Upper limit for SCR £ | Lower Limit for SCR £ |
|---|---|---|---|---|---|---|---|---|
| 1994 | 33 | 25 | - | 1/50 | - | - | 1,500,000 | 300,000 |
| 1995 | 33 | 25 | - | 1/50 | - | - | 1,500,000 | 300,000 |
| 1996 | 33 | 24 | - | 9/400 | - | - | 1,500,000 | 300,000 |
| 1997 | 31 | 21 | - | 1/40 | - | - | 1,500,000 | 300,000 |
| 1998 | 31 | 21 | - | 1/40 | - | - | 1,500,000 | 300,000 |
| 1999 | 30 | 20 | - | 1/40 | - | - | 1,500,000 | 300,000 |
| 2000 | 30 | 20 | 10 | 1/40 | 10,000 | 50,000 | 1,500,000 | 300,000 |

2    *Marginal relief*

$$(M - P) \times I/P \times \text{Marginal relief fraction}$$

3    *Capital allowances*

|  | % |
|---|---|
| Plant and machinery |  |
|   Writing down allowance | 25 |
|   First year allowance (acquisitions 2.7.97 - 1.7.98) | 50 |
|   First year allowance (acquisitions after 2.7.98) | 40 |
|   First year allowance (information and communication technology equipment - period 1.4.00 - 31.3.03) | 100 |
| Industrial buildings allowance |  |
|   Writing down allowance:   post 5.11.62 | 4 |
|       pre 6.11.62 | 2 |

C    VALUE ADDED TAX

1    *Registration and deregistration limits*

|  | *To 31.3.00* | *From 1.4.00* |
|---|---|---|
| Registration limit | £51,000 | £52,000 |
| Deregistration limit | £49,000 | £50,000 |

2    *Scale charges for private motoring*

2000/2001 (VAT inclusive)

|  | *Quarterly* | |
|---|---|---|
|  | *Petrol* | *Diesel* |
| Up to 1400 cc | 256 | 232 |
| 1401 to 2000 cc | 325 | 232 |
| Over 2000cc | 478 | 295 |

## D CAPITAL GAINS TAX

1 *Lease percentage table*

| Years | Percentage | Years | Percentage | Years | Percentage |
|---|---|---|---|---|---|
| 50 or more | 100.000 | 33 | 90.280 | 16 | 64.116 |
| 49 | 99.657 | 32 | 89.354 | 15 | 61.617 |
| 48 | 99.289 | 31 | 88.371 | 14 | 58.971 |
| 47 | 98.902 | 30 | 87.330 | 13 | 56.167 |
| 46 | 98.490 | 29 | 86.226 | 12 | 53.191 |
| 45 | 98.059 | 28 | 85.053 | 11 | 50.038 |
| 44 | 97.595 | 27 | 83.816 | 10 | 46.695 |
| 43 | 97.107 | 26 | 82.496 | 9 | 43.154 |
| 42 | 96.593 | 25 | 81.100 | 8 | 39.399 |
| 41 | 96.041 | 24 | 79.622 | 7 | 35.414 |
| 40 | 95.457 | 23 | 78.055 | 6 | 31.195 |
| 39 | 94.842 | 22 | 76.399 | 5 | 26.722 |
| 38 | 94.189 | 21 | 74.635 | 4 | 21.983 |
| 37 | 93.497 | 20 | 72.770 | 3 | 16.959 |
| 36 | 92.761 | 19 | 70.791 | 2 | 11.629 |
| 35 | 91.981 | 18 | 68.697 | 1 | 5.983 |
| 34 | 91.156 | 17 | 66.470 | 0 | 0.000 |

2 *Retail prices index (January 1987 = 100.0)*

| | 1982 | 1983 | 1984 | 1985 | 1986 | 1987 | 1988 | 1989 | 1990 |
|---|---|---|---|---|---|---|---|---|---|
| Jan | | 82.6 | 86.8 | 91.2 | 96.2 | 100.0 | 103.3 | 111.0 | 119.5 |
| Feb | | 83.0 | 87.2 | 91.9 | 96.6 | 100.4 | 103.7 | 111.8 | 120.2 |
| Mar | 79.4 | 83.1 | 87.5 | 92.8 | 96.7 | 100.6 | 104.1 | 112.3 | 121.4 |
| Apr | 81.0 | 84.3 | 88.6 | 94.8 | 97.7 | 101.8 | 105.8 | 114.3 | 125.1 |
| May | 81.6 | 84.6 | 89.0 | 95.2 | 97.8 | 101.9 | 106.2 | 115.0 | 126.2 |
| Jun | 81.9 | 84.8 | 89.2 | 95.4 | 97.8 | 101.9 | 106.6 | 115.4 | 126.7 |
| Jul | 81.9 | 85.3 | 89.1 | 95.2 | 97.5 | 101.8 | 106.7 | 115.5 | 126.8 |
| Aug | 81.9 | 85.7 | 89.9 | 95.5 | 97.8 | 102.1 | 107.9 | 115.8 | 128.1 |
| Sept | 81.9 | 86.1 | 90.1 | 95.4 | 98.3 | 102.4 | 108.4 | 116.6 | 129.3 |
| Oct | 82.3 | 86.4 | 90.7 | 95.6 | 98.5 | 102.9 | 109.5 | 117.5 | 130.3 |
| Nov | 82.7 | 86.7 | 91.0 | 95.9 | 99.3 | 103.4 | 110.0 | 118.5 | 130.0 |
| Dec | 82.5 | 86.9 | 90.9 | 96.0 | 99.6 | 103.3 | 110.3 | 118.8 | 129.9 |

| | 1991 | 1992 | 1993 | 1994 | 1995 | 1996 | 1997 | 1998 | 1999 | 2000★ | 2001★ |
|---|---|---|---|---|---|---|---|---|---|---|---|
| Jan | 130.2 | 135.6 | 137.9 | 141.3 | 146.0 | 150.2 | 154.4 | 159.5 | 163.4 | 167.5 | 173.5 |
| Feb | 130.9 | 136.3 | 138.8 | 142.1 | 146.9 | 150.9 | 155.0 | 160.3 | 163.7 | 168.0 | 174.0 |
| Mar | 131.4 | 136.7 | 139.3 | 142.5 | 147.5 | 151.5 | 154.4 | 160.8 | 164.1 | 168.5 | 174.5 |
| Apr | 133.1 | 138.8 | 140.6 | 144.2 | 149.0 | 152.6 | 156.3 | 162.6 | 165.2 | 169.0 | 175.0 |
| May | 133.5 | 139.3 | 141.1 | 144.7 | 149.6 | 152.9 | 156.9 | 163.5 | 165.6 | 169.5 | 175.5 |
| Jun | 134.1 | 139.3 | 141.0 | 144.7 | 149.8 | 153.0 | 157.5 | 163.4 | 165.6 | 170.0 | 176.0 |
| Jul | 133.8 | 138.8 | 140.7 | 144.0 | 149.1 | 152.4 | 157.5 | 163.0 | 165.1 | 170.5 | 176.5 |
| Aug | 134.1 | 138.9 | 141.3 | 144.7 | 149.9 | 153.1 | 158.5 | 163.7 | 165.5 | 171.0 | 177.0 |
| Sept | 134.6 | 139.4 | 141.9 | 145.0 | 150.6 | 153.8 | 159.3 | 164.4 | 166.2 | 171.5 | 177.5 |
| Oct | 135.1 | 139.9 | 141.8 | 145.2 | 149.8 | 153.8 | 159.6 | 164.5 | 166.5 | 172.0 | 178.0 |
| Nov | 135.6 | 139.7 | 141.6 | 145.3 | 149.8 | 153.9 | 159.6 | 164.4 | 166.7 | 172.5 | 178.5 |
| Dec | 135.7 | 139.2 | 141.9 | 146.0 | 150.7 | 154.4 | 160.0 | 164.4 | 167.3 | 173.0 | 179.0 |

★ Estimated figures.

E    NATIONAL INSURANCE (NOT CONTRACTED OUT RATES) 2000/01

*Class 1 contributions*

|  |  | £ |
|---|---|---|
| **Employee** | | |
| Primary threshold | | 3,952 (£76 pw) |
| Upper earnings limit (UEL) | | 27,820 (£535 pw) |
| **Employer** | | |
| Secondary threshold | | 4,385 (£84 pw) |

Employee contributions    10% on earnings between the primary threshold and the UEL (8.4% if contracted out)

Employer contributions    12.2% on earnings above secondary threshold (Reduced rates on earnings between secondary threshold and UEL of £28,820 if contracted out)

*Class 1A and Class 1B contributions - Rate 12.2%*

## REVIEW FORM & FREE PRIZE DRAW

All original review forms from the entire BPP range, completed with genuine comments, will be entered into one of two draws on 31 July 2001 and 31 January 2002. The names on the first four forms picked out on each occasion will be sent a cheque for £50.

Name: _____     Address: _____

_____

Date: _____     _____

### How have you used this Kit?
*(Tick one box only)*

☐ Self study (book only)

☐ On a course: college (please state)_____

_____

☐ With 'correspondence' package

☐ Other _____

### Why did you decide to purchase this Kit?
*(Tick one box only)*

☐ Have used the complementary Study Text

☐ Have used other BPP products in the past

☐ Recommendation by friend/colleague

☐ Recommendation by a lecturer at college

☐ Saw advertising in journals

☐ Saw website

☐ Other _____

### During the past six months do you recall seeing/receiving any of the following?
*(Tick as many boxes as are relevant)*

☐ Our advertisement in *CIMA Insider*

☐ Our advertisement in *Financial Management*

☐ Our advertisement in *Pass*

☐ Our brochure with a letter through the post

☐ Our website

### Which (if any) aspects of our advertising do you find useful?
*(Tick as many boxes as are relevant)*

☐ Prices and publication dates of new editions

☐ Information on product content

☐ Facility to order books off-the-page

☐ None of the above

When did you sit the exam? _____

### Which of the following BPP products have you used for this paper?

☐ Study Text  ☐ MCQ Cards  ☑ Kit  ☐ Passcards  ☐ Success Tape  ☐ Breakthrough Video

Your ratings, comments and suggestions would be appreciated on the following areas of this Kit.

|  | Very useful | Useful | Not useful |
|---|---|---|---|
| 'Question search tools' | ☐ | ☐ | ☐ |
| 'The exam' | ☐ | ☐ | ☐ |
| 'Background | ☐ | ☐ | ☐ |
| Preparation questions | ☐ | ☐ | ☐ |
| Exam standard questions | ☐ | ☐ | ☐ |
| 'Pass marks' section in answers | ☐ | ☐ | ☐ |
| Content and structure of answers | ☐ | ☐ | ☐ |
| Mock exams | ☐ | ☐ | ☐ |
| 'Plan of attack' | ☐ | ☐ | ☐ |
| Mock exam answers | ☐ | ☐ | ☐ |

|  | Excellent | Good | Adequate | Poor |
|---|---|---|---|---|
| Overall opinion of this Kit | ☐ | ☐ | ☐ | ☐ |

Do you intend to continue using BPP products?     ☐ Yes   ☐ No

**Please note any further comments and suggestions/errors on the reverse of this page. The BPP author of this edition can be e-mailed at: alisonmchugh@bpp.com**

**Please return this form to: Alison McHugh, CIMA range manager, BPP Publishing Ltd, FREEPOST, London, W12 8BR**

## REVIEW FORM & FREE PRIZE DRAW (continued)

**Please note any further comments and suggestions/errors below.**

**FREE PRIZE DRAW RULES**

1   Closing date for 31 July 2001 draw is 30 June 2001. Closing date for 31 January 2002 draw is 31 December 2001.

2   Restricted to entries with UK and Eire addresses only. BPP employees, their families and business associates are excluded.

3   No purchase necessary. Entry forms are available upon request from BPP Publishing. No more than one entry per title, per person. Draw restricted to persons aged 16 and over.

4   Winners will be notified by post and receive their cheques not later than 6 weeks after the relevant draw date.

5   The decision of the promoter in all matters is final and binding. No correspondence will be entered into.

See overleaf for information on other
BPP products and how to order

# CIMA Order

To BPP Publishing Ltd, Aldine Place, London W12 8AW
Tel: 020 8740 2211.  Fax: 020 8740 1184
www.bpp.com

Mr/Mrs/Ms (Full name)

Daytime delivery address

Postcode

Daytime Tel          E-mail          Date of exam (month/year)

| | 7/00 Texts | 1/01 Kits | 1/01 Passcards | 9/00 Tapes | 7/00 Videos | MCQ cards** |
|---|---|---|---|---|---|---|
| **FOUNDATION *** | | | | | | |
| 1 Financial Accounting Fundamentals | £19.95 | £10.95 | £5.95 | £12.95 | £25.00 | £4.50 |
| 2 Management Accounting Fundamentals | £19.95 | £10.95 | £5.95 | £12.95 | £25.00 | £4.50 |
| 3A Economics for Business | £19.95 | £10.95 | £5.95 | £12.95 | £25.00 | £4.50 |
| 3B Business Law | £19.95 | £10.95 | £5.95 | £12.95 | £25.00 | £4.50 |
| 3C Business Mathematics | £19.95 | £10.95 | £5.95 | £12.95 | £25.00 | £4.50 |
| **INTERMEDIATE *** | | | | | | |
| 4 Finance | £19.95 | £10.95 | £5.95 | £12.95 | £25.00 | £4.50 |
| 5 Business Tax (FA 2000) | £19.95 (9/00) | £10.95 | £5.95 | £12.95 | £25.00 | £3.50 |
| 6 Financial Accounting | £19.95 | £10.95 | £5.95 | £12.95 | £25.00 | |
| 6I Financial Accounting International | £19.95 | £10.95 | £5.95 | | £25.00 | |
| 7 Financial Reporting | £19.95 | £10.95 | £5.95 | £12.95 | £25.00 | |
| 7I Financial Reporting International | £19.95 | £10.95 | £5.95 | | | |
| 8 Management Accounting - Performance Mgmt | £19.95 | £10.95 | £5.95 | £12.95 | £25.00 | £3.50 |
| 9 Management Accounting - Decision Making | £19.95 | £10.95 | £5.95 | £12.95 | £25.00 | £3.50 |
| 10 Systems and Project Management | £19.95 | £10.95 | £5.95 | £12.95 | £25.00 | |
| 11 Organisational Management | £19.95 | £10.95 | £5.95 | £12.95 | £25.00 | |
| **FINAL** | | | | | | |
| 12 Management Accounting - Business Strategy | £20.95 | £10.95 | £5.95 | £12.95 | £25.00 | |
| 13 Management Accounting - Financial Strategy | £20.95 | £10.95 | £5.95 | £12.95 | £25.00 | |
| 14 Management Accounting - Information Strategy | £20.95 | £10.95 | £5.95 | £12.95 | £25.00 | |
| 15 Case Study | £15.95 (1) | £15.95 (2) | | £15.95 (12/00) | £15.95 (12/00) | |

(1) Workbook    (2) Case Question Bank

* There will also be a selection of Master CDs available in 2001
** (FREE WITH TEXT)

## POSTAGE & PACKING

### Study Texts
| | First | Each extra | |
|---|---|---|---|
| UK | £3.00 | £2.00 | £ |
| Europe*** | £5.00 | £4.00 | £ |
| Rest of world | £20.00 | £10.00 | £ |

### Kits/Passcards/Success Tapes
| | First | Each extra | |
|---|---|---|---|
| UK | £2.00 | £1.00 | £ |
| Europe*** | £2.50 | £1.00 | £ |
| Rest of world | £15.00 | £8.00 | £ |

### Master CDs(2001)/Breakthrough Videos
| | First | Each extra | |
|---|---|---|---|
| UK | £2.00 | £2.00 | £ |
| Europe*** | £2.00 | £2.00 | £ |
| Rest of world | £20.00 | £10.00 | £ |
| MCQ cards | £1.00 | £1.00 | £ |

**Grand Total** (Cheques to *BPP Publishing*) I enclose a cheque for (incl. Postage) £

Or charge to Access/Visa/Switch

Card Number

Expiry date          Start Date

Issue Number (Switch Only)

Signature

We aim to deliver to all UK addresses inside 5 working days. A signature will be required. Orders to all EU addresses should be delivered within 6 working days. All other orders to overseas addresses should be delivered within 8 working days.